To Establish Justice,
to Insure
Domestic Tranquility

A NEW YORK TIMES BOOK

To Establish Justice,
to Insure
Domestic Tranquility

THE FINAL REPORT OF
THE NATIONAL COMMISSION
ON THE CAUSES AND PREVENTION
OF VIOLENCE

Special Introduction by James Reston of
The New York Times

plus 32 pages of photographs

PRAEGER PUBLISHERS
New York • Washington • London

PRAEGER PUBLISHERS
111 Fourth Avenue, New York, N.Y. 10003, U.S.A.
5, Cromwell Place, London, S.W.7, England

Published in the United States of America in 1970
by Praeger Publishers, Inc.

Second printing, 1971

PHOTO CREDITS FOR PICTORIAL INSERT
("a" indicates top of page, "b" the bottom)

1 Library of Congress / 2 The John Carter Brown Library / 3-5 Library of Congress / 6a Frank Leslie's Illustrated Weekly / 6b Library of Congress / 7 Kansas State Historical Society / 9 Kansas State Historical Society / 10a Kansas State Historical Society / 10b Denver Public Library Western Collection / 11 United Press International / 12-13 Library of Congress / 14 National Archives / 15 Smithsonian Institution / 16 Library of Congress / 17a National Archives / 17b Harper's Weekly / 18-19 Library of Congress / 20a Frank Leslie's Illustrated Weekly / 21a Frank Leslie's Illustrated Weekly / 20-21b Library of Congress / 22-23a Denver Public Library Western Collection / 23b Library of Congress / 24 Harper's Weekly / 25 National Archives / 26 Rutherford B. Hayes Library / 27 Harper's Weekly / 28-29 Library of Congress / 30-31 Chicago Historical Society / 32a United Press International / 32b Wide World Photo

Library of Congress Catalog Card Number: 74-115422

Produced in cooperation with Bantam Books, Inc.

PRINTED IN THE UNITED STATES OF AMERICA

CONTENTS

SPECIAL INTRODUCTION

by James Reston

This report on violence in America was written for the President of the United States after the murders of Martin Luther King, Jr., and Robert F. Kennedy. It was commissioned by President Lyndon Johnson and submitted to President Nixon, who released it for publication on the theory that crime is not only a common fear but a common responsibility.

Accordingly, the reader now has a chance to look at a national problem as it is presented to the President by the experts on the subject. The conclusions presented here do not always agree with the wishes or interests of the White House.

In fact, President Johnson was so disturbed by some of the inquiries of his Commission that the Commission staff had great difficulty in obtaining previously committed funds midway through the investigation. And President Nixon finally was presented with a report that went against many of his own conclusions about how to deal with crime and violence in the country. He could have shelved or suppressed it, but he made it public in the belief that the American people were entitled to the facts.

The questions now are whether the people will read the report and whether the President will act on the recommendations of the Commission. Both points are in doubt. The record suggests that the American people are better at committing crime than reading about it. And President Nixon, unlike the Commission, puts his emphasis on suppressing criminals rather than on removing the causes of crime.

It should be clear to the reader, as he studies this report to the President, that the facts are not in dispute. Mr. Nixon defined them precisely in a speech made in New York during the presidential campaign of 1968—and the Commission supports his words.

In the last seven years, while the population of this country was rising some 10 percent, crime in the United States rose a staggering 88 percent. If the present rate of new crime continues, the number of rapes and robberies and assaults and thefts will double by the end of 1972.

That is a prospect America cannot accept. If we allow it to happen, then the city jungle will cease to be a metaphor. It will become a barbaric reality, and the brutal society that now flourishes in the core cities of America will annex the affluent suburbs. This nation will then be what it is fast becoming—an armed camp of 200 million of Americans living in fear.

The National Commission on the Causes and Prevention of Violence says the same thing in this volume, only in different words:

The United States is the clear leader among modern, stable democratic nations in its rates of homicide, assault, rape, and robbery, and it is at least among the highest in incidence of group violence and assassination . . . it is disfiguring our society—making fortresses of portions of our cities and dividing our people into armed camps . . .

To keep these melancholy observations in perspective, it should probably be remembered that crime and violence are not something new in American life. The independence of the nation was created by a violent revolution, and the continental United States was conquered by violent men. And always, the writers about America have been gloomy about the violence and corruption of our national life.

Walt Whitman, the poetic optimist of 19th-century America, writing exactly 100 years ago about the condition of American life, makes both President Nixon and the Violence Commission sound far too hopeful. He thought, when he wrote *Democratic Vistas* in 1870, that the great American experiment was lost in violence and corruption.

viii

Never was there, perhaps, more hollowness at heart than at present, and here in the United States. Genuine belief seems to have left us. The underlying principles of the States are not honestly believ'd in (for all this hectic glow, and these melodramatic screamings), nor is humanity itself believ'd in. What penetrating eye does not everywhere see through the mask? The spectacle is appalling. We live in an atmosphere of hypocrisy throughout. The men believe not in the women, nor the women in the men. A scornful superciliousness rules in literature. . . . The depravity of the business classes of our country is not less than has been supposed, but infinitely greater. The official services of America, national, state, and municipal, in all their branches and departments, except the judiciary, are saturated in corruption, bribery, falsehood, maladministration; and the judiciary is tainted. The great cities reek with respectable as much as non-respectable robbery and scoundrelism. . . .

The special value of this report, however, is that it goes beyond personal opinion. The 13 members of the Commission, under the chairmanship of Dr. Milton S. Eisenhower, President Emeritus of Johns Hopkins University, had the help of 200 leading scholars and an excellent staff under Lloyd N. Cutler; after a year and a half of hearings and discussion, they reached unanimous agreement on all but two comparatively minor points.

More important, they not only have looked at the history of violence in America, but have analyzed the causes of violent crime, group violence, civil disobedience, assassination, campus disorders, violence on television, and the relationship between violence and the easy availability of firearms in America.

In short, they have put the contemporary problem of violence into the perspective of the Constitution, and have made specific recommendations about how "to establish justice, to insure domestic tranquility."

Perhaps their most striking conclusion is that violence within the United States is as great a threat to the serenity of the nation as any probable combination of external dangers.

When in man's long history other great nations fell, it was less often from external assault than from internal decay. Our own civilization has shown a remarkable capacity for responding to crises and for emerging to higher pinnacles of power and achievement. But our most serious challenges to date have been external—the kind this strong and resourceful country could unite against.

While serious external dangers remain, the graver threats today are internal: haphazard urbanization, racial discrimination, disfiguring of the environment, unprecedented interdependence, the dislocation of human identity and motivation created by an affluent society—all resulting in a rising tide of individual and group violence.

It is interesting that Abraham Lincoln reached much the same conclusion in a famous speech at the Young Men's Lyceum in Springfield, Illinois in 1837: "At what point shall we Americans expect the approach of danger? . . . I answer, if it ever reach us, it must spring up amongst us; it cannot come from abroad. If destruction be our lot, we must ourselves be its author and finisher . . ."

The federal budget of the United States, for example, still reflects the opposite conclusion, namely, that the first priority of the nation is defense against threats from abroad. It is generally agreed, both by the Nixon Administration and by the Eisenhower Commission, that more attention and more money must be given to the causes of internal disorder, and also to the vigilant suppression of crime; but the Commission seems to give more emphasis to poverty and inequality as causes of crime than does the Nixon Administration.

"The way in which we can make the great progress toward reducing violence in America," the Eisenhower Commission says, "is by taking the actions necessary to improve the conditions of family and community life for all who live in our cities, and especially for the poor who are concentrated in the ghetto slums. It is the ghetto slum that is disproportionately responsible for violent crime, by far the most acute aspect of the problem of violence in the United States today."

The Nixon Administration, without specifically denying this conclusion, puts the emphasis the other way. Both agree on removing the causes of violence and suppressing the criminal and that, as the Commission says, "the twin objectives of the social order must be to make violence both unnecessary and unrewarding," but the administration tends to concentrate more on suppressing crime—making it unrewarding—than on removing the causes of crime, making it unnecessary.

This difference of emphasis is really the key point of this report. For while the Commission wants to spend more on the police and the courts, and the President wants to spend more on removing poverty, the administration is still concentrating on external defense and on punishing crime, while the Commission wants to concentrate on internal security and on removing the economic causes of crime.

During the presidential election campaign in 1968, Mr. Nixon indicated his approach to the problem:

> We cannot explain away crime in this country by charging it off to poverty—and we would not rid ourselves of the crime problem even if we succeeded overnight in lifting everybody above the poverty level. The role of poverty as a cause of the crime upsurge in America has been grossly exaggerated . . . In recent years, this nation has grown wealthier and its riches have been more widely distributed than in any other country in the world. And yet crime has been going up about three times as rapidly as the gross national product.

Even after a year in the White House, President Nixon still felt much the same way, and a great many Americans were even more unwilling to reorder the priorities and reallocate the resources of the nation to put social problems first. Thus, there was considerable opposition to racial integration, to the high costs of taxation and welfare programs, and particularly to the militancy of the Negroes and young intellectuals, who were also demanding an end to the war and transfer of vast sums from the military to the general welfare budget (health, labor, education, housing, pollution and law enforcement).

The Eisenhower Commission did not suggest that the problem of violence could be removed merely by passing vast new appropriations bills, in addition to increasing the general welfare budget by about $20 billion a year after the Vietnam War, but it made a long catalogue of specific recommendations to the President, including the following: double the national investment in the criminal justice process; increase day and night foot patrols of slum areas by inter-racial police teams; experiment with providing low cost drugs to criminal addicts so that they are not compelled to resort to robbery to meet the needs of their addiction;

bring all concealable handguns under a system of restrictive licensing.

To deal with the problems of mass demonstrations or group violence, the Commission proposed that all aggrieved groups in the nation have the right to speak out publicly and that their protests be given a fair hearing, but that efforts to coerce public authorities by mob action be condemned and put down by lawful means.

In addition, it was suggested that television and the newspapers reevaluate their practices to make sure that they were not contributing to an atmosphere of violence. The Commission was obviously concerned that presidential candidates minimize the risks of campaigning, and that all schools and universities pay more attention to teaching respect for the law. The Commission said:

We believe that candid examination of what is occurring in the United States today will lead to the conclusion that disobedience to valid law as a tactic of protest by discontented groups is not contributing to the emergence of a more liberal and humane society, but is, on the contrary, producing an opposite tendency.

The fears and resentments created by symbolic law violation have strengthened the political power of some of the most destructive elements in American society . . .

No doubt, there are many other observations and proposals in this report that are open to sharp debate and disagreement—the suggestion that the voting age be lowered to 18, for example, and that the marijuana laws be amended.

The main question, however, is whether the report will be taken seriously by the White House, the Congress and the educational institutions of the country. In a way, this will be a test of the value of these presidential commissions. In recent years, they have demonstrated that diverse groups of influential and experienced private citizens, aided by competent paid staffs, are often able to make deeper and more objective studies of national problems than committees of the Congress, the state legislatures or the federal or state executives.

The educational function of their work is valuable, and in many cases their recommendations have been the basis of new and important public welfare legislation. But often, too, they have been used as a device not to solve problems but to evade them.

It will not be easy, however, to evade this particular report, for it is a superlative study of a subject that is very much on the public mind. Anybody interested in either justice or domestic order, in the rising drug culture in America, in the contention between the sexes and the generations, in the turmoil in the universities or the decline in respect for public and private authority will find a great deal here to think about.

Beyond this lies the main post-Vietnam question: will the threat of public disorder be made the first order of business by the federal government? Will the resources of the nation be reallocated to "establish justice, to insure domestic tranquility?" The Eisenhower Commission has clearly challenged President Nixon to do just that.

January, 1970

NATIONAL COMMISSION ON THE CAUSES AND PREVENTION OF VIOLENCE

726 JACKSON PL., N.W., WASHINGTON, D.C. 20506

December 10, 1969

Dear Mr. President:

I transmit herewith the Final Report of the National Commission on the Causes and Prevention of Violence.

This Commission was created by President Johnson in an Executive Order dated June 10, 1968. Nearly a year later you asked us to continue our work and so extended the Commission's life for an additional six months. We are grateful for the support and encouragement that two Presidents and their staffs have given us.

Our Report is based on penetrating research by two hundred leading scholars and on eighteen months of hearings, conferences, and some sixty days of arduous working sessions by members of the Commission.

The Commission's findings and recommendations are presented to you in a single volume. The detailed data and findings of the scholars who helped us are set forth in more than fifteen volumes of printed reports. These reports provide a solid base for further study and research.

XV

We believe our Report will be of value to you, to the Congress, and to the American people. It sheds much light on the complex forces that tend to increase the level of violence in our rapidly changing society.

It suggests what the federal government, the state governments, and private associations and individuals can do to reduce the incidence of violence.

With one or two notable exceptions, our findings and recommendations have been unanimously agreed to by the thirteen members of this Commission. This is remarkable, for we are a diverse group of citizens; black and white, male and female, young and old, and Republican and Democratic—from the fields of education, law, religion, politics, psychology, history, labor and philosophy, and from every region of the United States.

I wish to emphasize that the solution to the problem of violence in our society will require manifold actions by individuals, by families, by many private organizations, as well as by every level of government. Hence, the public educational value of our report is surely as important as its use in formulating legislation.

Respectfully yours,

Milton S. Eisenhower,
Chairman

THE NATIONAL COMMISSION ON THE CAUSES AND PREVENTION OF VIOLENCE

Milton S. Eisenhower, *Chairman*

President Emeritus of Johns Hopkins University; former President, Pennsylvania State University and Kansas State University; former Special Ambassador and Presidential Representative for Latin American affairs.

A. Leon Higginbotham, *Vice-Chairman*

U.S. District Court Judge, Eastern District of Pennsylvania; former Commissioner, Federal Trade Commission; former Member, President's Committee to Fulfill These Rights (White House Conference on Civil Rights); Member, Commission on Reform of U.S. Criminal Law.

Hale Boggs

Majority Whip, House of Representatives; U.S. Representative from 2nd Congressional District, Louisiana; former Member, Warren Commission.

Terence Cardinal Cooke

Archbishop of New York; Military Vicar to the Armed Forces of the United States; Member, Presidential Task Force on International Development.

Philip A. Hart

U.S. Senator from Michigan; Member, Judiciary and Commerce Committees; Chairman, Judiciary Anti-Trust and Monopoly Subcommittee; Chairman, Commerce Subcommittee on Energy, Natural Resources, and Environment; Member, Democratic Policy Committee.

Eric Hoffer

Longshoreman; migratory worker; author; philosopher.

STAFF OFFICERS OF THE COMMISSION

Lloyd N. Cutler, *Executive Director*

Thomas D. Barr,
Deputy Director

James S. Campbell,
General Counsel

James F. Short, Jr.,
Marvin E. Wolfgang,
Co-Directors of Research

William G. McDonald,
Administrative Officer

Joseph Laitin,
Director of Information

SPECIAL ASSISTANTS TO THE COMMISSIONERS

Ronald A. Wolk, Anthony E. Neville
(Dr. Milton S. Eisenhower)
Monsignor James Murray (Terence Cardinal Cooke)
Gerald J. Kabel (Senator Philip A. Hart)
Richard Nelson, Wallace H. Johnson
(Senator Roman Hruska)
The Commission expresses its appreciation to the Federal
Bureau of Investigation and in particular to Robert Haynes
of FBI-Liaison.

COMMISSION STAFF

EDITORIAL/RESEARCH/ WRITING STAFF

Anthony F. Abell
Paul L. Briand, Jr.
Steffen W. Graae
Judy Harkison
Dale L. Smith

ADMINISTRATIVE STAFF

Lois A. Brooks,
Asst. Adm. Officer
Anne Horvath
R. Christine McKenzie
Gordon G. Mulcahy
John J. O'Neill

EXECUTIVE SECRETARIES

Frances L. Adams
Stephen M. D'Alessio
Mildred F. Dolan
Alyce Estrada-Palma
Audrey B. Habermann

Gertrude K. Holland
Carol A. Honus
Katherine Kaplan
Margaret A. Story
Barbara G. Windon

DIRECTORS OF TASK FORCES
AND STUDY TEAMS

TASK FORCE REPORTS

Violence in America
Hugh Davis Graham
Ted Robert Gurr

The Politics of Protest
Jerome Skolnick

Firearms and Violence in American Life
George D. Newton, Jr.
Franklin E. Zimring

Mass Media and Violence
Robert K. Baker
Sandra J. Ball

Crimes of Violence
Donald J. Mulvihill
Melvin M. Tumin
Lynn A. Curtis

Assassination and Political Violence
James F. Kirkham
Sheldon G. Levy
William J. Crotty

Law and Order Reconsidered
James S. Campbell
Joseph R. Sahid
David P. Stang

SPECIAL INVESTIGATIVE REPORTS

Rights in Conflict
Daniel Walker

Miami Report
Louis J. Hector
Paul L. E. Helliwell

Shoot-Out in Cleveland
Louis H. Masotti
Jerome R. Corsi

Rights in Concord
Joseph R. Sahid

Shut It Down! A College In Crisis
William H. Orrick, Jr.

STUDENT SUPPORT PANEL

Kenneth N. Cowden
Laurent A. DeLaine
George L. Gorse
Brian P. Jenney
E. Kelsey Kauffman
James J. Knicely
Edward F. Lopez

Leslie A. Pickering
Alan M. Rosen
Jay E. Silberman
David I. Tevelin
Robert S. Tigner
Alan D. Wiener
B. John Williams, Jr.

xx

We the People of the United States,
in order to form a more perfect Union,
establish Justice, insure domestic Tranquility,
provide for the common defence,
promote the general Welfare,
and secure the Blessings of Liberty
to ourselves and our Posterity, do ordain and establish
this Constitution
for the United States of America.

INTRODUCTION

This Commission was created by the President in June, 1968, to determine the causes of violence in the United States and to recommend methods of prevention.

Last January we issued a Progress Report, stressing the enormous complexities involved in understanding this vexing and multi-faceted problem.[1] We noted that to understand violence, we had to study American society itself, past and present, and the traditions and institutions which accept or condemn, generate or reduce the various forms of violence in our society. We indicated, too, that rather than depending solely on our own knowledge and preconceptions, we had found it necessary to enlist the assistance of more than two hundred of the nation's leading scholars in criminology, psychology, history, political science, sociology, and law.

We have now completed our study. We present the results in this Report. The full scope of our endeavor will be apparent to those who study not only what we say here but also the work of our seven research task forces and five investigatory study teams. Their reports to us fill fifteen volumes.[2] We also held a series of hearings and conferences, receiving the views of more than 150 public officials, scholars, educators, religious leaders, and private citizens from media executives to young students. We are publishing the transcript of six days of hearings on the mass media; transcripts of the other hearings will be available for study in the National Archives.

Extensive as our study was, it could not embrace every

VIOLENT CRIME

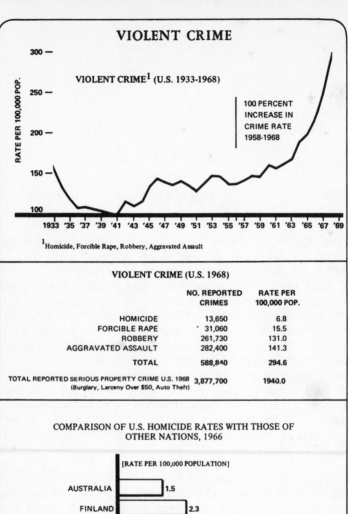

VIOLENT CRIME[1] (U.S. 1933-1968)

RATE PER 100,000 POP.

300 —

250 —

200 —

150 —

100

100 PERCENT
INCREASE IN
CRIME RATE
1958-1968

1933 '35 '37 '39 '41 '43 '45 '47 '49 '51 '53 '55 '57 '59 '61 '63 '65 '67 '69

[1]Homicide, Forcible Rape, Robbery, Aggravated Assault

VIOLENT CRIME (U.S. 1968)

	NO. REPORTED CRIMES	RATE PER 100,000 POP.
HOMICIDE	13,650	6.8
FORCIBLE RAPE	31,060	15.5
ROBBERY	261,730	131.0
AGGRAVATED ASSAULT	282,400	141.3
TOTAL	**588,840**	**294.6**
TOTAL REPORTED SERIOUS PROPERTY CRIME U.S. 1968 (Burglary, Larceny Over $50, Auto Theft)	3,877,700	1940.0

COMPARISON OF U.S. HOMICIDE RATES WITH THOSE OF OTHER NATIONS, 1966

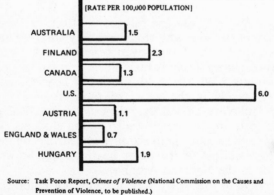

[RATE PER 100,000 POPULATION]

AUSTRALIA 1.5

FINLAND 2.3

CANADA 1.3

U.S. 6.0

AUSTRIA 1.1

ENGLAND & WALES 0.7

HUNGARY 1.9

Source: Task Force Report, *Crimes of Violence* (National Commission on the Causes and Prevention of Violence, to be published.)

aspect of such a complex problem. Others must build on our work, just as we have built on work that preceded ours. But within the confines of the time and resources available to us, we believe we have gained some valuable insights. We believe we have identified the causes of much of the violence that plagues contemporary America. We are convinced that most of this violence can be prevented, for our work has illuminated for us the strengths of this great nation, as well as its shortcomings. Our institutions and the spirit of our people are equal to this challenge, no less than to the challenges we have met in the past.[3]

Violence in the United States has risen to alarmingly high levels. Whether one considers assassination, group violence, or individual acts of violence, the decade of the 1960s was considerably more violent than the several decades preceding it and ranks among the most violent in our history. The United States is the clear leader among modern, stable democratic nations in its rates of homicide, assault, rape, and robbery, and it is at least among the highest in incidence of group violence and assassination.

This high level of violence is dangerous to our society. It is disfiguring our society—making fortresses of portions of our cities and dividing our people into armed camps. It is jeopardizing some of our most precious institutions, among them our schools and universities—poisoning the spirit of trust and cooperation that is essential to their proper functioning. It is corroding the central political processes of our democratic society—substituting force and fear for argument and accommodation.

We have endured and survived other cycles of violence in our history. Today, however, we are more vulnerable to violence than ever before. Two-thirds of our people live in urban areas, where violence especially thrives. Individual and group specializations have intensified our dependence on one another. Men are no longer capable of solitary living and individual self-defense; men must live together and depend upon one another to observe the laws and keep the peace.

The American people know the threat. They demand that violence be brought to a halt. Violence must be brought under control—to safeguard life and property, and to make possible the creation of the understanding and cooperation needed to remedy underlying causes. No society can remain free, much less deal effectively with its fundamental problems, if its people live in fear of their fellow citizens; it is ancient wisdom that a house divided against itself cannot stand.

In this Report we suggest a number of specific measures for the better control of violence. We urge, for example, that the nation should double its investment in the prevention of crime and the administration of justice, as rapidly as that investment can be wisely planned and utilized. We recommend that central offices of criminal justice be created at the metropolitan level to make all parts of the criminal justice process—police, courts, corrections—function more effectively, and that private citizens' organizations be formed to work as counterparts of these offices in every major city in the nation. We urge that public officials, including law enforcement officers, intensify their efforts to develop more effective tactics in handling both peaceful demonstrations and violent disturbances. As we show by comparing successful and unsuccessful strategies of control of major mass demonstrations of the past few years, official behavior may determine whether protest remains peaceful or erupts into serious violence.

Further, we recommend the adoption of a national firearms policy that will limit the general availability of handguns.

Necessary as measures of control are, they are only a part of the answer. They do not cure the basic causes of violence. Violence is like a fever in the body politic: it is but the symptom of some more basic pathology which must be cured before the fever will disappear.

Indeed, if measures of control were this society's only response to violence, they would in the long run exacerbate the problem. The pyramiding of control measures could turn us into a repressive society, where the peace is kept primarily through official coercion rather than through willing obedience to law. That kind of society, where law is more feared than respected, where individual expression and movement are curtailed, is violent too—and it nurtures within itself the seeds of its own violent destruction.

VIOLENT CRIME IN THE CITY

VIOLENT CRIME BY CITY SIZE (U.S. 1960 and 1968)

	[RATES PER 100,000 POP.]	
CITIES:	1960	1968
OVER 250,000	293.7	773.2
100,000–250,000	154.0	325.3
50,000–100,000	104.3	220.5
25,000–50,000	70.1	150.8
10,000–25,000	57.3	126.6
UNDER 10,000	47.7	111.4
SUBURBAN	N.A.	145.5
RURAL	N.A.	96.5

REPORTED URBAN ARREST RATES FOR VIOLENT CRIMES BY AGE

RATE PER 100,000 POPULATION U.S. 1967	AGE	INCREASE IN RATE 1958 TO 1967
123.0	10-14	222.0%
408.2	15-17	102.5%
222.1	10-17	138.8%
436.1	18-24	45.5%
127.3	25+	41.1%
189.1	ALL AGES (10+)	65.7%

■ Violent crime in the city is overwhelmingly committed by males.

■ Violent crime in the city is concentrated especially among youths between the ages of fifteen and twenty-four.

■ Violent crime in the city is committed primarily by individuals at the lower end of the occupational scale.

■ Violent crime in the cities stems disproportionately from the ghetto slum where most Negroes live.

■ The victims of assaultive violence in the cities generally have the same characteristics as the offenders: victimization rates are generally highest for males, youths, poor persons, and blacks. Robbery victims, however, are very often older whites.

Source: Task Force Report, *Crimes of Violence* (National Commission on the Causes and Prevention of Violence, to be published.)

In this Report, we analyze basic causes which underlie the chief varieties of contemporary violence. We make a number of recommendations directed to removing these causes. They cannot be eliminated entirely; even in a perfectly just society in which all have a fair and nondiscriminatory stake, there will always be some violent individuals, in rural as well as in urban areas, and measures of control will always be required to restrain them. But we can improve the conditions and opportunities of life for all citizens and thus reduce sharply the number who will commit violent acts.

Thus, we urge that young people must be given a greater

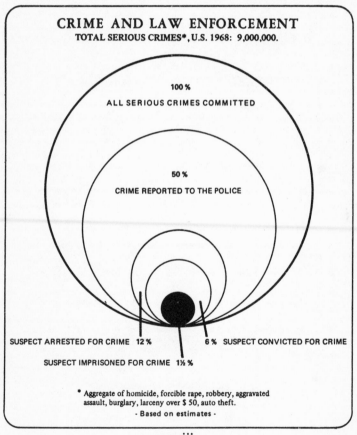

CRIME AND LAW ENFORCEMENT
TOTAL SERIOUS CRIMES*, U.S. 1968: 9,000,000.

100 %
ALL SERIOUS CRIMES COMMITTED

50 %
CRIME REPORTED TO THE POLICE

SUSPECT ARRESTED FOR CRIME 12 %   6 % SUSPECT CONVICTED FOR CRIME
SUSPECT IMPRISONED FOR CRIME 1½ %

* Aggregate of homicide, forcible rape, robbery, aggravated assault, burglary, larceny over $ 50, auto theft.
- Based on estimates -

GROUP VIOLENCE

COMPARATIVE LEVELS OF POLITICAL VIOLENCE (U.S. 1819-1968)

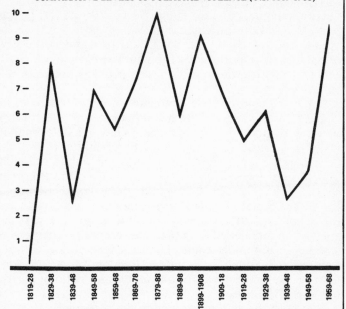

Rate of Incidents of Political Violence (Excluding War) Adjusted for Population, 10-Year Intervals
[Based on Sampling of Newspapers]

Source: Task Force Report, *Assassination and Political Violence* (National Commission on the Causes
and Prevention of Violence, Nov. 1969).

DEMONSTRATIONS, RIOTS AND INDIVIDUAL VIOLENT CRIMES
(U.S. JUNE 1963—MAY 1968)

	POLITICAL DEMONSTRATIONS AND PROTESTS INVOLVING MORE THAN 100 PERSONS [1]	URBAN RIOTS [2]	INDIVIDUAL ACTS OF VIOLENT CRIME [3] HOMICIDE	AGGRAVATED ASSAULT
POPULATION	2,000,000 PARTICIPANTS	200,000 PARTICIPANTS	195,000,000 CITIZENS	195,000,000 CITIZENS
INJURIES	1,100	8,000	————	1,124,200
DEATHS	NONE	190	53,200	————
ARRESTS	21,000	50,000	39,000	457,500

[1] Civil Rights Demonstrations, Antiwar Demonstrations, Student Protests on
Campus Issues, School Anti-Integration Demonstrations, Segregationist
Clashes and Counter-Demonstrations. 642 Events Identified.

[2] 239 Events Identified.

[3] Based on *Uniform Crime Reports*, FBI, Adjusted for Mid-1963 to Mid-1968.

Source: Task Force Report, *Violence in America* (National Commission on the
Causes and Prevention of Violence, June 1969)

role in determining their own destiny and in shaping the future course of our society. Responsible participation in decision-making may, for many, be a substitute for the violence that is born in frustration. We propose lowering the voting age, reforming the draft, and providing a massive expansion in opportunities for youth to engage in public service activities whose goals young people wholeheartedly embrace.

While we categorically condemn all illegal violence, including group violence,[4] as incompatible with the survival of a just, democratic, and humane society, we state emphatically that aggrieved groups must be permitted to exercise their constitutional rights of protest and public presentation of grievances. Accordingly, we believe the President should seek legislation that would confer jurisdiction upon the United States District Courts to grant injunctions, upon the request of the Attorney General or private persons, against the threatened or actual interference by any person, whether or not under color of state or federal law, with the rights of individuals or groups to freedom of speech, freedom of the press, peaceful assembly, and petition for redress of grievances.

We must have the perception to recognize injustices when they are called to our attention, and we must have the institutional flexibility to correct those injustices promptly. To enable the less affluent to obtain effective and peaceful redress of grievances, we recommend that additional steps should be taken to meet their needs for lawyers, and that state and local jurisdictions should be encouraged to experiment with the establishment of grievance agencies to serve all citizens.

The way in which we can make the greatest progress toward reducing violence in America is by taking the actions necessary to improve the conditions of family and community life for all who live in our cities, and especially for the poor who are concentrated in the ghetto slums. It is the ghetto slum that is disproportionately responsible for violent crime, by far the most acute aspect of the problem of violence in the United States today.

To be a young, poor male; to be undereducated and without means of escape from an oppressive urban environment; to want what the society claims is available (but mostly to others); to see around oneself illegitimate and often violent methods being used to achieve material gain; and to observe others using these means with impunity—all this is to be burdened with an enormous set of influences that pull many toward crime and delinquency. To be also a Negro, Puerto Rican or Mexican-American and subject to discrimination and segregation adds considerably to the pull of these other criminogenic forces.

Safety in our cities requires nothing less than progress in reconstructing urban life. We must meet the 1968 Housing Act's goal of a decent home for every American within a decade. We must take more effective steps to realize the goal, first set in the Employment Act of 1946, of a useful job at a reasonable wage for all who are able to work. We must provide better educational opportunities for all our children. We must act on current recommendations that those American families who cannot care for themselves receive a basic annual income. We must restructure our local governments, restore their fiscal vitality and accomplish a host of other major tasks of the kind discussed in this Report.

As these brief introductory comments indicate, we believe that the twin objectives of the social order must be to make violence both unnecessary and unrewarding. To make violence unnecessary, our institutions must be capable of providing justice for all who live under them—of giving all a satisfactory stake in the normal life of the community and the nation. To make violence unrewarding, our institutions must be able to control violence when it occurs, and to do so firmly, fairly, and within the law.

The Preamble of our Constitution does not speak merely of justice or merely of order; it embraces both. Two of the six purposes set forth in the Preamble are to "establish justice" and to "insure domestic tranquility." If we are to succeed in preventing and controlling violence, we must achieve both of these goals.

We are well aware that our recommendations for attaining these objectives—and the recommendations of other national commissions before us—will require far-reaching improvements in our institutions and unprecedented levels of public funding. We adopt as our own the

xxxi

ASSASSINATION ATTEMPTS AGAINST PRESIDENTS & PRESIDENTIAL CANDIDATES

Year	Victim	Assailant and professed or alleged reason	Method of attack and result	Location	Activity of victim at time of attack
1835	Andrew Jackson	Richard Lawrence; declared insane, said Jackson was preventing him from obtaining large sums of money.	pistol, misfired	Washington, D.C.	Attending funeral service in Capitol rotunda
1865	Abraham Lincoln	John W. Booth; loyalty to the Confederacy, revenge for defeat, slavery issue.	pistol, killed	Washington, D.C.	Attending theatrical performance in Ford Theatre
1881	James Garfield	Charles Guiteau; disgruntled office-seeker, supporter of opposite faction of Republican Party.	pistol, killed	Washington, D.C.	Passing through train station to go on vacation
1901	William McKinley	Leon F. Czolgosz; anarchist ideology	pistol, killed	Buffalo, N.Y.	Standing in reception line at Pan-American Exposition
1912	Theodore Roosevelt (Candidate)	John Schrank; declared insane, had vision that McKinley wanted him to avenge his death.	pistol, wounded	Milwaukee, Wisc.	Leaving hotel to deliver a campaign speech
1933	Franklin D. Roosevelt (President-Elect)	Guiseppe Zangara; hated rulers and capitalists.	pistol, bullets missed the President	Miami, Fla.	Leaving after delivering speech in Bayside Park
1950	Harry S. Truman	Oscar Collazo and Griselio Torresola; Puerto Rican independence.	automatic weapon, prevented from shooting at President	Washington, D.C.	Inside Blair House as assassins attempted to break in
1963	John F. Kennedy	Lee H. Oswald; motive unknown.	rifle, killed	Dallas, Tex.	Taking part in motorcade through Dallas streets
1968	Robert F. Kennedy (Candidate)	Sirhan Sirhan; opposition to U.S. mid-East policy.	pistol, killed	Los Angeles, Calif.	Leaving primary campaign headquarters through hotel kitchen after delivering speech

Source: Task Force Report, *Assassination and Political Violence* (National Commission on the Causes and Prevention of Violence, October, 1969)

xxxii

verdict which the Kerner Commission pronounced upon the scope and costs of its recommendations:

[T]hey neither probe deeper nor demand more than the problems which called them forth. There can be no higher priority for national action and no higher claim on the nation's conscience.

For the past three decades, the primary concerns of the federal government have been the national defense, the conduct of wars and foreign affairs, the growth of the economy, and, more recently, the conquest of space. These problems have consumed the major part of the public attention. They currently devour more than two-thirds of federal expenditures and approximately 50 percent of federal, state, and local expenditures combined.

Traditionally we have left the problems of social justice, provision of essential community services, and law enforcement primarily to the states and cities. In recent years, the federal government has made some major efforts in diverse fields such as rural development, civil rights, medical care, housing, employment, and education, but these efforts have been subordinated to the claims of the "national security."

Yet the federal government still collects the lion's share (about 65 percent) of all tax receipts. Tax revenue available to the states and cities falls woefully below what is needed to discharge their responsibilities. Each one percent rise in the Gross National Product increases the income of the federal government by one and one-half percent, while the normal income of state and city governments increases by less than half that percentage. Concentration on "national" and international problems at the expense of "local" and domestic concerns has left us with an enormous deficit of unmet social needs and deeply-felt social injustices.

Ironically, this gap has appeared despite rapidly accelerating technological, economic and social gains. For the first time in man's history, this nation is nearing the capability of releasing all citizens from the poverty and social privation that hitherto have been accepted as the inevitable lot of mankind. We have also achieved an enormous capacity to communicate: the poor, the black, and other deprived groups among us can see daily on their television sets what they are missing, and how near their release from bondage

xxxiii

can be. But our institutions have not yet made it possible for an expectant populace to achieve what our economy and technology are becoming capable of providing.

In our judgment, the time is upon us for a reordering of national priorities and for a greater investment of resources in the fulfillment of two basic purposes of our Constitution —to "establish justice" and to "insure domestic tranquility."

We solemnly declare our conviction that this nation is entering a period in which our people need to be as concerned by the internal dangers to our free society as by any probable combination of external threats. We recognize that substantial amounts of funds cannot be transferred from sterile war purposes to more productive ones until our participation in the Vietnam war is ended. We also recognize that to make our society essentially free of poverty and discrimination, and to make our sprawling urban areas fit to inhabit, will cost a great deal of money and will take a great length of time. We believe, however, that we can and should make a major decision now to reassess our national priorities by placing these objectives in the first rank of the nation's goals.

The decision that has the greatest effect on the level of our expenditures for these objectives is what we decide to spend on the national defense. For three decades, the national defense has ranked first by far in our scale of priorities, much of the time necessarily so. With occasional exceptions, whatever the Administration has requested for the Armed Forces has been readily granted. Since 1939 there have been a number of occasions when the Administration's budget requests for the Armed Forces have been exceeded by Congressional appropriations; for most other federal programs the opposite is true. For example, actual appropriations for the general welfare (health, labor, education, housing, pollution, and law enforcement) are currently running more than five billion dollars annually below the amounts previously authorized by the Congress.

Our Commission is not competent to recommend a specific level of national defense expenditures. We recognize that without the deterrent capability essential for security against external attack, internal freedom and se-

FIREARMS

1. TOTAL NUMBER OF FIREARMS IN CIVILIAN HANDS (U.S. 1968)

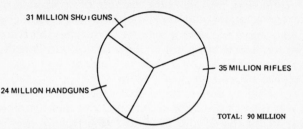

31 MILLION SHOTGUNS

35 MILLION RIFLES

24 MILLION HANDGUNS

TOTAL: 90 MILLION

2. ANNUAL INCREASE IN NUMBER OF FIREARMS IN CIVILIAN HANDS (U.S. 1962 vs. 1968)

RIFLES: 1962, **0.7** MILLION   1968, **1.4** MILLION
SHOTGUNS: 1962, **0.7** MILLION   1968, **1.4** MILLION
HANDGUNS: 1962, **0.6** MILLION   1968, **2.5** MILLION

TOTAL: 1962, **2.1** MILLION   1968, **5.3** MILLION

3. CRIMINAL USES OF FIREARMS (U.S. 1964 vs. 1967)

HOMICIDES: 1964, **55%** WITH FIREARMS   1967, **63%** WITH FIREARMS
AGGRAVATED ASSAULTS: 1964, **15%** WITH FIREARMS   1967, **21%** WITH FIREARMS
ROBBERIES: 1964, NOT AVAILABLE   1967, **37%** WITH FIREARMS

4. DEADLINESS OF FIREARMS ATTACK VS. KNIFE ATTACKS (U.S. 1967)

FIREARMS ATTACKS RESULTING IN DEATH: **12.8 %**
KNIFE ATTACKS RESULTING IN DEATH: **2.9 %**

FIREARMS ATTACKS ARE THUS 4.4 TIMES AS DEADLY AS KNIFE ATTACKS.

5. TYPE OF GUN USED IN CRIMES COMMITTED WITH FIREARMS (LARGE U.S. CITIES 1967)

HOMICIDE   **AGGRAVATED ASSAULT**   **ROBBERY**

92% HANDGUNS   86% HANDGUNS   96% HANDGUNS

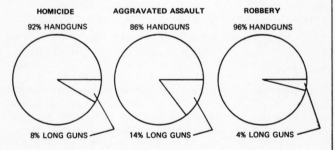

8% LONG GUNS   14% LONG GUNS   4% LONG GUNS

Source: Task Force Report, *Firearms and Violence in American Life* (National Commission on the Causes and Prevention of Violence, July, 1969).

curity would not be possible. It is to be expected that our military leaders will, like other government officials, stress the extreme urgency of the programs under their charge. But we believe the time has come to question whether expenditures for the general welfare should continue to be subordinated to those for national defense.

Defense expenditures, stated in 1968 prices, fell from about 78 billion dollars in 1953 (at the end of the Korean War) to about 60 billion dollars in 1954 and remained at that level for the decade 1955 to 1964. But by 1968 they had risen again to the present 81 billion dollar annual level as the result of our major commitment of troops to Vietnam.[5]

Federal expenditures for the general welfare, while they have increased substantially over the past several years, are now approximately 60 billion dollars, of which $25 billion represents social security payments.

As a first step, we should try to reverse this relationship. When our participation in the Vietnam War is concluded, we recommend increasing annual general welfare expenditures by about 20 billion dollars (stated in 1968 dollars), partly by reducing military expenditures and partly by use of increased tax revenues resulting from the growth of the Gross National Product. We suggest this only as an initial goal; as the Gross National Product and tax revenues continue to rise, we should strive to keep military expenditures level (in constant dollars), while general welfare expenditures should continue to increase until essential social goals are achieved.[6]

Based on estimates of the Council of Economic Advisers,[7] the funds needed to achieve this goal without inflationary consequences could be obtained from two sources:

1. The end of the Vietnam war should reduce defense expenditures by 19 billion dollars annually. The Council anticipates that this reduction will be offset in part by war-end program adjustments and deferred weapons programs. Hence, defense expenditures should go down to about 65 billion dollars (at 1968 prices).[8]

2. The Gross National Product is expected to increase over the next decade (in constant dollars) at the rate of about four percent a year. The same should be true of federal tax reve-

nues, which should grow in real terms at an annual increment of approximately 15 billion dollars.[9] Of this amount, approximately half will be required to meet expected annual increases for "baseline" federal non-defense expenditures other than general welfare programs. Hence, about seven or eight billion dollars more each year than the preceding year should be available for new and expanded programs in the general welfare field.

Whether somewhat more or less than the amounts we have indicated should be provided to overcome social ills is not the important point.[10] What is important is that the people of this nation recognize both the possibilities and the need for choice. For an entire generation, we have necessarily been more aware of and responsive to the external dangers to our society than to the internal dangers. In this Commission's opinion, the internal dangers now demand a greater awareness and a more substantial response—one that can only be made if we face the need to reorder our priorities. It is time to balance the risks and precautions we take abroad against those we take here at home.

The Department of Health, Education, and Welfare has made a suggestion which merits careful consideration as a potentially valuable supplemental step toward reordering national priorities, namely, the preparation of an "Annual Social Report." [11] The Annual Social Report, comparable to the present Annual Economic Report, would provide us with a set of measurements—of "social indicators"—on how well we have done in providing housing, education, health care, public safety, and opportunities for the upward advancement of all sectors of our population. It would tell us whether the disadvantaged groups among us have been advancing at a rate sufficient to foster hope and to quiet the desperation that drives men to violence. It would significantly aid the nation and its leaders in establishing national priorities.

The Social Report would be prepared by social scientists recruited for stated periods of public service from among the nation's best scholars, just as the members and staff of the Council of Economic Advisers are today. They could be organized as a Council of Social Advisers, as are the Economic Advisers, or in some other visible and independent form. A major function of the social science staff would be to develop tools for measuring the comparative effectiveness of social programs. While we have learned a good deal about social stresses and the gross causative factors that require correction, we still know very little about whether particular remedial programs work at all, which ones work better than others, and why. We lack practicable means for measuring cost-benefit ratios, for establishing and observing parallel programs with significant variables, and for putting an end to programs which have failed to justify their continuance.[12] A central staff charged with this responsibility could do much to improve the accuracy of our social planning and the efficacy of on-going programs.

Two decades ago, the Council of Economic Advisers was created by the Full Employment Act of 1946, amid much skepticism about the "science" of economics and particularly about the wisdom and effect of governmental efforts to stimulate or restrain economic activity. Today we recognize the importance of the government's economic role and of national economic measurements, imprecise and imperfect as the economist's tools still are. The other social sciences may now have as much potential for informing wise government policy as economics had twenty years ago.

In a democratic society, the citizens possess the basic social power, and national priorities reflect the value judgments of the majority. Skeptics may thus take a pessimistic view of this Commission's recommendation that our national priorities be reordered. They will point, for example, to the reluctance of the public, despite the penetrating reports and the excellent recommendations of previous presidential commissions, to take the comprehensive actions needed to curb crime, eliminate racial discrimination, and alleviate the problems of the ghetto poor. They will point especially to middle-class America—to the "forgotten American" —and his concern over some consequences of racial integration, his rebellion against rising taxes, his distrust of dissent on the campus and protest movements in the capital. How realistic is it, they will ask, to think that the majority of Americans will support a reallocation of our national resources to deal with social problems?

Skepticism is understandable. But the majority of Americans have always responded constructively to national crises when they have been fully informed and responsibly led. The "silent majority," like most other Americans, do not wish to surrender any of the most important freedoms of our open society—freedom of movement, freedom from harm, freedom from fear. They stand to benefit from the programs necessary to retain these freedoms just as much as any disadvantaged minority. All Americans—the majority and our various minorities—must come to grips with the basic causes of violence in our society and do what must be done to achieve liberty and justice for all.

Some, with little faith in our nation, predict that majority indifference will result in a violent revolution of some kind. Indeed, nihilists and anarchists openly espouse this course. We see signs, however, that a peaceful revolution is already under way: a spirit of needed reform is rising steadily among the people and in the ranks of local and national leaders. We see a growing readiness to formulate new values, to set new priorities, and to make firm commitments now, to be honored as soon as resources are available.

Some ordinary citizens feel they can do nothing to influence the direction and the destiny of their nation. But more and more Americans are proving this to be a myth. A growing number of our citizens have found they need not stand idle while our cities rot, people live in fear, householders build individual fortresses, and human and financial resources flow to less urgent endeavors. A new generation of Americans is emerging, with the energy and the talent and the determination to fulfill the promise of the nation. As it ever was, the young—idealistic but earnest, inexperienced but dedicated—are the spearheads of the drive toward change, and increasing numbers of adult Americans are joining their ranks.

When in man's long history other great civilizations fell, it was less often from external assault than from internal decay. Our own civilization has shown a remarkable capacity for responding to crises and for emerging to higher pinnacles of power and achievement. But our most serious challenges to date have been external—the kind this strong and resourceful country could unite against. While serious external dangers remain, the graver threats today are internal: haphazard urbanization, racial discrimination, disfiguring of the environment, unprecedented interdependence, the dislocation of human identity and motivation created by an affluent society—all resulting in a rising tide of individual and group violence.

The greatness and durability of most civilizations has been finally determined by how they have responded to these challenges from within. Ours will be no exception.

---

1. The Progress Report is reproduced as Appendix 2 to this Report.

2. The contents of these reports are outlined in Appendix 4.

3. We have devoted an entire Chapter of this Report to "The Strengths of America."

4. In Chapter III we define group violence as the unlawful threat or use of force by any group that results or is intended to result in the injury or forcible restraints or intimidation of persons, or the destruction or forcible seizure of property.

5. For fiscal 1970, the budgeted figure is $77 billion.

6. Some experts believe that since military expenditures were successfully held to an annual level of 60 billion dollars (in 1968 prices) for the decade from 1955 to 1964, a comparable plateau can and should be maintained for the decade of the seventies. Indeed, it has been urged that, assuming the success of strategic arms limitation talks and a reevaluation of our foreign commitments, it would be feasible to hold the military budget for the early 1970s to 50 billion dollars (at 1969 prices). See Kaysen. "Military Strategy, Military Forces and Arms Control," in *Agenda for the Nation* (Washington, D.C.: Brookings Institution, 1969), p. 549.

7. Annual report of the Council of Economic Advisers, January, 1969, pp. 199-200.

8. At estimated 1972 prices, for example, actual outlays would be 73 billion. At this point, defense expenditures would be at seven percent of forecast GNP, as compared to perhaps eight percent at present. In other industrially advanced democratic countries, according to the Institute for Strategic Studies, defense expenditures (in 1966) were 6.4 percent of GNP for the United Kingdom, 4.4 percent in France, 3.6 percent in West Germany, 3.3 percent in Italy, 2.2 percent in Canada and 1.1 percent in Japan. For Soviet Russia, the estimated figure is 8.9 percent, but this represents a total 1966 defense outlay of less than 30 billion dollars as compared to about 68 billion dollars for the United States.

9. This estimate assumes that the present 10 percent surcharge will have been repealed, but that other tax reform measures will be neutral in their effect on aggregate revenues. Any substantial reduction in federal tax revenues incidental to tax reform will make it more difficult to reorder our priorities as we have proposed.

10. We further note that the same point can be strongly made for other nonmilitary categories of expenditure that have been built into the federal budget, including agricultural and maritime subsidies, the postal service as presently structured, and space exploration. See Schultze, "Budget Alternatives After Vietnam," in *Agenda for the Nation* (Brookings, 1969), p. 44.

11. *Toward a Social Report*, Government Printing Office, 1969.

12. Daniel P. Moynihan. *Maximum Feasible Misunderstanding* (New York: MacMillan, 1968), pp. 190-203.

*To Establish Justice,
to Insure
Domestic Tranquility*

I ● VIOLENCE IN AMERICAN HISTORY

Because we believe that the past has much to tell us about the present and the future, this Commission has studied the history of violence in America. We wanted to know whether Americans are more violent today than they have been in the past. We studied historical events which parallel current events in hopes of finding basic principles that might guide us toward solutions. Most of all, however, we sought the broad perspective which would help us and our fellow citizens to understand better the nature, the character, and the dilemma of contemporary America.

This study of history has illuminated for us the causes of violence in this nation and some of the ways to reduce it:

1. America has always been a relatively violent nation. Considering the tumultuous historical forces that have shaped the United States, it would be astonishing were it otherwise.

2. Since rapid social change in America has produced different forms of violence with widely varying patterns of motivation, aggression, and victimization, violence in America has waxed and waned with the social tides. The decade just ending, for example, has been one of our most violent eras—although probably not the most violent.

3. Exclusive emphasis in a society on law enforcement rather than on a sensible balance of remedial action and enforcement tends to lead to a decaying cycle in which resistance grows and becomes ever more violent.

4. For remedial social change to be an effective moderator of violence, the changes must command a wide measure of support throughout the community. Official efforts to impose change that is resisted by a dominant majority frequently prompt counter-violence.

5. Finally, Americans have been, paradoxically, both a turbulent people but have enjoyed a relatively stable republic. Our liberal and pluralistic system has historically both generated and accommodated itself to a high level of unrest, and

1

our turmoil has reflected far more demonstration and protest than conspiracy and revolution.

These are a few of the conclusions we have drawn from our study of American history. It is a source of partial consolation and reassurance that our present pattern of violence falls largely within that tradition and that traditionally violence has subsided as political and social institutions gradually responded to the underlying social dislocations and injustices that caused it. But it is a source of great concern that the very velocity of historical change itself has been vastly accelerated by modern technology. Technological progress causes enormous dislocation and demands for social change; our techniques of instant communications intensify these demands manyfold. Whether our political and social institutions can respond as rapidly as new demands arise will largely determine how much violence we are about to experience.

If we are wise—if we listen carefully and watch closely—we will realize that violence is a social bellwether: dramatic rises in its level and modifications in its form (as is the case today) tell us that something important is happening in our political and social systems.

ONE • HISTORICAL ROOTS OF THE AMERICAN CONSENSUS

Our current eruption of violence must appear paradoxical to a generation of Americans who witnessed the emergence from depression to unparalleled affluence of a nation they regarded as the world's moral leader in defense of freedom. Only a decade ago America's historians and behavioral scientists were celebrating the emergence of a unique society, one sustained by a burgeoning prosperity and solidly grounded in a broad political consensus. This "consensus" school of American scholars, and particularly of her historians, was reacting against an older view that had pictured America as a crucible of conflict—colonials against the British, Jeffersonians against the Federalists, Jacksonians against the Bank, North against South, East against West, capital against labor, Republican against Democrat. While regarded as morally as well as materially superior to Eu-

2

rope, America in this older discordant view nonetheless functioned according to a common Western dynamic of class and ideological warfare.

Not so, said the consensus scholars of the 1950s. Rather, America had evolved as a truly unique society in which class, party and sectional divisions only served superficially to blind us to a far greater and distinctive commonality. We were told—and the implications were reassuring—that our uniqueness was derived from a progression of fundamental historical experiences which, mutually reinforcing one another, had joined to propel us toward a manifestly benevolent destiny.

We were, first, a nation of immigrants, culturally enriched by the variety of mankind. From America's melting-pot would emerge a new and superior synthesis of mankind—what Hector St. John de Crévecoeur called "the American, this new man." It is hard, from the perspective of the latter third of the 20th century, to recapture the grandeur of this noble dream—as did Emma Lazarus, writing a century earlier in "The New Colossus":

> Give me your tired, your poor,
> Your huddled masses yearning to breathe free,
> The wretched refuse of your teeming shore,
> Send these, the homeless, tempest-tossed, to me:
> I lift my lamp beside the golden door.

In the introduction to his Pulitzer Prize-winning book on American immigrants, *The Uprooted,* Oscar Handlin wrote: "Once I thought to write a history of the immigrants in America. Then I discovered that the immigrants *were* American history."

What did these millions of immigrants encounter upon their arrival in the New World? They found a vast and rich continent, thinly populated by native "Indians" who were themselves Asian immigrants from millenia past. In the extraordinary three-century process of exploring and settling this fertile wilderness, the American immigrants and their progeny were themselves transformed into the unique American democrat. The frontier, in the view of its most celebrated historian, Frederick Jackson Turner, lured the discontented and the dispossessed, the restive and the ambitious. This second formative influence encouraged ingenuity, demanded self-reliance, broke down class distinc-

3

tions, nurtured opposition to governmental coercion, reinforced the sanctity of private property and contract, and fostered political individualism. Though many were illiterate, America's immigrants insisted upon universal education as a prerequisite for an informed and productive citizenry. Universal education profoundly shaped the American character, thus contributing to America's uniqueness, power, and creative enterprise.

These distinctive traits, the American democratic ethos, were probably more reflected in than molded by the third historical source of our unique commonality: the American Revolution. We were told by the consensus historians that our revolution was essentially a *conservative* revolution, in that it achieved independence, through a surgical separation from Britain, for a "nation" that had already evolved its liberal ethos and lacked only the acute self-awareness that anti-colonial revolution inevitably brings.

Hence the new Federal Constitution and government forged by the founding fathers rested squarely upon a common ideology of Lockean-Jeffersonian liberalism, our fourth historic well-spring of American uniqueness. This liberal creed was shared by virtually all Americans, whether self-consciously or not—whether Federalist, Whig, Democrat or Republican—for a revealingly *negative* reason: America lacked a feudal past. In the Old World, encumbered as it was by an ancient feudal tradition, the fires of social revolution raged in societies deeply cleft by divisions of class and ideology. Hence, in Europe, the ideological spectrum would remain broad, and legions on the far left and the far right would make socialism and communism and fascism possible. But in pragmatic and no-feudal America, ideological loyalties remained tightly clustered around the liberal center and extremist politics could find no sizeable constituency.

This celebration of the American liberal consensus must be qualified historically by acknowledging the prominent exception of the "reactionary enlightenment" of the southern slavocracy. But every schoolboy knows that this near-fatal flaw was purged by the Civil War, and that this cancerous contradiction between the Declaration of Independence and the Constitution was at last resolved in favor of the former by the addition to the latter of the

4

13th, 14th, and 15th Amendments. During Reconstruction the South also was committed to provide free public education to all citizens, thereby belatedly embracing the crucial American doctrine that democracy depends upon a literate and informed as well as a free electorate.

Hence, also when the next major historical transformation swept America, the urban-industrial revolution, America accomplished it with turbulence but without Marx. Whereas labor in Europe, given the Old World's feudal legacy of acute class consciousness, had rather automatically gone socialist, American workers virtually ignored socialism and produced instead the solidly capitalist AF of L and CIO. Given "Americanism," who needed socialism —or any other "ism?" American workers did not hate Andrew Carnegie; they wanted to *become* an Andrew Carnegie. And, uniquely in rags-to-riches America, that seemed possible, for America was clearly destined to become the richest nation in the world.

Affluence, then, was perhaps the climactic historical source of American uniqueness. According to the foremost historian of the American national character, David M. Potter, Americans have been most characteristically a "people of plenty." American abundance was perhaps the keystone of the unique American arch. It made viable the pressure-relieving, rags-to-riches dream of upward mobility. It made the two-party system stable and workable by guaranteeing that transitions in power—between two parties that did not differ ideologically very much anyway— would also make relatively small difference in the distribution of property. (Abundance thereby afforded America the luxury of apathetic voters.) Indeed, abundance probably made democracy itself possible, by cushioning the abrasions inherent in an aggressive society bent on maximizing both the exercise of rights and the accumulation of property. The system was admittedly imperfect; for liberal, pluralistic societies inherently tolerate a measure of inequity as the price extracted by equality of opportunity. But the established system had produced in the aggregate a democratic nation unmatched in longevity of Constitution and currency, two-party stability, exercise of civil liberties, and standard of living.

It was a just and proud legacy, one which seemed to

5

make sense in the relatively tranquil 1950s. America could still vividly remember then that even when the Great Depression had devastated the Western world and so much of Europe had turned in desperation to extreme ideologies of the left and right, America had simply once again switched leaders and parties. Turning her back, as ever, on red flags and brown shirts, she had shored up her rickety capitalism by reforming it through the New Deal. Changes were wrought which legitimized the power of government to shape economic forces in the interests of the general welfare, reduced the power of the capitalist elite, and broadened the popular base of participation in the economic system. Concurrently, America muddled through until World War II brought both recovery and—characteristically for America—victory. Indeed, the consensus view of the American past seemed ideally constructed to ratify the present: locked in a Cold War with totalitarian communism, the United States represented not only the powerful and self-acknowledged leader of the free world, but also a politically stable and democratic model society that the rest of the world might seek to emulate.

TWO • THE ROOTS OF AMERICAN DISCONTENT

With the 1960s came shock and frustration. It was a decade against itself: the students of affluence were marching in the streets; the nation that had never lost a war to any power was mired in a seemingly endless, unpopular, and possibly unwinnable land war in Asia; the national consciousness was shocked by savage assassinations; and Negro Americans were responding to ostensible victories in civil rights and to their collectively unprecedented prosperity with a paradoxical venting of outrage. It seemed as if America, so long especially blessed by the fates, had suddenly been cheated. Emerging victorious from the world war against fascism, she faced not a century of Pax Americana (as had her British counterparts faced a century of Pax Britannica) but, instead, frustrating cold and hot war abroad and turmoil at home. How could the violent 1960s be explained in the light of our past?

Historical analysis of our national experience and char-

6

acter would suggest that the seeds of our contemporary discontent were to a large extent deeply embedded in those same ostensibly benevolent forces which had contributed to our uniqueness. First, we are indeed a nation of immigrants, but one in which the original dominant immigrant group, the so-called Anglo-Saxons, effectively preempted the crucial levers of economic and political power in government, commerce, and the professions. This elite group has consistently resisted—though by no means with uniform success—the upward strivings of successive "ethnic" immigrant waves. The resultant competitive hierarchy of immigrants has always been highly conducive to violence, but this violence has taken different forms. The Anglo-Americans used their access to the levers of power to maintain their dominance, using legal force surrounded by an aura of legitimacy for such ends as economic exploitation; the restriction of immigration by a national-origin quota system which clearly branded later immigrants from southern and eastern Europe and from Asia as culturally undesirable; the confinement of the original Indian immigrants largely to barren reservations; and the restriction of blacks first to slavery, then to a degraded caste. Periodically in times of national crisis, dominant Anglo-Americans rallied to "nativist" movements that directed violence toward "ethnic" scapegoats: in the 1790s with the Alien and Sedition Acts; in the 1850s with the sectional split; in the decade 1886–96 with unrestricted immigration and labor and racial unrest; in World War I with the Red Scare; in World War II with the Nisei.

But the system was also conducive to violence among competing racial and ethnic groups themselves. The massive New York draft riots of 1863 prompted thousands of poor Irish, who felt the brunt of an inequitable conscription that allowed wealthy men to purchase substitutes, to vent their wrath upon New York's Negroes. Much of the inter-ethnic hostility has flowed from genuine economic competition among lower class Americans, and this source of ethnic antagonism has historically been exacerbated by the tendency of American industrialists to combat union organizers by employing black "scabs" and strikebreakers. This practice most clearly linked two mutually supportive sources of social anxiety: economic threat and status frus-

7

tration. Given America's unprecedented ethnic pluralism, simply being born American conferred no automatic and equal citizenship in the eyes of the larger society. In the face of such reservations, ethnic minorities had constantly to affirm their Americanism through a kind of patriotic ritual which intensified the ethnic competition for status and invited severe and abiding conflict.

The second major formative historical experience was America's prolonged encounter with the frontier. While the frontier experience indubitably strengthened the mettle of the American character, it also witnessed the brutal and brutalizing ousting of the Indians and the forceful incorporation of Mexican and other original inhabitants, and fastened into the American character a tenacious habit of wastefully exploiting our natural resources. Further, it concomitantly created an environment in which, owing to the paucity of law enforcement agencies, a tradition of vigilante "justice" was legitimized. Originally prompted by frontier lawlessness and inspired—or at least rationalized—by the doctrines of self-preservation, the right of revolution, popular sovereignty and the Higher Law, American vigilantism has historically enjoyed powerful ideological support. Vigilantism has persisted as a socially malleable instrument long after the disappearance of the frontier environment that gave it birth, and it has proved quite congenial to an urban setting. The longevity of the Ku Klux Klan and the vitality both of contemporary urban rioting and of the stiffening resistance to it owe much to this tradition.

Third, the revolutionary doctrine that our Declaration of Independence proudly proclaims is mistakenly cited as a model for legitimate violence by contemporary groups such as militant Negroes and radical students who confront a system of both public and private government that they regard as contemptuous of their consent. Entranced by the resurgence of revolution in the underdeveloped world and of international university unrest, radical students and blacks seize upon our early doctrine of the inherent right of revolution and self-determination to justify their rebellion. That their analogies are fatefully problematical in no way dilutes the majesty of our own proud Declaration.

The fourth historic legacy, our consensual political philosophy of Lockean-Jeffersonian liberalism, was premised

8

upon a pervasive fear of governmental power and has reinforced the tendency to define freedom negatively as freedom *from*. As a consequence, conservatives have been able paradoxically to invoke the doctrines of Jefferson in resistance to legislative reforms, and the Sumnerian imperative that "stateways cannot change folkways" has historically enjoyed a wide and not altogether unjustified allegiance in the public eye. Its implicit corollary has been that forceful, and, if necessary, violent local and state resistance to unpopular federal stateways is a legitimate response; both Calhoun and Wallace could confidently repair to a strict construction of the same document invoked by Lincoln and the Warren court.

This ability of the American liberal consensus to encompass widely divergent social views within a common framework of constitutionalism was clearly demonstrated by the failure of Reconstruction following the Civil War. While the taut prohibition of the 13th Amendment permitted no ambiguity concerning slavery, the conservative Supreme Court of the post-war years consistently demonstrated the extraordinary flexibility of judicial construction in largely eviscerating the substance and perverting the purpose of the 14th and 15th Amendments and the social reform of Reconstruction law. The resultant hypocrisy for generations made a mockery of liberal rhetoric and fueled the fires of alienation. Black education became separate and manifestly unequal, yet for a century the local bias of Jeffersonian liberalism effectively blocked federal assistance or intervention. The massive expansion of public education in recent years, together with the social reform of the Second Reconstruction, has to some extent bolstered public faith in the contemporary efficacy and relevance of the American liberal tradition and particularly its commitment to free public education. But this proud commitment has too often been advanced as a panacea wherein America's schools are expected somehow to solve her most deeply-rooted social problems.

The next historic source both of our modern society and our current plight, following Civil War and Reconstruction, has been our industrial revolution and the great internal migration from the countryside to the city. Yet the process occurred with such astonishing rapidity that it

9

produced widespread socioeconomic dislocation in an environment in which the internal controls of the American social structure were loose and the external controls were weak. Urban historian Richard Wade has observed that—

The cities inherited no system of police control adequate to the numbers or to the rapid increase of the urban centers. The modern police force is the creation of the 20th century; the establishment of genuinely professional systems is historically a very recent thing. Throughout the 18th and 19th century, the force was small, untrained, poorly paid, and part of the political system. In case of any sizeable disorder, it was hopelessly inadequate; and rioters sometimes routed the constabulary in the first confrontation.

Organized labor's protracted and bloody battles for recognition and power occurred during these years of minimal control and maximal social upheaval. The violence of workers' confrontation with their employers was partly the result of a lack of consensus on the legitimacy of workers' protests, partly the result of the lack of means of social control. Workers used force to press their grievances, employers organized violent resistance, and repeatedly state or federal troops had to be summoned to restore order.

The final distinctive characteristic—in many ways perhaps our most distinctive—has been our unmatched prosperity. Ranked celestially with life and liberty in the sacrosanct Lockean trilogy, property has generated a quest and prompted a devotion in the American character that has matched our devotion to equality and, in a fundamental sense, has transformed the idea of equality from the radical leveling of the European democratic tradition into a typically American insistence upon equality of *opportunity*. In an acquisitive society of individuals with unequal talents and groups with unequal advantages, this had resulted in an unequal distribution of the rapid accumulation of abundance that, especially since World War II, has promised widespread participation in the affluent society to a degree unprecedented in history. Central to the notion of "revolutions of rising expectations" is the assumption that improved economic rewards can coincide with and often obscure a degree of *relative* deprivation that generates frustration and can prompt men toward violent protest despite measurable gains. Revolutions have not historically occurred in stagnant and utterly destitute nations; rather, they have occurred in nations in which rising but uneven prosperity at once inspired hope and intensified frustrations and impatience with the old order.

THREE • VIOLENCE IN THE AMERICAN TRADITION

Our historical evolution, then, has given our national character a dual nature: we strive for both liberty and equality, which can be—and often in practice are—quite contradictory goals. This is not to suggest that American society is grounded in a fatal contradiction. For all the conflict inherent in a simultaneous quest for liberty and equality, American history is replete with dramatic instances of the successful adjustment of "the system" to the demands of disparate protesting groups. An historical appraisal of these genuine achievements should give pause to contemporary Cassandras who bemoan in self-flagellation how hopelessly wretched we all are. To be sure, these radically disillusioned social critics can find abundant evil in our historical legacy: centuries of Negro slavery, the cultural deracination and near extinction of the Indians, our initiation of atomic destruction—*ad infinitum*. But these radical new social critics in their overcompensations tend to distort the American experience in much the same fashion, although in an opposite direction, as have the more familiar superpatriotic celebrants of American virtuosity. Even so, a careful and honest historical appraisal should remind us that violence has been far more intrinsic to our past than we should like to think.

Although violence has been a disagreeably persistent characteristic of American social life, this recurrent theme of violence has taken different forms in response to America's rapidly changing social context. Historical analysis suggests that while much of the American violence was prompted by environmental conditions that no longer exist, many of the social tensions that produced violence are recurrent and remain of contemporary relevance.

Perhaps the historically violent American episode that is least relevant to our contemporary concerns is the family

11

feud. The famous and colorful clan feuding of Hatfields versus McCoys and Suttons versus Taylors seems to have been triggered by the Civil War in border areas where loyalties were sharply divided and where the large extended family of the 19th century provided both a focus for intense loyalties and a ready instrument of aggression. But this tradition has waned with the fading of the peculiar circumstances that conditioned its birth. It is arguable, however, that the brutalizing traditions associated with the Indian wars have left their callous imprint on our national character long after the estimated 850,000 to one million American Indians had been ruthlessly reduced by 1950 to 400,000. Similarly, the violence associated with the American Revolution, the Civil War, and the two Reconstructions has surely reinforced the ancient notion that the end justifies the means.

Whether the long association with violence of agrarian uprising and the labor movement has permanently faded with changing modern circumstances is fervently to be hoped, but by no means certain. Employer acceptance of unions during and after the New Deal suggests that that long and bloody conflict is largely behind us. But the growing guild-like defensiveness and exclusiveness of especially those unions threatened by automation, together with the persistent reality that the majority of American laborers—especially black workers—remain outside the unions, invite a resurgence of intramural labor unrest. Also, the stubborn persistence of rural poverty constitutes a latent invitation to a resurgence of latter-day populism.

Two other sordid American traditions that have largely waned but that recently have shown some signs of revival are vigilantism and lynching. If vigilantism is defined broadly to include regional and even national movements as well as local organizations, then America's preeminent vigilante movement has been the Ku Klux Klan—or rather, the Ku Klux Klans, for there have essentially been three of them. The original Klan arose in the South in response to radical Reconstruction and, through terror and intimidation, was instrumental in the "redemption" of the southern state governments by white conservatives. The second Klan, by far the largest, was resurrected in Atlanta in 1915 and boomed nationally in the 1920s. Strong in the Midwest and Far West as well as in the South, and making inroads even in the cities, the Klan of the 1920s—despite its traditional racist and xenophobic rhetoric—focused its chastisement less upon Negroes, Catholics, and Jews than upon white Protestants who were adjudged guilty of violating smalltown America's Victorian moral code. The third Klan represented a proliferation of competing Klans in the South in response to the civil rights movement of the 1950s. Generally lacking the prestige and organizational strength of the earlier Klans, the groups of lower-class whites engaged in a period of unrestrained terrorism in the rural and smalltown Black Belt South in the 1950s and early 1960s, but have belatedly been brought under greater control.

Lynching, vigilantism's supreme instrument of terror and summary "justice," has been widely practiced in America since the Revolution era, when miscreant Tories were tarred and feathered, and worse. Although lynching is popularly associated with racial mob murder, this pattern is historically a relatively recent one, for prior to the late 19th century, white Americans perforce lynched one another—Negro slaves being far too valuable to squander at the stake. But lynching became predominantly racial from 1882 to 1903, when 1,985 Negroes were murdered in the tragic but successful effort of those years to forge a rigid system of biracial caste, most brutal and explicit in the South but generally reflective of national attitudes. Once the point that this was a white man's country was made, lynching gradually declined. Its recent resurgence in response to the civil rights movement is notorious, but it nowhere approximates its scale at the turn of the century.

The contemporary relevance of political assassination and freelance multiple murder needs no documentation to a nation that has so recently witnessed the murders of John and Robert Kennedy, Dr. Martin Luther King, and, on television, Lee Harvey Oswald—in addition to the chilling mass slaughtering sprees of Charles Whitman in Austin and Richard Speck in Chicago. Historically, political assassination has become a recurrent feature of the American political system only in the South during (the first) Reconstruction and in the New Mexico Territory. Although four American Presidents have been assassinated since 1865, prominent politicians and civil servants occupying

13

the myriad lesser levels of government have been largely immune. Whether the current spate of public murder is an endemic symptom of a new social malaise is a crucial question that history cannot yet answer, other than to observe that precedents in our past are minimal.

Similarly, historical precedents are few regarding massive student and anti-war protests. American students have historically engaged in food riots and succumbed to the annual spring throes of the panty-raid syndrome, but the current wave of campus confrontations is essentially an unprecedented phenomenon—as is the massive and prolonged opposition to the war in Vietnam. But the size of and sophistication of the contemporary college student body are also unprecedented. Now outnumbering America's farmers by almost three million, America's seven million college students confront, largely without votes, a society that nags the conscience of the best of them by sending younger non-college students off to an unpopular war in Asia, and threatens their security and careers by greeting them with the same grim summons upon graduation. We have lived with these harsh realities before—unpopular wars, inequitable conscription, threatened young men—but never in such potent combination. Unfortunately, in this regard, the past does not have much to tell us; we will have to make our history along uncharted and frightening ways.

But the past has much to tell us about the rioting and crime that have gripped our cities. Urban mobs are as old as the city itself. Colonial seaports frequently were rocked for days by roving mobs—groups of unruly and often drunken men whose energies were shrewdly put to political purpose as Liberty Boys in the American Revolution. Indeed, our two principal instruments of physical control evolved directly in response to 19th-century urban turmoil. The professional city police system replaced the inadequate constabulary and watch-and-ward in response to the urban rioting of the 1840s and 1850s, largely in the Northeast. Similarly, the national guard was organized in order to control the labor violence—or more appropriately, the anti-labor violence—of the 1880s and 1890s.

14

FOUR • CONCLUSION

Probably all nations are given to a kind of historical amnesia or selective recollection that masks unpleasant traumas of the past. Certainly, Americans since the Puritans have historically regarded themselves as a latter-day "Chosen People" sent on a holy errand to the wilderness, there to create a New Jerusalem. One beneficent side effect of our current turmoil may be to force a harder and more candid look at our past.

Violence has usually been the lava flowing from the top of a volcano fed by deeper fires of social dislocation and injustice; it has not been stopped solely by capping the top, but has usually subsided when our political and social institutions have managed to make the adjustments necessary to cool the fires below. If our future is to be more just, less violent, less crime-ridden, and free of fear, we obviously must do much better than we are now doing to speed social reform and simultaneously improve the effectiveness of the entire law enforcement system of the nation. Only in an orderly society can we achieve the advances which militants and moderates alike know are required.

II • VIOLENT CRIME: HOMICIDE, ASSAULT, RAPE, ROBBERY*

When citizens express concern about high levels of violence in the United States, they have in mind a number of different types of events: homicides and assaults, rioting and looting, clashes between demonstrators and police, student seizures of university buildings, violence in the entertainment media, assassinations of national leaders. Foremost in their minds, no doubt, is what appears to be a rising tide of individual acts of violent crime, especially "crime in the streets."

Only a fraction of all crime is violent, of course. Major

*An edited version of statement issued November 24, 1969.

15

crimes of violence—homicide, rape, robbery, and assault —represent only 13 percent (or 588,000) of the Federal Bureau of Investigation's Index of reported serious crimes (about 4.5 million in 1968).[1] Moreover, deaths and personal injuries from violent crime cause only a small part of the pain and suffering which we experience: one is five times more likely to die in an auto accident than to be criminally slain, and one hundred times more likely to be injured in a home accident than in a serious assault.

But to suffer deliberate violence is different from experiencing an accident, illness or other misfortune. In violent crime man becomes a wolf to man, threatening or destroying the personal safety of his victim in a terrifying act. Violent crime (particularly street crime) engenders fear—the deep-seated fear of the hunted in the presence of the hunter. Today this fear is gnawing at the vitals of urban America.

In a recent national survey, half of the women and one-fifth of the men said they were afraid to walk outdoors at night, even near their homes. One-third of American householders keep guns in the hope that they will provide protection against intruders. In some urban neighborhoods, nearly one-third of the residents wish to move because of high rates of crime, and very large numbers have moved for that reason. In fear of crime, bus drivers in many cities do not carry change, cab drivers in some areas are in scarce supply, and some merchants are closing their businesses. Vigilante-like groups have sprung up in some areas.

Fear of crime is destroying some of the basic human freedoms which any society is supposed to safeguard— freedom of movement, freedom from harm, freedom from fear itself. Is there a basis for this fear? Is there an unprecedented increase in violent crime in this country? Who and where are most of the violent criminals and what makes them violent? What can we do to eliminate the causes of that violence?

ONE • PROFILE OF VIOLENT CRIME

Between 1960 and 1968, the national rate of criminal homicide per 100,000 population increased 36 percent,

16

the rate of forcible rape 65 percent, of aggravated assault 67 percent, and of robbery 119 percent. These figures are from the *Uniform Crime Reports* published by the Federal Bureau of Investigation. These Reports are the only national indicators we have of crime in America. But, as the FBI recognizes, they must be used with caution.

There is a large gap between the reported rates and the true rates. In 1967 the President's Commission on Law Enforcement and Administration of Justice stated that the true rate of total major violent crime was roughly twice as high as the reported rate.[2] This ratio has probably been a changing one. Decreasing public tolerance of crime is seemingly causing more crimes to be reported. Changes in police practices, such as better recording procedures and more intensive patrolling, are causing police statistics to dip deeper into the large well of unreported crime. Hence, some part of the increase in reported rates of violent crime is no doubt due to a fuller disclosure of the violent crimes actually committed.

Moreover, while current rates compare unfavorably, even alarmingly, with those of the 1950s, fragmentary information available indicates that at the beginning of this century there was an upsurge in violent crime which probably equaled today's levels. In 1916, the city of Memphis reported a homicide rate more than seven times its present rate. Studies in Boston, Chicago and New York during the years of the First World War and the 1920s showed violent crime rates considerably higher than those evident in the first published national crime statistics in 1933.

Despite all these factors, it is still clear that *significant and disturbing increases in the true rates of homicide and, especially, of assault and robbery have occurred over the last decade.*

While the reported incidence of forcible rape has also increased, reporting difficulties associated with this crime are too great to permit any firm conclusion on the true rate of increase.

Violent crimes are not evenly distributed throughout the nation. Using new data from a Victim-Offender Survey conducted by our staff Task Force on Individual Acts of

17

Violence, standard data from the FBI, and facts from other recent studies, we can sketch a more accurate profile of violent crime in the United States than has hitherto been possible. We note, however, that our information about crime is still unsatisfactory and that many critical details in the profile of violent crime remain obscure. Moreover, we strongly urge all who study this profile to keep two facts constantly in mind. First, violent crime is to be found in all regions of the country, and among all groups of the population—not just in the areas and groups of greatest concentration to which we draw attention. Second, despite heavy concentrations of crime in certain groups, the overwhelming majority of individuals in these groups are law-abiding citizens.

1. *Violent crime in the United States is primarily a phenomenon of large cities. This is a fact of central importance.*

The 26 cities with 500,000 or more residents and containing about 17 percent of our total population contribute about 45 percent of the total reported major violent crimes. Six cities with one million or more residents and having ten percent of our total population contribute 30 percent of the total reported major violent crimes.

Large cities uniformly have the highest reported violent crime levels per unit of population.[3] Smaller cities, suburbs and rural areas have lower levels. The average rate of major violent offenses in cities of over 250,000 inhabitants is eleven times greater than in rural areas, eight times greater than in suburban areas, and five and one-half times greater than in cities with 50,000 to 100,000 inhabitants.

For cities of all sizes, as well as for suburbs and rural areas, there has been a recent upward trend in violent crime; the increase in the city rate has been much more dramatic than that for the other areas and subdivisions.

The result in our larger cities is a growing risk of victimization: in Baltimore, the nation's leader in violent crime, the risk of being the victim of a reported violent crime is one in 49 per year. Thus, in the context of major violent crimes, the popular phrase "urban crisis" is pregnant with meaning.

2. *Violent crime in the city is overwhelmingly committed by males.*

18

Judgments about overall trends and levels of violent crime, and about variations in violent crime according to city size, can be based upon reported offense data. But conclusions about the sex, age, race and socioeconomic status of violent offenders can be based only on arrest data. Besides the gap previously mentioned between true offense rates and reported offense rates, we must now deal also with the even larger gap between *offenses reported* and *arrests made*. Accordingly, conclusions in these areas must be drawn with extreme care, especially since arrests, as distinguished from convictions, are made by policemen whose decisions in apprehending suspects thus determine the nature of arrest statistics.[4]

In spite of the possibly wide margins of error, however, one fact is clearly indisputable: violent crimes in urban areas are disproportionately caused by male offenders. To the extent that females are involved, they are more likely to commit the more "intimate" violent crimes like homicide than the "street crimes" like robbery. Thus, the 1968 reported male homicide rate was five times higher than the female rate; the robbery rate twenty times higher.

3. *Violent crime in the city is concentrated especially among youths between the ages of fifteen and twenty-four.*

Urban arrest rates for homicide are much higher among the 18-24 age group than among any other; for rape, robbery and aggravated assault, arrests in the 15-24 age group far outstrip those of any other group. Moreover, it is in these age groups that the greatest increases in all arrest rates have occurred. Surprisingly, however, there have also been dramatic and disturbing increases in arrest rates of the 10-14 age group for two categories—a 300 percent increase in assault between 1958 and 1967, and 200 percent in robbery in the same period.

4. *Violent crime in the city is committed primarily by individuals at the lower end of the occupational scale.*

Although there are no regularly collected national data on the socioeconomic status of violent offenders, local studies indicate that poor and uneducated individuals with few employment skills are much more likely to commit serious violence than persons higher on the socioeconomic

19

ladder. A forthcoming University of Pennsylvania study of youthful male offenders in Philadelphia, for example, will show that boys from lower income areas in the city have delinquency rates for assaultive crimes nearly five times the rates of boys from higher income areas; delinquency rates for robbery are six times higher.[5] Other studies have found higher involvement in violence by persons at the lower end of the occupational scale. A succession of studies at the University of Pennsylvania, using Philadelphia police data, show that persons ranging from skilled laborers to the unemployed constitute about 90-95 percent of the criminal homicide offenders, 90 percent of the rape offenders and 92-97 percent of the robbery offenders. A St. Louis study of aggravated assault found that blue collar workers predominate as offenders. The District of Columbia Crime Commission found more than 40 percent of the major violent crime offenders to be unemployed.

5. *Violent crime in the cities stems disproportionately from the ghetto slum where most Negroes live.*

Reported national urban arrests rates are much higher for Negroes than for whites in all four major violent crime categories, ranging from ten or eleven times higher for assault and rape to sixteen or seventeen times higher for robbery and homicide.[6] As we shall show, these differences in urban violent crime rates are not, in fact, racial; they are primarily a result of conditions of life in the ghetto slum. The gap between Negro and white crime rates can be expected to close as the opportunity gap between Negro and white also closes—a development which has not yet occurred.

The large national urban differentials between Negroes and whites are also found in the more intensive Philadelphia study previously cited. Of 10,000 boys born in 1945, some 50 percent of the three thousand non-whites had had at least one police contact by age 18, compared with 20 percent of the seven thousand whites. (A police contact means that the subject was taken into custody for an offense other than a traffic violation and a report recording his alleged offense was prepared and retained in police files.) The differences were most pronounced for the major violent offenses: of fourteen juveniles who had police con-

20

tacts for homicide, all were non-whites; of 44 who had police contacts for rape, 86 percent were non-whites and fourteen percent whites; of 193 who had police contacts for robbery, 90 percent were non-whites and ten percent whites; and of 220 who had police contacts for aggravated assault, 82 percent were non-whites and eighteen percent whites. When the three sets of figures for rape, robbery and assault are related to the number of non-whites and whites, respectively, in the total group studies (3,000 vs. 7,000), the differences between the resulting ratios closely reflect the differentials in the national urban arrest rates of non-whites and whites in the 10-17 age group.

6. *The victims of assaultive violence in the cities generally have the same characteristics as the offenders: victimization rates are generally highest for males, youths, poor persons, and blacks. Robbery victims, however, are very often older whites.*

There is a widespread public misconception that most violent crime is committed by black offenders against white victims. This is not true. Our Task Force Victim-Offender Survey covering seventeen cities has confirmed other evidence that serious assaultive violence in the city—homicide, aggravated assault and rape—is predominantly between white offenders and white victims and black offenders and black victims. The majority of these crimes involves blacks attacking blacks, while most of the remainder involve whites victimizing whites. Indeed, our Survey found that 90 percent of urban homicide, aggravated assaults and rapes involve victims and offenders of the same race.

In two-thirds of homicides and aggravated assaults in the city, and in three-fifths of the rapes, the victim is a Negro. Rape victims tend strongly to be younger women; the victims of homicide and aggravated assault are usually young males but include a high proportion of older persons. Nearly four-fifths of homicide victims and two-thirds of the assault victims are male. Generalizing from these data, we may say that the typical victim of a violent assaultive crime is a young Negro male, or in the case of rape, a young Negro woman.

Robbery, on the other hand, is the one major violent crime in the city with a high inter-racial component: although about 38 percent of robberies in the Survey involve

21

Negro offenders and victims, 45 percent involve Negroes robbing whites—very often young black males robbing somewhat older white males. In three-fifths of all robberies the victim is white and nearly two-thirds of the time he or she is age 26 or over. Four-fifths of the time the victim is a man.

Data collected by the Crime Commission indicate that victimization rates for violent crimes are much higher in the lower-income groups. This is clearly true for robbery and rape, where persons with incomes under $6,000 were found to be victimized three to five times more often than persons with incomes over $6,000. The same relation held, but less strongly, for aggravated assault, while homicide victimization rates by income could not be computed under the investigative techniques used.

7. *Unlike robbery, the other violent crimes of homicide, assault and rape tend to be acts of passion among intimates and acquaintances.*

The Victim-Offender Survey shows that homicide and assault usually occur between relatives, friends or acquaintances (about two-thirds to three-fourths of the cases in which the relationship is known). They occur in the home or other indoor locations about 50-60 percent of the time. Rape is more likely to be perpetrated by a stranger (slightly over half of the cases), usually in the home or other indoor location (about two-thirds of the time). By contrast, robbery is usually committed outside (two-thirds of the cases) by a stranger (more than 80 percent of the cases).

The victim, the offender, or both are likely to have been drinking prior to homicide, assault, and rape, and the victim often provokes or otherwise helps precipitate the crime. The ostensible motives in homicide and assault are often relatively trivial, usually involving spontaneous altercations, family quarrels, jealous rages, and the like. The two crimes are similar; there is often no reason to believe that the person guilty of homicide sets out with any more intention to harm than the one who commits an aggravated assault. Except for the seriousness of the final outcomes, the major distinction is that homicides most often involve handguns while knives are most common in assault.[7]

8. *By far the greatest proportion of all serious violence is committed by repeaters.*

While the number of hard-core repeaters is small compared to the number of one-time offenders, the former group has a much higher rate of violence and inflicts considerably more serious injury. In the Philadelphia study, 627 of the 10,000 boys were chronic offenders, having five or more police contacts. Though they represented only six percent of the boys in the study, they accounted for 53 percent of the police contacts for personal attacks—homicide, rape and assault—and 71 percent of the contacts for robberies.

Offenders arrested for major criminal violence generally have long criminal histories, but these careers are mainly filled with offenses other than the final serious acts. Generally, though there are many exceptions, the more serious the crime committed, the less chance it will be repeated.

9. *Americans generally are no strangers to violent crime.*

Although it is impossible to determine accurately how many Americans commit violent crimes each year,[8] the data that are available suggest that the number is substantial, ranging from perhaps 600,000 to 1,000,000—or somewhere between one in every 300 and one in every 150 persons. Undoubtedly, a far greater number commit a serious violent crime at some time in their lives. The Philadelphia study found that of about 10,000 boys 35 percent (3475) were taken into police custody for delinquency, and of the delinquents ten percent (363) were apprehended once or more for a major crime of violence before age eighteen.

A comparison of reported violent crime rates in this country with those in other modern, stable nations shows the United States to be the clear leader. Our homicide rate is more than twice that of our closest competitor, Finland, and from four to twelve times higher than the rates in a dozen other advanced countries including Japan, Canada, England and Norway. Similar patterns are found in the rates of other violent crimes: averages computed for the years 1963-1967 show the United States rape rate to be twelve times that of England and Wales and three times that of Canada; our robbery rate is nine times that of Eng-

23

land and Wales and double that of Canada; our aggravated assault rate is double that of England and Wales and eighteen times that of Canada.

TWO • CAUSES OF VIOLENT CRIME

Violent crime occurs in many places and among all races, but we have just shown that it is heavily concentrated in large cities and especially among poor black young men in the ghettos. We must therefore focus on the conditions of life for the youth of the inner-city to find the root causes of a high percentage of violent crime.

Much has been written about inner-city slums where crime and delinquency are bred.[9] Social scientists have analyzed slum conditions and their casual link to crime and violence, writers and artists have dramatized the sordidness and the frustrations of life in the inner cities, and a number of Commissions prior to this one have produced comprehensive reports on this subject. In its 1967 Report the Crime Commission described the linkage between violent crime and slum conditions in large cities as "one of the most fully documented facts about crime." Referring to numerous studies conducted over a period of years, the Commission found that violent crime, its offenders and its victims are found most often in urban areas characterized by:

- low income
- physical deterioration
- dependency
- racial and ethnic concentrations
- broken homes
- working mothers
- low levels of education and vocational skills
- high unemployment
- high proportions of single males
- overcrowded and substandard housing
- low rates of home ownership or single family dwellings
- mixed land use
- high population density.[10]

A series of studies by Clifford Shaw and Henry McKay remains the classic investigation of these ecological patterns.[11] Extensive data on the distribution of delinquency among neighborhoods were collected in a number of large American cities, and the results for Chicago have recently been updated to cover the period from 1900 through 1965. Finding uniformly high correlations between delinquency and areas having the characteristics listed above, Shaw and McKay focused on the process of change in the communities studied.

Neighborhoods disrupted by population movements and social change contained high proportions of delinquents. Although the same central core areas tended to experience social change and high delinquent rates over time, high or low delinquent rates were not permanently associated with any particular ethnic or racial group. The newest immigrant or migrant groups tended to settle initially in the core areas and be responsible for the highest delinquency rates in each city; yet the rates for these groups went down as the groups either moved outward to better areas or achieved a more stable community structure. In Chicago, first the Germans and Irish, then the Poles and Italians, and finally southern Negroes and Spanish-speaking people replaced one another as the newest groups settling in the inner-city producing the highest delinquency rates. Consistent with these findings has been a regular decline in delinquency rates from the innermost to the outermost areas around the centers of each city examined.[12] Crime and delinquency are thus seen as associated with the disorganization and deprivation experienced by new immigrant or migrant groups as they strive to gain a foothold in the economic and social life of the city.

Negroes, however, have not been able, even when they have improved their economic condition, to move freely from the central cities. Therefore, movement of Negroes with higher income has tended merely to extend the ghetto periphery. The southern Negro migrants who have now been concentrated in the cities for two generations—as well as Negroes who have been living under conditions of urban segregation even longer—have experienced the same disorganizing forces as the earlier European settlers, but there are a number of reasons why the impact of these forces has been more destructive in the case of the Negro. Discrimination by race in housing, employment and education has been harder to overcome than discrimination based on language or ethnic background. With changes in the economy, there has been less demand for the Negro's unskilled labor than for that of the earlier immigrants. The urban political machines which furthered the political and economic interests of earlier immigrants had declined in power by the time the Negroes arrived in large numbers. The cultural experience which Negroes brought with them from the segregation and discrimination of the rural South was of less utility in the process of adaptation to urban life than was the cultural experience of many of the European immigrants. The net effect of these differences is that urban slums have tended to become *ghetto* slums from which escape has been increasingly difficult.

The National Commission on Urban Problems observed in its Report last year that "one has to see and touch and smell a slum before one appreciates the real urgency of the problem." Some of the urgency comes through, however, even in the simple verbal description of the facts and figures of slum life. Before presenting this description (much of which is drawn from the Reports of the Crime Commission and the Kerner Commission), we emphasize again that many slum residents manage to live peaceful and decent lives despite the conditions that surround them, and that the characterizations which follow are typical only of the ghetto core and those who fall into delinquency. They do not describe all neighborhoods or all residents of the inner city.

The Home. If the slums in the United States were defined strictly on the basis of dilapidated housing, inadequate sanitary facilities, and overcrowding, more than five million families could be classified as slum inhabitants.[13] To the inner-city child, home is often characterized by a set of rooms shared by a shifting group of relatives and acquaintances, furniture shabby and sparse, many children in one bed, plumbing in disrepair, plaster falling, roaches and sometimes rats, hallways dark or dimly lighted, stairways littered, air dank and foul.

In such circumstances, home has little holding power for a child, adolescent or young adult. Physically unpleasant and unattractive, it is not a place to bring friends; it is not even very much the reassuring gathering place of

26

one's own family. Indeed, the absence of parental super-vision early in the slum child's life is not unusual, a fact partly due to the condition of the home.

The Family. Inner-city families are often large. Many are fatherless, permanently or intermittently; others involve a conflict-ridden marital relationship; in either instance the parents may communicate to their offspring little sense of permanence and few precepts essential to an orderly, peaceful life.

Loosely organized, often with a female focus, many inner-city families bestow upon their children what has been termed "premature autonomy." Their children do not experience adults as being genuinely interested or caring persons. These children may, rather, experience adults as more interested in their own satisfactions than those of their children. Consequent resentment of authority figures, such as policemen and teachers, is not surprising. With a lack of consistent, genuine concern for children who are a burden to them, the parents may vacillate from being unduly permissive to becoming overly stern. Child rearing problems are exacerbated where the father is sometimes or frequently absent, intoxicated, or replaced by another man; where coping with everyday life with too little money for the size of the family leaves little time or energy for discipline; or where children have arrived so early and unbidden that parents are too immature to put their child's needs above their personal pleasure.

The seeds of delinquency in young boys are sown, studies suggest,[14] in families where there is an absence of consistent affection from both parents and where consistent parental direction is lacking. Identification of the boy with a stable positive male image is difficult when the father is frequently absent, erratic in his behavior, often unemployed, unfair in his discipline, or treated without respect by others. Conversely, studies indicate that a stable integrated family life can do much to counteract powerful external influences that pull young men toward delinquency.[15] If the inner-city family, particularly the ghetto black family, were stronger and more secure, with good family relationships, more of its offspring could avoid criminal behavior. However, even where there is a stable family which wishes to avoid the problems of slum-ghetto

27

life, continuing racial discrimination makes it difficult for them to remove themselves and their children from the pernicious influences of the slums.

The Neighborhood. In many center city alleys are broken bottles and snoring "winos"—homeless, broken men, drunk constantly on cheap wine. Yards, if any, are littered and dirty. Fighting and drunkenness are everyday occurrences. Drug addiction and prostitution are rampant. Living is crowded, often anonymous. Predominantly white store ownership and white police patrols in predominantly black neighborhoods are frequently resented, reviled, and attacked, verbally and physically. Municipal services such as garbage collection, street repairs and utilities maintenance and the like are inadequate and, at times, all but nonexistent.

Many ghetto slum children spend much of their time—when they are not watching television—on the streets of this violent, poverty-stricken world. Frequently, their image of success is not the solid citizen, the responsible, hard-working husband and father. Rather, the "successful" man is the cynical hustler who promotes his own interests by exploiting others—through dope selling, numbers, robbery and other crimes. Exploitation and hustling become a way of life.

The School. The low-income ghetto child lives in a home in which books and other artifacts of intellectual interest are rare. His parents usually are themselves too poorly schooled to give him the help and encouragement he needs. They have not had the time—even had they the knowledge—to teach him basic skills that are routinely acquired by most middle-class youngsters: telling time, counting, learning the alphabet and colors, using crayons and paper and paint. He is unaccustomed to verbalizing concepts or ideas. Written communication is probably rare in his experience.

The educational system in the slums is generally poorly equipped. Most schools in the slums have outdated and dilapidated buildings, few text and library books, the least qualified teachers and substitute teachers, the most overcrowded classrooms, and the least developed counseling and guidance services. These deficiencies are so acute that the school cannot hold the slum child's interests. To him

28

it is boring, dull, and apparently useless, to be endured for awhile and then abandoned.

The school experience often represents the last opportunity to counteract forces in a child's life that are influencing him toward crime and violence. The public school program has always been viewed as a major force for the transmission of legitimate values and goals, and some studies have identified a good school experience as a key factor in the development of "good boys out of bad environments." The link between school failure and delinquency is not completely known, but there is evidence that youth who fail in school contribute disproportionately to delinquency. One estimate is that the incidence of delinquency among dropouts is ten times higher than among youths who stay in school.[16]

The Job. Getting a good job is harder than it used to be for those without preparation, for an increasing proportion of all positions require an even higher level of education and training. To be a Negro, an 18-year-old, a school dropout, a resident of the slums of a large city, is to have many times more chances of being unemployed than a white 18-year-old high school graduate living a few blocks away. Seventy-one percent of all Negro workers are concentrated in the lowest paying and lowest skilled occupations. They are the last to be hired. Union practices, particularly in the building trades, have always been unduly restrictive toward new apprentices (except those related to union members), and this exclusionary policy has a major impact on young blacks. The unemployment rate, generally down in the last few years, remains twice as high for non-whites as for whites; and for black teenagers in central cities in 1968 the unemployment rate was 30 percent, up a third over 1960.

Success in job hunting is dependent on information about available positions. Family and friends in middle-class communities are good sources for obtaining information about employment. In the ghetto, however, information about job openings is limited by restricted contact with the job market. The slum resident is largely confined to his own neighborhood, where there are few new plants and business offices, and unfortunately State Employment Services have been generally ineffective even when used.

Most undereducated youngsters do not choose a job.

29

Rather, they drift into one. Since such jobs rarely meet applicants' aspirations, frustration typically results. Some find their way back to school or into a job training program. Some drift fortuitously among low paying jobs. Others try crime and, if successful, make it their regular livelihood; others lack aptitude and become failures in the illegal as well as the legal world—habitués of our jails and prisons. And there are those who give up, retreat from conventional society, and search for a better world in the private fantasies induced by drink and drugs.

The realities of the employment problem faced by ghetto Negroes are reflected in the data on family income. Negro family income in the cities is only sixty-eight percent of the median white family income. One-third of Negro families in cities live on $4,000 a year or less, while only sixteen percent of the whites do so.

When poverty, dilapidated housing, high unemployment, poor education, over-population, and broken homes are combined, an inter-related complex of powerful criminogenic forces is produced by the ghetto environment. These social forces for crime are intensified by the inferiority-inducing attitudes of the larger American society—attitudes that today view ghetto blacks as being suspended between slavery and the full rights and dignity of free men.

The competitive road to success is accorded great emphasis in American life. Achievement often tends to be measured largely in material terms. Our consumer-oriented culture pressures us to desire goods and services and to feel successful if one obtains them, unsuccessful if one does not. The network of mass communications spreads a culture of consumer desires over a vast audience. Happiness, we are endlessly reminded, is obtaining and having things. Most Americans operate on the premise that in the race to material success all men have an equal chance at the starting line, and that anyone who falls behind has only himself to blame. Yet not all can be at the front of the pack, especially not those who started far behind in the first place. And the race has different rules for different participants.

There are many ways of coping with the frustration of failure. Some take solace in the fact that others are even further behind. Some withdraw entirely from the race: alcohol, drugs, mental illness even suicide are avenues of escape. Others, especially college youth whose parents have succeeded in the race, experiment with "alternative life-styles" such as those associated with the hippie phenomenon. In the inner city, where the chances of success are less, many adopt illegal means in the effort to achieve their goals of securing more money and higher status among their peers.

To be a young, poor male; to be undereducated and without means of escape from an oppressive urban environment; to want what the society claims is available (but mostly to others); to see around oneself illegitimate and often violent methods being used to achieve material success; and to observe others using these means with impunity —all this is to be burdened with an enormous set of influences that pull many toward crime and delinquency. To be also a Negro, Mexican or Puerto Rican American and subject to discrimination and segregation adds considerably to the pull of these other criminogenic forces.

Believing they have no stake in the system, the ghetto young men see little to gain by playing according to society's rules and little to lose by not. They believe the odds against their success by legitimate means are greater than the odds against success by crime. The step to violence is not great, for in an effort to obtain material goods and services beyond those available by legitimate means, lower-class persons without work skills and education resort to crimes for which force or threat of force has a functional utility, especially robbery, the principal street crime.

But the slum ghetto does more than generate frustration that expresses itself in violent acquisitive crime. It also produces a "subculture" within the dominant American middle-class culture in which aggressive violence tends to be accepted as normal in everyday life, not necessarily illicit. In the contemporary American city we find the necessary conditions not only for the birth but also for the accelerated development of violent subcultures, and it is in these settings that most violent aggressive crimes in fact occur.[17]

From the perspective of dominant middle-class standards, the motives in most criminal homicides and other assaults—altercations, family quarrels, jealousy—are cheap issues for which people give their lives or suffer serious

31

injury. Similarly, the transient gratifications to be obtained from the rape or the robbery do not seem to warrant the risk of punishment or the burden of guilt that is presumably involved. Yet these events are much more reasonable to those in the ghetto slum subculture of violence, where a wide range of situations is perceived as justifying violent responses. An altercation with overtones threatening a young man's masculinity, a misunderstanding between husband and wife, competition for a sexual partner, the need to get hold of a few dollars—these "trivial" events can readily elicit a violent response in an environment that accepts violence as a norm, allows easy access to weapons, is physically and culturally isolated from the rest of the wider American community, and has limited social controls—including inadequate law enforcement.[18]

Violence is actually often used to enable a young man to become a successful member of ghetto society. In the subculture of violence, proving masculinity may require frequent rehearsal of the toughness, the exploitation of women, and the quick aggressive responses that are characteristic of the lower-class adult male. Those who engage in subcultural violence are often not burdened by conscious guilt, because their victims are likely to belong to the same subculture or to a group they believe has exploited them. Thus, when victims see their assaulters as agents of the same kind of aggression they themselves represent, violent retaliation is readily legitimized.

Moreover, if the poor, young, black male is conditioned in the ways of violence by his immediate subculture, he is also under the influence of many forces from the general, dominant culture. As we have said in another statement, violence is a pervasive theme in the mass media. The frequency of violent themes in myriad forms in the media tends to foster permissive attitudes toward violence. Much the same can be said about guns in American society. The highest gun-to-population ratio in the world, the glorification of guns in our culture, and the television and movie displays of guns by heroes surely contribute to the scope and extent of urban violence.

Taking all the foregoing facts and circumstances into account, perhaps we should marvel that there is not more violent crime in the cities of our nation.

THREE • THE RISE IN VIOLENT CRIME

If, as we believe, the conditions of life for inner-city populations are responsible for the sharp difference in violent
crime rates between these populations and other groups in
our society, there remains a puzzling paradox to be considered: Why, we must ask, have urban violent crime rates
increased substantially during the past decade when the
conditions that are supposed to cause violent crime have
not worsened—have, indeed, generally improved?

The Bureau of the Census, in its latest report on trends
in social and economic conditions in metropolitan areas,
states that most "indicators of well-being point toward
progress in the cities since 1960."[19] Thus, for example, the
proportion of blacks in cities who completed high school
rose from 43 percent in 1960 to 61 percent in 1968; unemployment rates dropped significantly between 1960 and
1968; the median income of families living in cities rose by
16 percent between 1959 and 1967 (from $6,720 to
$7,813), and the median family income of blacks in cities
increased from 61 per cent to 68 percent of the median
white family income during the same period. Also during
the same period the number of persons living below the
legally-defined poverty level in cities declined from 11.3
million to 8.3 million.

There are some important counter-trends. The unemployment rate for blacks, though lower, continued to be
about twice that for whites; and, as previously noted, unemployment among black teenagers in cities increased by a
third between 1960 and 1968 (to 30 percent, two and
one-half times the urban white teenager rate). Moreover,
figures indicating a closing of the family income gap between blacks and whites in the 1960s do not reflect a number of critical details, such as the fact that in cities black
men who worked the year round in 1967 earned about
seven-tenths as much as white workers and that this fraction was unchanged since 1959, or the fact that the "dependency ratio"—the number of children per thousand
adult males—for blacks is nearly twice that for whites, and
the gap widened sharply in the 1960s.[20] The degree of

33

poverty among the Negro poor in metropolitan areas remained severe, half the families reporting incomes $1,000 or more below the Social Security Administration's poverty budget of $3,335 for a family of four. We also find a significant increase in the number of children growing up in broken homes, especially among Negroes and lower income families in the cities. Among Negroes in the cities in 1968 with incomes below $4,000, only one-fourth of all children were living with both parents, as compared to one-half for white families of the same income level. Significantly, for families with incomes of $10,000 per year, this difference between white and black families disappears.

Whatever may be the correct over-all judgment on the change in inner-city living conditions over the past ten years, it is clear, however, that the change has been less dramatic than the change in violent crime rates during this period. How is this discrepancy to be explained?

In seeking an acceptable answer, we must keep in mind two qualifications which to a degree mitigate the seriousness of the discrepancy: first, while, as we have said, serious increases have occurred in major crimes involving violence, these increases are not so dramatic as FBI data suggest. Undoubtedly our crime reporting system is gradually dipping deeper into the well of previously unreported crime. Second, substantial portions of such increases as have occurred are to some extent attributable to demographic shifts in the population, particularly increases in the young population and increasing urbanization of the population.[21]

Even with these two factors taken into account, however, an important part of the original question remains. Why, if a high percentage of the crime in our cities is caused by factors such as poverty and racial discrimination, has it increased in a period of unprecedented prosperity for most Americans and in a time of painfully slow and uneven but genuine progress toward racial equality? These questions are not susceptible to precise scientific answers, but it is possible to offer informed judgments about them. In our considered opinion, the following factors have been significantly operative in the increasing levels of violent crime in the inner cities:

(1) The United States has been changing with bewildering rapidity—scientifically, technologically, socially, and

34

politically. Americans literally are changing how we work, how we live, how we think, how we manage our vast enterprise. Other rapidly changing nations—Israel, Japan, Western European countries—also have experienced rapid rises in crime rates, though at a much lower level than ours. Sociologists and anthropologists have long observed that rapid social change leads to a breakdown of traditional social roles and institutional controls over the behavior of young and old alike—but particularly the young, who, because of the social change, are less likely to be socialized into traditional ways of doing things (and not doing them) and, hence, ineffectively constrained by these traditional ways. This process includes the breakdown in traditional notions of civility, respect for elders and the institutions and patterns of conduct they represent, property rights, ways of settling disputes, relations between the sexes and many other matters.

With economic and technical progress in the United States has come increased affluence for most—but not all— of the members of our society. This combination of rapid social change and unevenly distributed affluence is devastating. At a time when established ways of doing things, traditions of morality, and attitudes about personal and property rights are changing, rising levels of affluence, interacting with public promises of a better life and television displays of still more affluence, have created expectations that have outstripped reality, particularly among the poor and especially the poor black. Rising income statistics look reassuring until one focuses on the continuing gap between black and white incomes.

We have in this country what has been referred to as a "revolution of rising expectations" born of unprecedented prosperity, changes in the law, wars on poverty, space spectaculars, and a host of other features of contemporary life. But, as one of the research contributions in this Commission's Task Force on Historical and Comparative Perspectives points out,[22] a rapid increase in human expectations followed by obvious failure to meet those expectations has been and continues to be a prescription for violence. Disappointment has manifested itself not only in riots and violent demonstrations—but may also be reflected in the increasing levels of violent crime.

35

(2) Our agencies of law enforcement have not been strengthened sufficiently to contain the violence that normally accompanies rapid social change and the failure to fulfill human expectations. The criminal justice process, suffering from an insufficiency of resources and a lack of management, has become less effective as a deterrent to crime and as an instrument for rehabilitating those who are apprehended and convicted.

As we analyze in other parts of our reports, we are allowing law enforcement to falter, the handgun census to approach 25 million, and an increasing number of crimes to go unpunished. Every successful crime is an inducement to further crime: it advertises society's inability to enforce generally accepted rules of conduct. Weaknesses of our criminal justice system have had a multiplier effect upon the rise of violent crime.

(3) Public order in a free society does not and cannot rest solely on applications or threats of force by the authorities. It must also rest on the people's acceptance of the legitimacy of the rule-making institutions of the political and social order and of the rules these institutions make. Persons obey the rules of society when the groups with which they identify approve those who abide by the rules and disapprove those who violate them. Such expressions of approval and disapproval are forthcoming only if the group believes that the rule-making institutions are in fact entitled to rule—that is, are "legitimate." What weakens the legitimacy of social and political institutions contributes to law-breaking, including violent crime.

In recent years a number of forces have converged to weaken the legitimacy of our institutions. We repeat what said elsewhere: the spectacle of governors defying court orders, police unlawfully beating demonstrators, looters and rioters going unapprehended and unpunished, and college youth attacking society's rules and values, makes it easier, even more "logical," for disadvantaged young people, whose attachment to law-abiding behavior already is tenuous, to slip into law-breaking behavior when the opportunity presents itself. Too, the pervasive suspicion that personal greed and corruption are prevalent among even the highest public officials has fed the idea among the poor

36

that nearly everyone is "on the take," and that the real crime is getting caught.

The beliefs that some claim to be widely held among poor young ghetto males—that the "system" in the United States is collectively guilty of "white racism" and of prosecuting an "immoral" war in Vietnam—have also tended to impair the moral impact upon them of our nation's institutions and laws and weakened the sense of guilt that otherwise would have restrained the commission of violent crimes against society.

These three factors—disappointments of minorities in the revolution of rising expectations, the weakening of law enforcement, and the loss of institutional legitimacy in the view of many—have had their effects on crime rates throughout our society. It is not surprising, however, that their greatest impact has been in the inner cities, among the young, the poor, the male, the black. It is there that reality most frustrates expectations, that law enforcement provides the least protection, and that the social and political institutions of society serve the needs of the individual least effectively. It is in the inner city that a subculture of violence, already flourishing, is further strengthened by the blockage of aspirations whose fulfillment would lead out of the subcultural, by the failure of a criminal justice system that would deter adherence to undesirable subculture, values, and by the weakness of institutions which would inculcate a competing set of values and attitudes.

FOUR ● THE PREVENTION OF
VIOLENT CRIME

For the past three decades, the primary concerns of our nation have been (a) the national defense, mutual security, and world peace, (b) the growth of the economy, and, (c) more recently, the conquest of space. These challenges have devoured more than two-thirds of all federal expenditures, approximately one-half of federal, state and local expenditures. We have staked out vast projects to promote the general domestic welfare and to overcome some of the problems we have here analyzed—but in view of dangerous inflationary trends and an already unprecedented level of federal, state and local taxation, we have not been able to obtain funds to support such projects in a volume and manner consistent with their lofty aims. The contemporary consequence of this pattern of resource allocation is an enormous deficit of unsatisfied needs and aspirations. Nowhere is this deficit more clearly apparent than in our crime-plagued metropolitan areas, where 65 percent of our people are now living.

In the absence of the massive action that seems to be needed to overcome this deficit, our cities are being misshaped in other ways by actions of more affluent citizens who desire safety for themselves, their families, and their investments. The safety they are getting is not the safety without fear that comes from ameliorating the causes of violent crime; rather it is the precarious safety obtained through individual efforts at self-defense. Thus the way in which we have so far chosen to deal with the deepening problem of violent crime begins to revise the future shape of our cities. In a few more years, lacking effective public action, this is how these cities will likely look:

• Central business districts in the heart of the city, surrounded by mixed areas of accelerating deterioration, will be partially protected by large numbers of people shopping or working in commercial buildings during daytime hours, plus a substantial police presence, and will be largely deserted except for police patrols during night-time hours.

• High-rise apartment buildings and residential compounds protected by private guards and security devices will be fortified cells for upper-middle and high-income populations living at prime locations in the city.

• Suburban neighborhoods, geographically far removed from the central city, will be protected mainly by economic homogeneity and by distance from population groups with the highest propensities to commit crimes.

• Lacking a sharp change in federal and state policies, ownership of guns will be almost universal in the suburbs, homes will be fortified by an array of devices from window grills to electronic surveillance equipment, armed citizen volunteers in cars will supplement inadequate police patrols in neighborhoods closer to the central city, and extreme left-wing and right-wing groups will have tremendous armories of weapons which could be brought into play with or without any provocation.

• High-speed, patrolled expressways will be sanitized corridors connecting safe areas, and private automobiles, taxicabs, and commercial vehicles will be routinely equipped with unbreakable glass, light armor, and other security features. Inside garages or valet parking will be available at safe buildings in or near the central city. Armed guards will "ride shotgun" on all forms of public transportation.

• Streets and residential neighborhoods in the central city will be unsafe in differing degrees, and the ghetto slum neighborhoods will be places of terror with widespread crime, perhaps entirely out of police control during night-time hours. Armed guards will protect all public facilities such as schools, libraries and playgrounds in these areas.

• Between the unsafe, deteriorating central city on the one hand and the network of safe, prosperous areas and sanitized corridors on the other, there will be, not unnaturally, intensifying hatred and deepening division. Violence will increase further, and the defensive response of the affluent will become still more elaborate.

Individually and to a considerable extent unintentionally, we are closing ourselves into fortresses when collectively we should be building the great, open, humane city-societies of which we are capable. Public and private action must guarantee safety, security, and justice for every citizen in our metropolitan areas without sacrificing the quality of life and the other values of a free society. If the nation is not in a position to launch a full-scale war on domestic ills, especially urban ills, at this moment, because of the difficulty in freeing ourselves quickly from other obligations, we should now legally make the essential commitments and then carry them out as quickly as funds can be obtained.

What do our cities require in order to become safe from violent crime?

They surely require a modern, effective system of criminal justice of the kind we recommend in Chapter 6, "Violence and Law Enforcement." All levels of our criminal justice process are underfunded and most are uncoordinated. Police protection and community relations are poorest in the high crime slum neighborhoods where they should be the best. Lower courts are impossibly overburdened and badly managed, while juvenile courts have failed to live up to their original rehabilitative ideal. Correctional institutions are generally the most neglected part

39

of the criminal justice process. *We reiterate our previous recommendations that we double our national investment in the criminal justice process, that central offices of criminal justice be created at the metropolitan level, and that complementary private citizen groups be formed.*

In addition to other long-run solutions that we suggest, other immediate steps must be taken to reduce the opportunity and incentive to commit crimes of violence. The President's Commission on Law Enforcement and Administration of Justice made many suggestions which we endorse. In particular, we emphasize the need for actions such as the following (some of which are new):

Increased day and night foot-patrols of slum ghetto areas by interracial police teams, in order to discourage street crime against both blacks and whites; improved street lighting to deprive criminals of hiding places from which to ambush victims; increase in numbers and use of community neighborhood centers that provide activity so that city streets are not deserted in early evening hours.

Increased police-community relations activity in slum ghetto areas in order to secure greater understanding of ghetto residents by police, and of police by ghetto residents. Police should be encouraged to establish their residences in the cities in order to be a part of the community which they serve.

Further experimentation with carefully controlled programs that provide low cost drugs such as methadone to addicts who register, so that addicts are not compelled to resort to robbery and burglary in order to meet the needs of their addiction; increased education about the dangers of addictives and other drugs in order to reduce their use.

Identification of specific violence-prone individuals for analysis and treatment in order to reduce the likelihood of repetition; provision of special schools for education of young people with violence-prone histories, special psychiatric services and employment programs for parolees and released offenders with a history of violent criminal acts.[23]

Concealable hand-guns, a common weapon used in violent crimes, must be brought under a system of restrictive licensing as we have recommended in Chapter VII.

But safety without fear cannot be secured alone by well-trained police, efficient courts, modern correctional practices, and hand-gun licensing. True security will come only when the vast majority of our citizens voluntarily accept society's rules of conduct as binding on them. Such acceptance will prevail widely among those who enjoy by legitimate means the benefits and pleasures of life to which they believe they are entitled—who have, in short, a satisfactory stake in the system. Today the stake of our impatient urban poor is more substantial than it used to be, but unrealized expectations and needs are massive. To ensure safety in our cities, we must take effective steps toward improving the conditions of life for all the people who live there.

Safety in our cities requires nothing less than progress in reconstructing urban life.

It is not within the purpose or the competence of this Commission to detail specific programs that will contribute to this fundamentally important national goal—the goal of reconstruction of urban life. Such programs must be worked out in the normal functioning of our political processes. Many important ideas have been put forth in the reports of the National Advisory Commission on Civil Disorders, the Urban Problems Commission, the Urban Housing Committee[24] and other groups which have made the city the focal point of their studies. Indeed, as the Urban Problems Commission observed, we already have on the national agenda much of the legislation and the programs needed to do the job. Examples are the Housing Act of 1968, the Juvenile Delinquency Prevention and Control Act, the Civil Rights laws of recent years, the President's welfare reform proposal, and many other existing and proposed enactments.

What we urge, from the standpoint of our concern, is that early and accelerated progress toward the reconstruction of urban life be made if there is to be a remission in the cancerous growth of violent crime. The programs and the proposals must be backed by a commitment of resources commensurate with the magnitude and the importance of the goal and with the expectations which have been irreversibly raised by the small start already made.

Dr. Daniel P. Moynihan has recently outlined a ten-point national urban policy that embraces many of the recommendations of earlier Commissions and which this Commission, while not in a position to endorse in detail,

41

believes to merit careful consideration.[25] The essentials of the ten points, together with some enlargements of our own, are as follows:

(1) *The poverty and social isolation of minority groups in central cities is the single most serious problem of the American city today.* In the words of the Kerner Commission, this problem must be attacked by national action that is "compassionate, massive, and sustained, backed by the resources of the most powerful and the richest nation on this earth." We must meet the 1968 Housing Act's goal of a decent home for every American within a decade; we must take more effective steps to realize the goal, first set in the Employment Act of 1946, of a useful job at a reasonable wage for all who are able to work; and we must act on current proposals that the federal government pay a basic income to those American families who cannot care for themselves.[26]

(2) *Economic and social forces in urban areas are not self-balancing.* There is evidence that some federal programs, such as the highway program, have produced sharp imbalances in the "ecology" of cities, and that others, such as urban renewal, have sometimes accomplished the opposite of what was intended.[27] A more sophisticated understanding and appreciation of the complexity of the urban social system is required—and this will in turn require the development of new, dependable and lasting partnerships between government, private industry, social and cultural associations and organized groups of affected citizens. Without such partnerships even the best-intentioned programs will fail or produce unforeseen disruptive effects.

(3) *At least part of the relative ineffectiveness of the efforts of urban government to respond to urban problems derives from the fragmented and obsolescent structure of urban government itself.* At the present time most of our metropolitan areas are mis-governed by a vast number of smaller, independent local governmental units—yet effective action on certain critical problems such as law enforcement, housing and zoning, and revenue-raising requires governmental units coterminous with metropolitan areas. At the same time, however, many city governments suffer

42

from being too large to be responsive to citizens, especially disadvantaged groups with special needs for public services and for increased political participation.

A dual strategy for restructuring local governments is thus required. On the one hand, steps must be taken to vest certain functions, such as the power to tax and to zone, in a higher tier of true metropolitan governments, each exercising jurisdiction over an entire metropolitan area. On the other hand, our cities must also develop a lower tier of modular neighborhood political units, operating under the direction of representatives elected by residents of the neighborhood and with the authority to determine some of the policies and to operate at the neighborhood center some of the services presently performed by city-wide agencies.[28] To provide new insights and new momentum for urban government restructuring, we suggest that the President might profitably convene an Urban Convention of delegates from all the states and major cities, as well as the national government, to advise the nation on the steps that should be taken to increase urban efficiency and accountability through structural changes in local government.

(4) *A primary object of federal urban policy must be to restore the fiscal vitality of urban government, with the particular object of ensuring that local governments normally have enough resources on hand or available to make local initiative in public affairs a reality.* Local governments that try to meet their responsibilities lurch from one fiscal crisis to another. Each one percent rise in the gross national product increases the income of the federal government by one and one-half percent, while the normal income of city governments increases only one-half to three quarters percent at most. Yet federal aid to state and local governments is only 17 percent of state-local revenue, a figure which should be substantially increased as soon as possible. We also believe it is essential to insure that the cities that are most in need of federal funding will obtain their fair share from the states which receive the federal payments.

The President's revenue-sharing proposal is one way to increase state and local revenues. However, it is limited both in the amounts envisioned and in the way they are

43

proposed to be channeled. As an alternate to federal sharing of its tax revenue, consideration might be given to a plan by which a full credit against federal income taxes would be given for all state and municipal taxes up to some maximum percentage of a taxpayer's income. To prevent encroachment by state governments upon the municipal tax base, separate ceilings could be fixed for state tax credits and for municipal tax credits. Such a tax-credit plan for revenue-sharing would be simple to execute, would channel more funds directly to cities, and would eliminate competition among neighboring states and communities to lower tax rates as a means of attracting businesses and upper income residents.

(5) *Federal urban policy should seek to equalize the provision of public services as among different jurisdiction in metropolitan areas.* This includes, at the top of the list, public education and public safety. Not only are both of these vital parts of the public sector severely underfunded, but the available resources are not equitably distributed between, for example, the inner city and suburban areas. What constitutes an equitable distribution may not be an easy question to answer, but it is at least clear that the kinds of inner city-suburban disparities in educational expenditures and police protection reported by the Kerner Commission are *not* equitable.[29] Federal aid programs should include standards to insure that equitable allocation policies are maintained.

(6) *The federal government must assert a specific interest in the movement of people, displaced by technology or driven by poverty, from rural to urban areas, and also in the movement from densely populated central cities to suburban areas.* Much of the present urban crisis derives from the almost total absence of positive policies to cope with the large-scale migration of southern Negroes into northern and western cities over the past half century, when the number of Negroes living in cities rose from 2.7 million to 14.8 million. In the next 30 years our metropolitan areas will grow both absolutely and in proportion to the total population as this nation of 200 million persons becomes a nation of 300 million persons. We must do the planning and take the action—*e.g.,* maintenance of a flexible and open housing market, creation of "new towns"—

44

that are necessary if future urban growth is to be less productive of social and human problems than has been true of past urban growth.

(7) *State government has an indispensible role in the management of urban affairs, and must be supported and encouraged by the federal government in the performance of this role.* City boundaries, jurisdictions and powers are subject to the control of state governments, and the federal government must work with state governments to encourage a more progressive, responsible exercise of the state role in this process.

(8) *The federal government must develop and put into practice far more effective incentive systems than now exist whereby state and local governments, and private interests too, can be led to achieve the goals of federal programs.* In recent years Congress has enacted legislation under which the federal government has funded an increasing number of venturesome programs aimed at broadening the scope of individual opportunity for educational and economic achievements. Under many of these new enactments, grants-in-aid to implement the federal policies in health, education, employment and other areas of human welfare have been given not only to state and local authorities, but also to universities, private industries and a host of specially created non-profit corporations. Although these grants have been made pursuant to specified standards of performance, the results have often been disappointing, in part because there have been inadequate incentives for successful performance and inadequate evaluative mechanisms for determining which specific programs are most efficiently and effectively achieving the federal goals.

It is thus increasingly agreed that the federal government should sponsor and subsequently evaluate alternative—in a sense "competing"—approaches to problems whose methods of spurring improvement in the delivery of federally-supported services include the provisions of incentives to deliver the services at the lowest possible cost (as in current efforts with regard to Medicare), and the granting of the federal assistance directly to the consumers of the programs concerned, thus enabling them to choose among competing suppliers of the goods or services that the program is designed to provide (as in the GI Bill and other federal scholarship programs).

(9) *The federal government must provide more and better information concerning urban affairs, and should sponsor extensive and sustained research into urban problems.* Social science research is increasingly able to supply policy-makers and the public with empirical indicators of the nature of social problems and the success or failure of efforts to solve these problems. The time is at hand when these indicators should be systematically collected and disseminated in aid of public policy at all levels.

(10) *The federal government, by its own example, and by incentives, should seek the development of a far heightened sense of the finite resources of the natural environment, and the fundamental importance of aesthetics in successful urban growth.* Many American cities have grown to be ugly and inhumane largely because of an unrestrained technological exploitation of the resources of land, air and water by the economically most efficient means. That there has been too little restraint is not surprising in view of the over-all American cultural context in which the natural environment was perceived as an inexhaustible frontier impervious to human harm. Today, however, the critical cultural context seems to be changing, and the "frontier spirit" is giving way to a new conservation ethic more appropriate to a crowded urban society. Government should take the lead in encouraging, and in acting consistently with, the development of this new ethic.

FIVE • CONCLUSION

To summarize our basic findings:

• Violent crimes are chiefly a problem of the cities of the nation, and there violent crimes are committed mainly by the young, poor, male inhabitants of the ghetto slum.

• In the slums increasingly powerful social forces are generating rising levels of violent crime which, unless checked, threaten to turn our cities into defensive, fearful societies.

• An improved criminal justice system is required to contain the growth of violent crime, but only progress toward urban reconstruction can reduce the strength of the crime-causing forces in the inner city and thus reverse the direction of present crime trends.

Our confidence in the correctness of these findings is strengthened by the support of the findings of the President's Commission on Law Enforcement and Administration of Justice and by subsequent events. At the end of its monumental work, in February of 1967, that Commission not only called for scores of improvements in the effectiveness and fairness of the law enforcement process, it also identified the same basic causes of violent crime and said this about their cure:

Warring on poverty, inadequate housing and unemployment, is warring on crime. A civil rights law is a law against crime. Money for schools is money against crime. Medical, psychiatric, and family-counseling services are services against crime. More broadly and most importantly, every effort to improve life in America's "inner cities" is an effort against crime.

---

1. The FBI Index of Reported Crime classifies seven offenses as "serious crimes"—homicide, forcible rape, robbery, aggravated assault, burglary, larceny of more than $50 and auto theft. It classifies the first four—homicide, rape, robbery and assault—as "violent crimes" because they involve the doing or threatening of bodily injury.

2. Reasons for the gap include failure of citizens to report crimes because they believe police cannot be effective in solving them; others do not want to take the time to report, some do not know how to report, and others fear reprisals.

3. The direct correlation between city size and violent crime rates may not be as uniform in the South as in other regions. Available data indicate higher suburban violent crime rates relative to city rates in the South, suggesting the possibility that smaller city rates may also be higher relative to larger city rates in the South (although direct evidence on this point is not presently available). Also, it should be kept in mind that the relationships noted in the text are for cities within certain population ranges (*e.g.*, more than 250,000, 100,000–250,000, etc.), not for individual cities. Thus the five cities with the highest metropolitan violent crime rates in 1968—Baltimore, Newark, Washington, San Francisco and Detroit—had smaller populations than some very large cities with somewhat lower rates of violent crime.

4. According to the FBI *Uniform Crime Reports*, about half of all arrests for serious crimes result in pleas of guilty or convictions; in only 88 percent of all arrests does the prosecutor decide he has sufficient evidence to try the case, and of those cases that are prosecuted, only 62 percent result in a plea of guilty or a conviction, often for a lesser offense than the one originally charged. A wide margin of error thus exists between the making of an arrest and proof that the person arrested has committed an offense.

5. This is a study of 9945 males born in 1945 and who lived in Philadelphia at least from age 10 to 18. Of this group, 3475, or 35 percent, were taken into custody by the police for delinquent offenses other than traffic violations. Race, socioeconomic status and many other variables are analyzed in this study, supported by NIMH, to be published shortly by Thorsten Sellin and Marvin E. Wolfgang under the title, *Delinquency in a Birth Cohort*.

6. Because some police commonly associate crime with Negroes more than with whites, Negroes may be disproportionately arrested on suspicion, thus producing a higher reported Negro involvement in crime than is the true situation.

7. In Chapter 6, "Violence and Law Enforcement," this Commission indicates that gun attacks are fatal in one out of five cases, on the average; knife attacks are fatal in one out of twenty.

8. The FBI has reported that in 1968 588,000 violent crimes occurred. This is about 300 crimes of major violence per each 100,000 Americans. It is generally estimated that only about half of all violent crimes are reported; if this is true, the total number of violent crimes per year is in the range of 1,200,000 or 600 per 100,000 people. These are *offenses*, not *offenders*. Since violent crimes often involve several offenders committing a single crime—particularly among the large number of juvenile offenders—a fair guess might be that twice as many offenders (2,400,000) were involved. But some offenders account for more than one crime per year. If we assume the commission of two crimes per year per offender, the total number of offenders drops back to 1,200,000; if we assume the commission of four crimes per year per offender, the total number of offenders is 600,000. Thus the number of Americans who commit violent crimes each year appears to be somewhere between these figures—between one in every 150 and one in every 300 Americans. Since children under twelve and adults over 45 commit relatively few crimes, the rate for persons between 12 and 45 is even higher.

9. President's Commission on Law Enforcement and Administration of Justice, *The Challenge of Crime in a Free Society* (Washington, D.C.: Government Printing Office, 1967); *Report of the National Advisory Commission on Civil Disorders* (Washington, D.C.: Government Printing Office, 1968); National Commission on Urban Problems, *Building the American City* (Washington, D.C.: Government Printing Office, 1968).

10. *The Challenge of Crime in a Free Society, op. cit.,* p. 35.

11. Shaw and McKay, *Juvenile Delinquency and Urban Areas* (Chicago, 1969).

12. One expert testifying before this Commission reported his finding in Chicago: a person living in the inner-city faced a risk each year of 1 in 77 of being assaulted; a risk of only 1 in 2,000 in the better areas of the city, and 1 in 10,000 in the rich suburbs.

13. See Chapter 14 of *Crimes of Violence,* the Report of our Task Force on Individual Acts of Violence.

14. See studies cited in "The Family and Violence," Chapter 9 of *Law and Order Reconsidered,* the Report of this Commission's staff Task Force on Law and Law Enforcement (Washington, D.C.: Government Printing Office, 1969) and in "Juvenile Delinquency and the Family," Appendix L of the Crime Commission's *Task Force Report on Juvenile Delinquency* (Washington, D.C.: Government Printing Office, 1967).

15. *E.g.,* U.S. Dept. of Labor, Office of Policy Planning and Research, *The Negro Family: The Case for National Action* (Washington, D.C.: Government Printing Office, 1965), pp. 38-40.

16. See "Violence and Youth," Chapter 14 of *Crimes of Violence,* the Report of our staff Task Force on Individual Acts of Violence. Thirty-nine percent of Negroes and 23 percent of whites in cities fail to complete four years of high school.

17. The subculture of violence is not the product of our cities alone: the Thugs of India, the *vendetta barbaricina* in Sardinia, the *mafiosi* in Sicily and the Ku Klux Klan, for example, have existed for many years. Nor is violence absent from the established middle-class culture of the majority in our society. It is simply the greater frequency and approval of illegitimate violence that distinguishes the subculture of violence from the dominant cultural pattern.

18. We are here drawing upon Marvin E. Wolfgang and Franco Ferracuti, *The Subculture of Violence* (New York: Barnes and Noble; London: Tavistock Publications, 1967).

19. U.S. Bureau of the Census, "Trends in Social and Economic Conditions in Metropolitan Areas," *Current Population Reports* Series P-23, Special Studies (formerly Technical Studies), No. 27 (Washington, D.C.: Government Printing Office, 1969).

20. Also, such closing of the family income gap as has occurred all took place after 1965; for the previous 15 years there was no change. See *Law and Order Reconsidered, op. cit.,* p. 103.

21. Computations set forth in *Crimes of Violence,* the Report of our staff Task Force on Individual Acts of Violence, suggest that 18% of the increase in the volume of violent crime between 1950 and 1965 is attributable solely to urbanization, and 12% to age redistribution alone.

22. See James C. Davies, "The J-Curve of Rising and Declining Satisfactions as a Cause of Some Great Revolutions and a Contained Rebellion," in *Violence in America,* the Report of the Task Force on Historical and Comparative Perspectives (Washington, D.C.: Government Printing Office, 1969).

23. The Philadelphia cohort study cited above shows that out of the entire Philadelphia population of boys born in 1945 (about 10,000), less than six percent had five or more police contacts. Even though the age group from 15 to 24 includes ten such cohorts, the number of identifiable violence-prone youths in a major city such as Philadelphia is still small enough to be manageable.

48

24. These documents are available for purchase from the Superintendent of Documents, U.S. Government Printing Office, Washington, D.C. 20402.

25. Daniel P. Moynihan, "Toward a National Urban Policy," *The Public Interest* (No. 17, Fall 1969), p. 15. Dr. Moynihan has been Executive Director of the President's Urban Affairs Council and is now Counselor to the President.

26. The President has recently made such a proposal including a work incentive formula. A somewhat different proposal has been put forward in a recent report of the President's Commission on Income Maintenance Programs.

27. "Is the only answer to traffic congestion more and wider roads? Clearly in many localities, it is not. The dislocation of people and businesses, the distortion of land use, the erosion of the real property tax base, and the dollars and cents cost, make this an increasingly unacceptable solution." U.S. Dept. of Housing and Urban Development, *Tomorrow's Transportation: New Systems for the Urban Future* (Washington, D.C.: U.S. Government Printing Office, 1968), p. 18. See also Advisory Commission on Intergovernmental Relations, *Urban and Rural America: Policies for Future Growth* (Washington, D.C.: U.S. Government Printing Office, 1968), pp. 59-60.

28. From the standpoint of reducing violence, needed services which might be provided at the neighborhood level include job counseling and training; family counseling and planning advice; medical and psychiatric care; counseling on alcohol and drugs; citizen's grievance agencies; adult education; preschool training and child care for working mothers; psychological counseling for parents during the formative child rearing years; domestic quarrel teams; suicide prevention units; youth bureaus, including counseling of youth referred for non-police action by local Juvenile Squads and Gang Control Units; and legal advice.

29. *Report of the National Advisory Commission on Civil Disorders, op. cit.*, pp. 161-62, 241.

III ● GROUP VIOLENCE*

ONE ● CAUSES: HISTORICAL AND COMPARATIVE ASPECTS

We tend to think of group violence[1] as a major aberration in a democratic society, as a sickness that comes only in extraordinary times. A deeper reading of the past belies this notion. In man's political history, group violence has accompanied periods of serious social stress from Homer to this morning's newspaper. Group violence runs through the American experience, as it always has, in varying degrees and manifestations, for every society. Violence has been used by groups seeking power, by groups holding onto power, and by groups in the process of losing power. Violence has been pursued in the defense of order by the satisfied, in the name of justice by the oppressed, and in fear of displacement by the threatened.

At the outset, it must be made clear that group violence has no necessary relationship to group protest, although

---

*An edited version of statement issued December 3, 1969.

there continue to be those who decry the one as though it were the other. The right to protest is an indispensable element of a free society; the exercise of that right is essential to the health of the body politic and its ability to adapt itself to a changing environment. In this country, we have endowed the right of protest with constitutional status. The very first Amendment to the Constitution protects freedom of speech and press and "the right of the people peaceably to assemble and to petition the government for a redress of grievances." The Amendment protects much more than the individual right of dissent; it guarantees the right of groups to assemble and petition, or, in the modern phrase, to demonstrate.

Group violence, on the other hand, is dangerous to a free society. All too frequently, it is an effort not to persuade, but to compel. It has no protected legal status; indeed, one purpose of law is to prevent and control it. Nor is group violence a necessary consequence of group protest. The violence of the Ku Klux Klan—the lynching of Negroes at the rate of almost 100 per year from 1890 to 1910 —had little to do with protest; if anything, it was more a cause of protest than a response. The same may be said of the harsh treatment of Orientals on the Pacific frontier and the common use of violence to settle property and political disputes among competing groups in the early days of the American West.

It is true, of course, that group protest sometimes results in group violence. Violence may be committed by groups opposed to the aims of the protesters (as in the Southern murders of civil rights workers by groups of white militants); excessive force may be used by the public authorities, as in Selma in 1965; violence may be committed by some within the protesting group itself (as in the case of the Weatherman faction of the SDS). But the widely held belief that protesting groups usually behave violently is not supported by fact. Of the multitude of occasions when protesting groups exercise their rights of assembly and petition, only a small number result in violence.

Thus, our Task Force Report on Historical and Comparative Perspectives reports that over the five year period from mid-1963 to mid-1968, protests or counterprotests and ghetto riots involved more than two million persons. Civil rights demonstrations mobilized 1.1 million, anti-war demonstrations 680,000, and ghetto riots an estimated 200,000. Nine thousand casualties resulted, including some 200 deaths.[2] Ghetto riots were responsible for most of these casualties, including 191 deaths. Almost all other deaths, an estimated 23, resulted from white terrorism against blacks and civil rights workers. These casualty figures are for a five-year period, and apart from the ghetto riots, they are comparatively infinitesimal. While they are not to be condoned, in a country with 250,000 aggravated assaults and 12,000 homicides per year, group protest cannot be considered as accounting for a major part of the deliberate violence we experience.[3]

Do we have a greater amount of group violence today than in earlier periods of our history? While a precise quantitative answer cannot be provided, we may conclude with confidence that, while group violence in the 1960's was at a higher level than in the decades immediately preceding, several earlier decades of American history were marked by higher levels of group violence—in terms of casualties per 100,000 population—than has been true of the decade now ending.

Ever since the Boston Tea Party, occasional group violence has been a recurring—though not a continuous—feature of American political and social history.

● From 1740 to 1790, Appalachian farmers, protesting against debt and tax collectors from the seaboard centers of political and economic power, engaged in a series of violent disorders, of which the Whiskey Rebellion in Pennsylvania is best known.

● Southern landowners and northern Abolitionists engaged in a variety of skirmishes, from "bleeding Kansas" to John Brown's raid on Harper's Ferry, that were the violent prelude to the Civil War.

● During Reconstruction, The Ku Klux Klan and other elements of the defeated white majority in the South conducted a campaign of terrorism against the freed blacks, government officials and Southerners who cooperated with them.

● So-called "Native Americans" of the original colonial stocks resorted to group violence when they perceived their status as threatened by European Catholic and Jewish immigrants in the East and Orientals in the West; the immigrant

51

groups occasionally engaged in violence such as the New York Draft Riots in 1863.

• As the freed Negro migrants from the South began settling in border and Northern cities after the Civil War, white residents (including the most recent of the European immigrants) launched occasional attacks on black sections of the city.

• The growth of organized labor in the half century from 1880 to 1930 was marked by unusually severe episodes of violence in which employers, workers and public authorities were all occasional aggressors. In the three year period 1902-1904, about 200 persons were killed and 2,000 injured in the violence accompanying various strikes and lockouts.

During each of these episodes, most of the community continued to live in peace. The violent episodes themselves were sporadic. At any given time they probably involved minor percentages of the total population—certainly not more than a small fraction of the number who were then engaging in various sorts of group protest.

While it is probably true that protest by one or more groups seeking to advance or defend its status in society has been a continuous feature of American life, group violence has not. Indeed, it is group protest, not group violence, that is as American as cherry pie.

Do we have more group violence than other modern nations? Comparisons with other countries are difficult. Our Task Force Report shows a group violence casualty rate in seventeen other industrially advanced nations for the first half of this decade that is only one-fourth the United States rate.[4] (The average for all nations, however, was 40 times the United States rate.) Yet few advanced democratic nations are free from group violence, as the riots in France, Germany, Italy, Canada and Japan during the past two years and the continuing strife in Northern Ireland remind us. Unlike many other countries, (including some advanced ones) strife in the United States is usually aimed at particular policies, conditions or groups rather than at overthrow of the government; indeed, the United States has been free of anything resembling insurrection for more than a century. Except for Great Britain, this country has the longest record of government continuity in the world.

Why does group violence occur in an advanced democratic society? We may accept that men naturally possess

52

aggressive tendencies without concluding that group violence is inevitable. Nature provides us with the capacity for violence; material, social and political circumstances are the determinants of whether and how we exercise that capacity. Men's frustration over some of these circumstances is a necessary precondition of group protest. Whether that frustration will erupt into violence depends largely on the degree and consistency of social control and the extent to which social and political institutions afford peaceful alternatives for the redress of group grievances.

All societies generate some discontent because organized life by its very nature inhibits most human beings. Group violence occurs when expectations about rights and status are continually frustrated and when peaceful efforts to press these claims yield inadequate results. It also occurs when the claims of groups who feel disadvantaged are viewed as threats by other groups occupying a higher status in society. Greater expectations and frustrations for disadvantaged groups, and greater fears of threatened groups, are more likely to occur in times of rapid social change than in times of social stability.

America has always been a nation of rapid social change. We have proclaimed ourselves a modern promised land, and have brought millions of restless immigrants to our shores to partake in its fulfillment. Persistent demands by these groups—by the western farmers of the revolutionary period, later by the Irish, the Italians and the Slavs, and more recently by Puerto Rican, Mexican, and Negro Americans—and resistance to these demands by other groups, have accounted for most of the offensive and defensive group violence that marks our history.

This analysis, however, does not adequately explain why some upper class and middle class students engage in group violence. Some affluent students doubtless perceive themselves as disadvantaged—by the draft and forced service in the Vietnam war, by their small voice in college governance, by their lack of identity and purpose in what they perceive as a complex, computerized and highly materialistic urban society. But for many students, the causes that attract them most are not their own grievances but those of the other groups and problems of the society as a whole. To a high degree, they are motivated by a sense of guilt for being

53

privileged and by the desire of many young people to share with others in the experience of serving a noble cause. For most of those so motivated, participation in peaceful protest fulfills this need. Those few who are particularly impatient or cynical about the "system" or are committed to revolution resort to violence.

As we have noted, discontent is only one prerequisite of group violence. Whether violence actually occurs also depends on popular attitudes and how effectively political institutions respond to the threat of violence and to demands for the redress of group grievances. Although we have an open political and social system, more dedicated than most to the dream of individual and group advancement, the majority are sometimes unwilling either to hear or to redress the just grievances of particular minorities until violent advocacy or repression calls them to the forefront of our attention.

And for all our rhetoric to the contrary, we have never been a fully law-abiding nation. For example, some measure of public sympathy has often been with the nightriders who punished the transgressor of community mores and with the disadvantaged who sought to remedy obvious injustices by violent means. Lack of full respect for law and at least tacit support for violence in one's own interest have helped to make the United States, in the past as at present, somewhat more tumultuous than we would like it to be.

TWO • THE RATIONALE OF
GROUP VIOLENCE

Those who engage in group violence as a political tactic advance several reasons to support it. Some of the current justifications have been summarized by our Task Force on Violent Aspects of Protest and Confrontation.[5] They are stated as the militants themselves might make them.

1. Militants argue that the creation of turmoil and disorder can stimulate otherwise quiescent groups to take more forceful action in their own ways. Liberals may come to support radical demands while opposing their tactics; extreme tactics may shock moderates into self re-examination.

2. Militants point out that direct action is not intended to

win particular reforms or to influence decision makers, but rather to bring out a repressive response from authorities—a response rarely seen by most white Americans. When confrontation brings violent official response, uncommitted elements of the public can see for themselves the true nature of the "system." Confrontation, therefore, is a means of political education.

3. Militants believe that if the movement really seriously threatens the power of political authorities, efforts to repress the movement through police-state measures are inevitable. The development of resistant attitudes and action toward the police at the present time is a necessary preparation for more serious resistance in the future.

4. Militants state that educated, middle-class, non-violent styles of protest are poorly understood by working-class youth, black youth, and other "drop-outs." Contact with these other sectors of the youth population is essential and depends upon the adoption of a tough and aggressive stance to win respect from such youth.

5. Militants recognize that most middle-class students are shocked by aggressive or violent behavior. In the militant view, this cultural fear of violence is psychologically damaging and may be politically inhibiting. To be a serious revolutionary, they say, one must reject middle-class values, particularly deference toward authority. Militant confrontation gives resisters the experience of physically opposing institutional power, and it may force students to choose between "respectable" intellectual radicalism and serious commitment to revolution, violent or otherwise.

6. Militants respond to those who point to the possibility of repression as a reaction to confrontation tactics by accusing them of wishing to compromise demands and principles and dilute radicalism. Militants believe that repression will come in any case, and to diminish one's efforts in anticipation is to give up the game before it starts.

Somewhat different arguments are advanced by those among threatened groups to justify defensive private violence and the use of excessive force by public authorities. They believe that the disadvantaged group will cease to exert pressure only if protesters are firmly and decisively repressed and that strong evidence of superior force and willingness to use it will succeed in defending the status quo.

These arguments for group violence—offensive or defensive[6]—are not sustained by history, contemporary reality, logic or law. They are inconsistent with the basic principles of democratic government.

We put to one side the efficacy of violence in overturning a government or maintaining it in power, for this has not been the main thrust of American group violence. The thornier question—one that is more pertinent to American practitioners of group violence who usually aim not at seizing or defending the government but at altering or continuing its policies—is whether group violence is an effective, albeit illegal, tactic for winning or preventing a significant change of status.

History provides no ready answer to this question. There have been a great many protest movements marked by violence which eventually achieved some of their aims. But whether offensive violence by the protesting group helped or hindered the subsequent achievement remains a matter of conjecture, as does the question of whether defensive violence by the threatened group hindered or helped the eventual change. In the history of the American labor movement, for example, violence persistently accompanied the struggle of workingmen to gain decent working conditions and recognition for their unions; both ends were eventually achieved, but there are differences of opinion whether pro-labor violence helped the cause or whether anti-labor violence hindered it.[7] Labor leaders themselves doubted the effectiveness of violence, and no major labor organization in American history advocated violence as a policy. Typically, pro-labor violence was a response to the use of excessive force by militia or private police or strikebreakers. While violence proved to be a better short-run weapon for employers than for workers the escalation of counterviolence it produced was a factor in the passage of the laws that eventually established the rights of labor.

It is no doubt true that in the 1960s policy changes advantageous to dissident groups have sometimes followed in the wake of urban riots and campus disturbances. These gains, however, may have been attributable more to the validity of the protest goals than to the violent outbreaks when they came. Moreover, to the extent violence may have contributed to these gains, the use of excessive force against peaceful demonstrators—as in Birmingham—may have been more decisive than any violence by the demonstrators them-

56

selves. No one will ever know whether as much or more might have been won without resort to violence by either side. The advocacy and practice of deliberate violence by some radical black militants and some student and anti-war activists have certainly created antagonism and resulted in the loss of sympathy for these causes among large sectors of the public. Leaders of many protesting groups recognize the counterproductivity of violence; before the November Peace Mobilization in Washington, many of the protest leaders sought diligently to discourage violence by such groups as the Weatherman faction and the Youth International Party. When these factions did resort to violence, leaders of the Mobilization expressly disavowed and condemned them.

If the lessons of history are ambiguous on the short-term effectiveness of violence as a political tactic, they are clear on its long-term dangers. As we note in Chapter IX "Campus Disorder," violence tends to feed on itself, with one power group imposing its will on another until repressive elements succeed in reestablishing order. The violent cycles of the French and Russian Revolutions and the decade resulting in the Third Reich are dark abysses of history to ponder. Violence tends to become a style, with many eager followers. German students setting fire to cars in West Berlin chanted in English: "Burn, baby, burn." When students last year violently took control of the telephone system at Brandeis University, within ten days British, French, German and Italian students attempted to do the same thing. Violently disruptive tactics that began inappropriately in universities have been copied even more inappropriately in high schools and churches.

As our Task Force on Law and Law Enforcement has found, the danger of this contagion is that extreme, unlawful tactics will replace normal legal processes as the usual way of pressing demands. Given present trends, it is not impossible to imagine an America in which the accepted method for getting a traffic light installed will be to disrupt traffic by blocking the intersection, where complaints against businessmen will call for massive sit-ins, where unsatisfactory refuse collection will cause protesting citizens to dump garbage in the street. We do not believe that a healthy society can result from the widespread use of such techniques.

As our Task Force concluded, group violence as a tactic to advance or restrain protest by discontented groups does not contribute to the emergence of a more liberal and humane society but produces an opposite tendency. The fears and resentments created by these tactics have strengthened the political power of some of the most destructive elements in American society.

As one of this nation's most thoughtful leaders has observed:

No society can live in constant and destructive tumult. . . . The anarchist plays into the hands of the authoritarian. Those of us who find authoritarianism repugnant have a duty to speak out against all who destroy civil order. The time has come when the full weight of community opinion should be felt by those who break the peace or coerce through mob action.[8]

THREE • ELEMENTS OF PREVENTION AND CONTROL

What steps should a representative constitutional society take to prevent and control group violence? Our political institutions should be so framed and managed as to make violence as a political tactic both unnecessary and unrewarding. To make violence an unnecessary tactic, our institutions must be capable of providing political and social justice for all who live under them and of correcting injustice against any group by peaceful and lawful means. To make violence an unrewarding tactic, our political and social institutions must be able to cope with violence when it occurs and do so firmly, fairly, and within the law.

Our Constitution was written after the violent overthrow of a colonial government which followed one of these imperatives, but ignored the other. Its preamble does not speak merely of justice, or merely of order; it embraces both. Two of the six purposes set forth in the Preamble are to "establish justice" and to "insure domestic tranquility." The First Amendment sets forth a third and closely related goal—to protect the rights of free speech and peaceable assembly and the right to petition the government for re-

58

dress of grievances. If we are to succeed in controlling group violence, we must navigate by all three of these stars.

History is full of violent disasters that occurred because channels for peaceful presentation of grievances were blocked and because governments did not or could not act to correct the underlying injustices or to control disorder; history also contains examples of disasters that were averted by governments which kept the channels of protest open and applied a judicious combination of reform and control.

The French and Russian Revolutions reached extraordinary peaks of violence because absolutist governments concentrated on efforts to restore order and refused to redress grievances or transfer a sufficient share of power to the emerging lower classes. The British, on the other hand, averted a similar disaster by judicious measures of control and by more flexible development of their political institutions to accommodate the rights and needs of all their people.[9] In Germany, after World War I, the Weimar Republic was too weak either to control street fighting between right wing and left wing students and workers or to remedy their grievances; the emergence of Hitler to "restore order" proved to be a disaster for the entire world.

In our own country, we have on some occasions failed to take the necessary measures of reform and control; on other occasions we have succeeded. We proved unable to abolish the injustice of Negro slavery without a bloody war —a conflict which released currents of violence that continue to flow a century later. The Reconstruction governments in the southern states were too weak to enforce the newly won rights of black people against a hostile community or to prevent the Ku Klux Klan from reestablishing white supremacy by violence. The struggle of the labor unions was marked by extensive restrictions on peaceful protest and by repressive violence in the absence of laws to provide minimum standards of justice for working people and legal machinery for the resolution of disputes; the violence largely subsided after such laws were enacted. And in the wake of the Depression, after relatively few violent incidents such as the Bonus March and the farmers' defense of their lands against foreclosure, we averted further violence by fashioning major alterations in the rights of individuals to government assistance and in the responsibilities

59

of government for directing the course of our private enterprise economy.

When group violence occurs, it must be put down by lawful means, including the use of whatever force may be required. But when it occurs—better still, before it occurs —we must permit aggrieved groups to exercise their rights of protest and public presentation of grievances; we must have the perception to recognize injustices when they are called to our attention, and we must have the institutional flexibility to correct those injustices promptly.

We do not mean, of course, that the mere making of a demand entitles it to be granted, or that the particular remedy proposed by those aggrieved should be adopted. Some "non-negotiable" demands by students, by radical black militants, by anti-war demonstrators and others are unrealistic and unfair to the rights of others; some proposed remedies are self-defeating or administratively unworkable. What is essential is that when the basic justice of the underlying grievance is clear, an effort to take suitable measures of accommodation and correction must be made. The effort must be made even though other groups feel threatened by the proposed correction, and even though they may resort to violence to prevent it. We cannot "insure domestic tranquility" unless we "establish justice"—in a democratic society one is impossible without the other.

We therefore put forth our suggestions as to how these three goals—controlling disorder, keeping open the channels of protest, and correcting social injustices—can be more successfully pursued.

FOUR • STRATEGIES OF CONTROL

Many feel that rioters should be dealt with harshly. At least two-thirds of white Americans, according to one poll, believe that looters and fire-bombers should simply be shot down in the streets.[10] Many believe that even peaceful demonstrators are "agitators" or "anarchists." In a poll conducted for this Commission, 56 percent agreed that "any man who insults a policeman has no complaint if he gets roughed up in return."

As recent history illustrates, the prompt, prudent deployment of well-trained law enforcement personnel can extinguish a civil disorder in its incipiency. But history also demonstrates that excessive use of force is an unwise tactic for handling disorder. To the generalization made earlier, that violence is an always dangerous and sometimes ineffective tactic for dissident groups pressing their demands or for threatened groups resisting those demands, may be added this corollary: the use of excessive and illegal force is an always dangerous and usually ineffective tactic for authorities seeking to quell unrest. Both in the short and in the long run, the use of excessive force to repress group violence often has the effect of magnifying turmoil, not diminishing it.

It is useful to contrast the official response to the antiwar protest in Chicago during the Democratic National Convention of 1968 and the "counter-inaugural" in Washington on January 20, 1969. These two events were organized by many of the same protesting groups and attended by many of the same individuals, in roughly equal numbers. Yet the results of these events were markedly different. In Chicago, the authorities were restrictive in granting demonstration permits; some of the police, deliberately goaded by verbal and physical attacks of small militant groups, responded with excessive force not only against the provocateurs but also against peaceful demonstrators and passive bystanders. Their conduct, while it won the support of the majority, polarized substantial and previously neutral segments of the population against the authorities and in favor of the demonstrators.[11]

In Washington, demonstration permits were liberally issued. Although there was also provocative violence by some of the demonstrators, the police used only that force clearly necessary to maintain order. As a result, there was little criticism of police behavior. Our analysis leads to the conclusion that the amount of violence that occurred during these demonstrations and the resulting effects on public opinion were directly related to the kind of official response that greeted them.[12]

In both instances a small number—no more than a few hundred in either case—intended to provoke a "confrontation" with authorities by provocative acts, aimed especially at policemen. A majority of the participants intended to demonstrate peacefully and, in fact, did so.

In response to reports that violence and disruptive conduct would occur, Chicago authorities adopted tight, well-publicized security measures designed to dissuade protesters from coming to the city. To discourage the protesters further, they prolonged the negotiations for demonstration permits and exercised their discretionary powers restrictively. The limited, begrudging dialogue with protesting groups reduced the opportunity of the authorities to assess and separate the component groups in the demonstration (many of which intended to demonstrate peacefully) and to learn the details of their plans. This resistant posture served to discourage more mature and responsible protesters from coming while firing the determination of young militants to attend and confront. To some of the police and some Chicago citizens, the official posture of resistance signified that the protest activities as such were dangerous or illegitimate; they tended to view protesters as troublemakers and law-breakers, thus failing to discriminate between the small number of radicals seeking trouble and the great majority of peaceful citizens exercising their constitutional rights.

In preparation for the Inaugural in Washington five months later, intelligence reports were carefully evaluated. Genuine threats were sorted from theatric exaggerations. Troublemakers were identified and watched closely, but no attempt was made to interfere with the activities of the majority of peaceful demonstrators. Authorities negotiated conscientiously with protest leaders and arrived at agreements on the scope of permits for parades and meetings that were acceptable to all parties. The protest leaders, impressed with the reasonableness of the government spokesmen, made substantial efforts to cooperate with officials and ensure peace.

As the Chicago and Washington events differed in preparation, they differed in outcome. After minor skirmishes, trouble in Chicago escalated when throngs of demonstrators, having been denied permits to remain overnight, refused to leave Lincoln Park, their main gathering place. Dozens of police attempted to clear the park on three successive nights. In response to serious and deliberate provocations, but without coherent planning, some policemen

62

clubbed and teargassed guilty and innocent alike, chasing demonstrators through streets some distance from the park. Particularly on the side streets, some bystanders who had taken no part in the demonstrations were attacked by police officers. Several media representatives were clubbed and had their cameras smashed. Predictably, tensions and anger rose. Extremists who would otherwise have been ignored began to attract audiences. They urged demonstrators to fight back. The police were exposed to more and more jeers and obscenities and had to withstand heavier barrages of rocks and other missiles. During one of the first nights, fifteen policemen were injured; two nights later, 149 were injured.

In Washington, the cycle of escalating violence never got started. Both verbal and physical provocations by demonstrators were frequently intense, but they were met with restraint. Provocation by policemen was rare; when it occurred it was terminated by police and city officials who intervened quickly to restore discipline. In general, police withstood physical and verbal abuse with great calm. In the end, the behavior of Washington officials and the police won praise in newspaper editorials and from leaders of the demonstrations.

There were some radical leaders, however, who were more grateful for the official response in Chicago, for it appeared to validate their characterizations of government as being "reactionary" and "repressive" and to increase support from other protesting groups. The chaos at Chicago also gave solidarity to the ranks of those who regard all demonstrators, however peaceful, as irresponsible "punks." The overall effect was to increase polarization and unrest, not diminish them.

This comparison between Chicago in August of 1968 and Washington last January can be closed on two encouraging notes. Permits for peace marches in Chicago were sought and granted in October 1969. The marches were organized by the "Weatherman," an extremely militant faction of the Students for a Democratic Society. In the course of the demonstrations, Chicago police had to face four days of intense provocation and wanton violence. This time, however, the police acted with calm and restraint. No injuries to residents, bystanders or newsmen were re-

63

ported; on the contrary, the police took steps to safeguard bystanders from the violence. As a result of the professional conduct of Chicago police, violence was effectively contained, and blame for the damage and injuries that did occur fell squarely upon the violent group among the demonstrators, many of whom were arrested.

The Peace Moratorium Parade and assembly in Washington on November 15 was another example of intelligent and restrained official response. Although the government had reason to expect that some elements among the protesting groups were bent on violence, reasonable permits were ultimately negotiated with the responsible demonstration leaders, and ample police and military force were provided to preserve order if necessary. In the largest single protest demonstration in American history, the overwhelming majority of the participants behaved peacefully. Their activities were facilitated rather than restrained by the police. When the few extremists did attempt violent attacks on two occasions, the police responded quickly and firmly but, on the whole, without excessive force.[13] As a result, order was maintained, the right to protest was upheld, and it was possible to judge both the peaceful and the violent aspects of the protest in their true proportion.

Civil governments must, of course, act promptly and decisively against threats to public order. As the National Advisory Commission on Civil Disorders stated: "Individuals cannot be permitted to endanger the public peace and safety, and public officials have a duty to make it clear that all just and necessary means to protect both will be used."[14]

A parallel duty exists for colleges and universities: they must have firm, well-publicized plans for dealing swiftly and decisively with campus disorders. The practice of keeping rules fuzzy so that dissident groups are "kept off balance" has failed demonstrably. In chapter IX, "Campus Disorder," we recommend that students, faculty and administrators develop acceptable standards of conduct and responses appropriate to deviations from those standards, including the circumstances under which they will resort to (i) campus disciplinary procedures, (ii) campus police, (iii) court injunctions, (iv) other court sanctions, and (v)

64

the city police. We believe genuine progress is presently being made in this direction.

Police manuals recognize that when the police are needed—as in urban riots, demonstrations that threaten violence, and campus disorders in which court injunctions must be enforced—their behavior must be calm and impartial, however intense the provocation. Panic, overt expressions of anger, and inflammatory use of force are serious breaches of police discipline. The FBI riot control manual states that:

> The basic rule, when applying force, is to use only the minimum force necessary to effectively control the situation. Unwarranted application of force will incite the mob to further violence, as well as kindle seeds of resentment for police that, in turn, could cause a riot to recur.[15]

The National Advisory Commission on Civil Disorders has provided excellent, detailed prescriptions for improving police practices, especially in handling urban riots.[16] Despite notable progress since the Commission issued its report in March 1968, many police departments in American cities are still ill-prepared to handle riots and other civil disorders.

In a survey of 16 major cities, this Commission's Task Force on Law and Law Enforcement found that few city governments had established formal, dependable communication links with dissident groups. Few had adequate plans for dealing with disorders, and effective planning staffs were rare. Though all have added riot control to the curriculum of police training, the number of hours devoted to training per man has not increased significantly.

We therefore urge police departments throughout the nation to improve their preparations for anticipating, preventing and controlling group disorders, and to that end to study the approaches that have been employed successfully on the three most recent occasions in Washington and Chicago.[17]

FIVE • KEEPING OPEN THE CHANNELS OF PEACEFUL PROTEST

We have pointed out the fundamental distinction between protest and violence, the fact that there is no necessary connection between them, and the need to vindicate the former while opposing the latter. As we have noted, the First Amendment to the Constitution protects freedom of speech, freedom of the press, and the "right of the people peaceably to assemble and to petition the government for a redress of grievances." In the Supreme Court's words, the First Amendment entails a "profound national commitment to the principle that debate on public issues should be uninhibited, robust and wide open." [18]

Obstructions to peaceful speech and assembly—whether by public officials, policemen, or unruly mobs—abridge the fundamental right to free expression. On the other hand, speech, assembly and other forms of conduct that become coercive or intimidating invade the fundamental First Amendment rights of other citizens. When a mob forces a university to suspend classes, the rights of teachers to teach and students to learn are abridged; when a speaker is shouted down or forced from a platform, he is deprived of freedom to speak, and the great majority of the audience is deprived of freedom to listen.

Society's failure to afford full protection to the exercise of these rights is probably a major reason why protest sometimes results in violence. Although these rights are expressly safeguarded by the federal Constitution, the existing remedies available to aggrieved persons are not adequate. The only approximation to an effective remedy at the federal level is a court injunction authorized under 42 U.S.C. sec. 1983, a Reconstruction era civil rights statute that creates a private cause of action for the "deprivation of any rights, privileges, or immunities secured by the Constitution" by any person acting "under color of" state law. The relative ineffectiveness of this private remedy is indicated by the rarity with which injunctions have been sought in the thirty years since the statute was first interpreted to apply to interference with First Amendment rights. Moreover, state officials acting under color of state law are not alone in posing threats to First Amendment rights; on college campuses, for example, the protesters themselves have obstructed free speech and peaceful assembly. No present federal law affords a remedy for private abridgement of First Amendment rights.[19]

66

Accordingly, we recommend that the President seek legislation that would confer jurisdiction upon the United States District Courts to grant injunctions, upon the request of the Attorney General or private persons, against the threatened or actual interference by any person, whether or not under color of state or federal law, with the rights of individuals or groups to freedom of speech, freedom of the press, peaceful assembly and petition for redress of grievances.

Under present law private citizens can seek federal injunctions in instances where the complainant alleges unreasonable denial of permits for parades or meetings by state or federal officials or their issuance only on excessively restrictive conditions. Private persons can also obtain federal injunctive relief on proof of suppression by government agencies or their employees of publications or communications (including the seizure or destruction of newsmen's cameras or film) or the use by law enforcement officials of excessive or unauthorized force to arrest or disperse individuals who seek to make lawful expressions of their views. Our proposal would authorize the Attorney General, as well as private persons, to initiate such proceedings in appropriate cases involving state or federal action. It would also authorize suits for injunctions, both by the Attorney General and by private persons, against private obstruction of the exercise of free expression by pushing speakers off platforms, by the making of deliberately excessive noise—or by seizure of or denial of access to buildings or other facilities, streets and public areas—a type of interference with First Amendment rights not now covered by any federal statute.

The statute should also authorize suits for either damages or an injunction by the persons aggrieved and allow the Attorney General to intervene in such suits on request of the parties or the court or on his own motion. State and federal courts should be given concurrent jurisdiction to enforce the statute.

Our proposal suggests a greater federal role in preserving freedom of expression. We do so because federal district courts, which often deal with somewhat comparable provisions in other areas of federal law, are experienced in handling requests for injunctions expeditiously and fashioning careful and effective decrees. The use of federal court injunctions would also provide for greater uniformity in the judicial treatment of those infringing the constitutional rights of others. It would increase the likelihood that the experience of one community or institution would be readily available and useful in handling subsequent problems elsewhere.

State remedies against private misconduct involving infringement of First Amendment rights are usually based not on the First Amendment but on trespass statutes or disorderly conduct ordinances. Such laws were not written to deal with acts of physical obstruction, particularly those committed for demonstrative purposes, and are not always effective in handling such conduct. Moreover, where acts of violence or obstruction are committed in the name of righting fundamental grievances, those engaging in such conduct may find it harder to justify disobedience of court orders issued to uphold the First Amendment than would be true of orders based upon the laws against trespass and disorderly conduct.

In recent legislation, Congress has given the Attorney General an increasingly active role in protecting certain vital individual rights. This approach seems particularly appropriate for the protection of First Amendment rights, since the mechanism of peaceful dispute, debate, compromise, and change is so essential to the preservation of a just and orderly society and since private persons are often unable to protect their First Amendment rights without some assistance.

For speech, petition and assembly to be effective, they must be heard and seen. In 1789 this was a regular consequence of exercising one's First Amendment rights. In today's crowded and complex society, however, being seen and heard depends almost entirely upon the printed and electronic news media, which are necessarily selective in picking out the relatively few items in a day's or a week's events that can be fitted into the space or time available for reporting "news." The *New York Times* daily receives 1.25 to 1.5 million words of news material from its correspondents and news services; of that amount, only about one-tenth is printed.

Moreover, the number of separate, independent news "voices" has not kept up with the growing size and diversity

68

of the nation. Economic factors have forced down the number of regularly published daily newspapers and weekly magazines despite substantial population increases. The number of radio and television stations in any area is greater but still relatively small; more importantly, there is little difference among them in their reporting of the "news." Protesting groups can and do print their own newspapers and handbills, but their circulation is rarely extensive. All in all, the number of efforts to gain attention through the exercise of free speech and assembly far exceeds the number that impact upon the public consciousness as news. For example, the *New York Times* received over 37,000 letters to the editor last year; only six percent were published, though at least 85 percent were, in the words of the *Times* motto, considered "fit to print." Had they all been printed, they would have completely filled 135 daily issues of the newspaper.

The difficulties presented by today's society for those who want their protests and demonstrations to be seen and heard leave most people unaware of how deeply felt many grievances have become. A decade ago it would have been fair to say—as many thoughtful journalists have since admitted—that the press did too little reporting of the existence of social injustice and of the grievances of protesting groups. It was generally thought that open conflict—especially violent conflict—was the most important kind of news. Too few news reports went beyond a description of "who-what-when-where" into the "why" of social and political analysis. The national press, for example, has acknowledged its past shortcomings in covering the life and the problems of our black, Indian and Latin American minorities and their efforts to redress their grievances.

Today, in-depth analysis of underlying social conditions is now a regular and welcome part of the best of our print and broadcast media. Many responsible journalists now recognize more fully the challenge of their crucial role in creating the public understanding of complex modern problems that is a necessary precondition for informed democratic decisions on the timing and content of peaceful social and institutional change. Indeed, some critics—wrongly in our opinion—complain that the media now go too far in reporting protests and in commentary on their causes.

Like the Kerner Commission before us, this Commission has struggled with the question of what public or private measures a governmental body might recommend to improve the efforts of the press to report on the problems facing individuals and groups in American society and alternative means proposed for solving them, as well as on protest and its underlying causes. We have concluded the indispensable element of a free press is pluralism and diversity: we need more effective and different voices, not fewer and fewer standardized or homogenized ones.

Accordingly, we recommend that private and governmental institutions encourage the development of competing news media and discourage increased concentration of control over existing media.

Apart from such strictly limited measures of government intervention as the "fairness doctrine" for broadcasters who operate under public license—which deals not with the substance of broadcast speech but only with the broadcaster's duty to present all sides—we oppose official attempts to control how the media present and interpret the news. Governmental interference with the free press is no way to cure its defects. The need is rather for constant self-appraisal and for responsible, effective criticism of the media by private entities such as university schools of journalism and by any group or individual, public or private, aggrieved by any aspect of media performance.

We urge that the members of the journalism profession continue to improve and re-evaluate their standards and practices, and to strengthen their capacity for creative self-criticism, along the lines suggested in the staff report of our Media Task Force.[20]

An observer of the current journalistic scene has recently observed:

It ought to be plain, but seemingly it is not, that the quality of journalism depends primarily on journalists—not on government and not on the legal owners of media. . . .

Journalism will always need artistry to reach the public's mind and heart. Indeed, what is now required is a higher level of art, a boldness that will get journalism unstuck from forms of communication developed in and for a social context very different from the present. Nobody except journalists can develop such forms.[21]

70

SIX • ESTABLISHING JUSTICE

The third element in any program for reducing group violence is to see to it that our political and social institutions "establish justice" and that valid grievances of disadvantaged groups of citizens are redressed in a timely manner.

Man's progress has reached a stage in which several forces combine to create critical stresses in our social and political structure. First, technological advances and population growth have wrought profound and complex changes in our physical environment and our ability to control it so as to meet basic human needs. Second, an extended period of considerable progress in raising standards of living and education for all and in providing greater social justice for disadvantaged groups—however unevenly—has created rising expectations of still further progress and demands that it be brought about. Third, our political and social institutions and the programs they manage are not changing rapidly enough to keep up with the speed of change in the environment they are intended to control. Although we now have the technological and economic capability of releasing all our citizens from poverty and social deprivation, we have not been willing or able to fashion the changes in our political institutions and public programs that will bring to the disadvantaged the liberation that is almost within their grasp. This combination of forces creates demands for change that are not being met, and leads to protests that sometimes result in group violence.

To appreciate the magnitude of these forces and the stresses that result, we need look back no further than the beginning of this century. In 1900, within the memory of men still alive, we were a nation of 75 million people, of whom less than forty percent lived in metropolitan areas. We rode in carriages or trains. We communicated by mail and the printed word.

Today, within the same land space, we have almost tripled our number. Two-thirds of us live in urban concentrations. We motor at high speeds over a nation paved with freeways. We fly across and between the continents. We communicate by telephone, radio and television. Our resources and the demands we place upon them have increased enormously; so has our individual specialization of function and our dependence on one another for shelter and food, for personal safety, and even for the purity of the air we breathe.

But our political and social institutions and programs have not kept pace. We have achieved the phenomenal forward leap to the moon, but we have not managed the flow of traffic in New York. Most of us now live in metropolitan areas, but as noted in Chapter II, "Violent Crime," we have made few, if any, advances in the art of governing the urban environment. We desire peace, but we are now engaged in the fourth war of this century. Science has shown us how to provide so much food that surpluses embarrass us economically, yet millions are hungry. We boast of our dedication to the concept that all men are created equal, yet inequality of opportunity remains our most persistent problem.

Despite our special penchant for economic and technological innovation, we tend like other peoples to resist political and social change. Thomas Jefferson noted this phenomenon and its relationship to violence. After a lifetime of public service, he observed:

I am certainly not an advocate for frequent and untried changes in laws and constitutions. . . . But I know also, that laws and institutions must go hand in hand with progress of the human mind. As that becomes more developed, more enlightened, as new discoveries are made, new truths disclosed, and manners and opinions change with the change of circumstances, institutions must advance also and keep pace with the times. We might as well require a man to wear still the coat which fitted him when a boy, as civilized society to remain ever under the regimen of their barbarous ancestors. It is this preposterous idea which has lately deluged Europe in blood. Their monarchs, instead of wisely yielding to the gradual change of circumstances, of favoring progressive accommodation to progressive improvement, have clung to old abuses, entrenched themselves behind steady habits, and obliged their subjects to seek through blood and violence rash and ruinous innovations, which, had they been referred to the peaceful deliberations and collected wisdom of the nation, would have been put into acceptable and salutary forms.[22]

We strongly urge all Americans to reflect upon Jefferson's observations, and their special relevance to the causes and prevention of group violence. Today, the pace of change has become far more rapid than when Jefferson wrote, and the need for adapting our institutions to the changing environment has become greater still. Today, more than ever before, we need to strengthen and utilize our institutions for peaceful redress of grievances and peaceful accommodation to the quickening pace of social change.[23]

1. For present purposes we define group violence as the unlawful threat or use of force by any group that results or is intended to result in the injury or forcible restraint or intimidation of persons, or the destruction or forcible seizure of property.

2. Report of the Task Force on Historical and Comparative Perspectives, *Violence in America*, Vol. 2 (U.S. Government Printing Office: Washington, D.C., 1969), pp. 445-6. The Department of Justice recorded 22 deaths in civil disturbances in the last 6 months of 1968 and the first 3 months of 1969; 11 of these deaths occurred in a single disturbance—the Cleveland "shoot-out" in July of 1968. Similarly, while most of the nation's 2,300 college campuses probably experienced some kind of demonstrative protest during the academic year 1968-1969, the American Council on Education has found that only about six percent of the colleges experienced destruction of property or injury to persons. *Campus Disruption During 1968-1969*, ACE Research Reports, Vol. 4, No. 3 (1969), p. 8.

3. Comparative figures for property damage as the result of group protests are not available. But when measured against property damage resulting from more than 1,000,000 annual robberies and burglaries reported in crime statistics, it also seems likely that group protest accounts for a very small part of the deliberate property damage we experience.

4. *Violence in America*, p. 448. This comparison is based on available data that may not be fully comparable on a cross-national basis.

5. *The Politics of Protest* (U.S. Government Printing Office: Washington, D.C., 1969), pp. 81-82.

6. We use the term "offensive" violence as violence used to advance the cause of a protesting group, and the term "defensive" violence as violence used to defend the position of the group threatened by protest. Occasionally, a peacefully protesting group meeting defensive violence as so defined may engage in counter-violence as a means of self defense, as is true of the Negro Deacons for Defense in Mississippi and Alabama.

7. In *Violence in America*, p. 290, Philip Taft and Philip Ross conclude: "The effect of labor violence was almost always harmful to the union. There is little evidence that violence succeeded in gaining advantage for strikers."

8. John W. Gardner, *No Easy Victories* (New York: Harper and Row, 1968), p. 5.

9. See B. C. Roberts, "On the Origins and Resolution of English Working-Class Protest," in *Violence in America*, pp. 197-220.

10. Report of the Task Force on Law and Law Enforcement, *Law and Order Reconsidered* (U.S. Government Printing Office: Washington, D. C., 1969), p. 335.

11. The Democratic Convention and the possible desire of some demonstrators to influence its outcome by violence may have intensified the disorder in Chicago—a circumstance absent during the Washington Inaugural.

12. The Washington authorities had also dealt successfully with the large-scale antiwar march on the Pentagon in October 1967.

13. The bulk of the actual work of maintaining the peacefulness of the proceedings was performed by the demonstrators themselves. An estimated five thousand "marshals," recruited from among the demonstrators, flanked the crowds throughout. Their effectiveness was shown when they succeeded in stopping an attempt by the fringe radicals to leave the line of march in an effort to reach the White House during the Saturday parade.

Fringe groups among the demonstrators, numbering approximately 100, provoked two confrontations by throwing rocks at police on Friday night, November 14, as they unlawfully attempted to march on the Embassy of South Vietnam, and again on Saturday evening when rocks and paint bombs were used during an otherwise lawful assembly at the Justice Department. On both occasions, police used tear gas to disperse the crowds among which the extremists were mingled.

14. *Report of the National Advisory Commission on Civil Disorders* (U.S. Government Printing Office: Washington, D.C., 1968), p. 171.

15. *Law and Order Reconsidered,* p. 352.

16. *Report,* Chapter 12.

17. See generally, *Law and Order Reconsidered,* Chapters 15 and 16.

18. *New York Times* v. *Sullivan,* 376 U.S. 254.

19. The Supreme Court has suggested that federal statutory remedies against such private acts of interference are constitutional but that no statute yet enacted provides them. *United States* v. *Guest,* 383 U.S. 745.

20. These suggestions include more attention to in-depth, interpretive news reporting; hiring and training newsmen from minority groups and providing equivalent regular coverage of minority group activities including births and deaths, business promotions and social functions, as well as larger issues; and creation of vehicles for responsible criticism of news media performance, including internal grievance machinery within news organizations, community press councils, professional journalism reviews, and a national center for media study. See *Mass Media and Violence,* to be published.

21. Max Ways, "What's Wrong with News? It Isn't New Enough," *Fortune Magazine,* October 1969.

22. Letter to Samuel Kerchival, July 12, 1816. *Writings of Thomas Jefferson* (Lippincott, 1871), Vol. VII, p. 15.

23. We present our recommendations for achieving this goal throughout this report.

IV ● CIVIL DISOBEDIENCE*

(Section I of this chapter is adopted by a majority of the Commission: Commissioners Boggs, Hoffer, Hruska, Jaworski, Jenner, McCulloch and McFarland. Commissioners Eisenhower, Harris, Hart, Higginbotham and Menninger do not adopt Section I, but instead believe that such relationship as may exist between disobedience to law and the contemporary forms of violence occurring in the United States is more adequately and accurately discussed in Chapter 2 of the Task Force Report, *Law and Order Reconsidered,* which is incorporated herein as Section II of this Chapter. Cardinal Cooke does not join the majority statement in Section I but does approve of Section II. Thus, all Commissioners approve of Section II.

Four Commissioners have filed additional statements, appearing in Section III as follows: (A) additional statement of Cardinal Cooke, (B) additional statement of

---

*An edited version of statement issued December 8, 1969.

Ambassador Harris, (C) additional statement of Senator Hart, and (D) additional statement of Judge Higginbotham.)

ONE

In a Task Force Report, *Law and Order Reconsidered*, presented to our Commission, the authors found it impossible to present a discourse on law and law enforcement without including a discussion of civil disobedience as contemporarily practiced. We, too, regard the impact of civil disobedience practices so relevant to the problem of maintaining our society obedient to law, that, in addition to endorsing the Staff Report,[1] we feel impelled to add comments of our own.

Our concern with civil disobediences is not that they may involve acts of violence *per se*. Most of them do not. Rather, our concern is that erosion of the law is an inevitable consequence of widespread civil disobediences.

As observed by a legal scholar, . . . it is necessary to persuade those bent on civil disobedience that their conduct is fraught with danger, that violation of one law leads to violation of other laws, and eventually to a climate of lawlessness that by easy stages leads to violence.

Our Commission heard the testimony of a number of noted educators who described their experiences with and causes of campus disruptions. The head of one of the nation's largest universities summed up his views with this comment: "I think that civil disobediences are mainly responsible for the present lawbreaking on university campuses."

An analysis of widely publicized defiances of law antecedent to the eruption of campus disorders supports that conclusion. For several years, our youth has been exposed to dramatic demonstrations of disdain for law by persons from whom exemplary conduct was to be expected. Segregationist governors had disobeyed court orders and had proclaimed their defiance of judicial institutions; civil rights leaders had openly disobeyed court injunctions and had urged their followers to do likewise; striking teachers'

75

union members had contemptuously ignored judicial decrees. It was not surprising that college students, following adult example, destroyed scientific equipment and research data, interfered with the rights of others by occupying laboratories and classrooms, and in several instances temporarily closed their colleges.

The cancerous growth of disobediences has now reached many high schools and junior high schools of the nation.

Pointing out that force and repression are not the only threats to the rule of law, the dean of one of the nation's largest law schools observed:

> The danger also arises from those groups whose commitments to social reform and the eradication of injustices lead to the defiance of law and the creation of disorder. We are learning that the rule of law can be destroyed through lack of fidelity to the law by large numbers of citizens as well as through abuses of authority by governmental officials.[3]

In our democratic society, lawlessness cannot be justified on the grounds of individual belief. The spectrum of individual consciences encompasses social and political beliefs replete with discordant views. If, for example, the civil libertarian in good conscience becomes a disobeyer of law, the segregationist is endowed with the same choice of conscience, or vice versa. If this reasoning is carried to its logical conclusion, we must also make allowance for the grievances of numerous groups of citizens who regard themselves shackled by laws in which they do not believe. Is each group to be free to disregard due process and to violate laws considered objectionable? If personal or group selectivity of laws to be obeyed is to be the yardstick, we shall face nationwide disobedience of many laws and thus anarchy.

We regard the right of peaceful dissent to be fundamental, not only to the individual freedoms we enjoy, but to the social progress so essential to our nation. Yet, just as fundamental are the disciplines that must control our individual and group actions, without which individual freedoms would be threatened and social progress retarded.

The United States Supreme Court, in upholding convictions for contempt of court of civil rights leaders, admonished all our citizens in these words:

. . . no man can be judged in his own case, however exalted his station, however righteous his motives, and irrespective of his race, color, politics or religion. . . . One may sympathize with the petitioners' impatient commitment to their cause. But respect for judicial process is a small price to pay for the civilizing hand of law, which alone can give abiding meaning to constitutional freedom.[4]

Every time a court order is disobeyed, each time an injunction is violated, each occasion on which a court decision is flouted, the effectiveness of our judicial system is eroded. How much erosion can it tolerate? It takes no prophet to know that our judicial system cannot face wholesale violations of its orders and still retain its efficacy. Violators must ponder the fact that once they have weakened the judicial system, the very ends they sought to attain—and may have attained—cannot then be preserved. For the antagonist of the disobeyer's attained objectives most likely will proceed viciously to violate them and since judicial institutions would no longer possess essential authority and power, the "rights" initially gained could be quickly lost.

It is argued that in instances where disobeyers seek to test the constitutionality of a legislative enactment or a court decree, and are willing to accept punishment, their acts should be condoned. We suggest that if in good faith the constitutionality of a statute, ordinance or a court decree is to be challenged, it can be done effectively by one individual or a small group. While the judicial test is in progress, all other dissenters should abide by the law involved until it is declared unconstitutional.

We commend to our fellow citizens the words of Richard Cardinal Cushing:

. . . observance of law is the eternal safeguard of liberty, and defiance of law is the surest road to tyranny. . . . Even among lawabiding men, few laws are loved, but they are uniformly respected and not resisted.

If we are to maintain and improve our democratic society, the government, including the judiciary, must have the respect and the loyalty of its citizens.

TWO • DISOBEDIENCE TO LAW*

Over the past two decades increasing numbers of people seem to have embraced the idea that active disobedience to valid law—perhaps even violent disobedience—is justified for the purpose of achieving a desirable political goal. This idea found widespread support in the South as the white majority in that region resisted enforcement of the constitutionally defined rights of Negroes, and some such notion was probably not far from the minds of the Alabama State Troopers when they attacked Dr. King's peaceful demonstration at Selma in 1965. No doubt it was also prominent in the thinking of the Chicago policemen who administered punishment to the demonstrators in Chicago during the Democratic Convention of 1968.

The same idea—that disobedience to law is justified in a good cause which can be furthered in no other way—is also widely held by many students, black citizens and other groups pressing for social change in America today. It is the illegal and sometimes violent activities of these groups that have been most perplexing and disturbing to the great majority of Americans. Their actions have prompted the most intense interest in the ancient philosophical question of man's duty of obedience to the state. Business lunches and suburban cocktail parties have come to sound like freshman seminars in philosophy, as an older generation has argued back and forth over the rightness and the wrongness of "what the kids and the Negroes are doing."

When deliberate, active disobedience to duly enacted, constitutionally valid law is widely engaged in as a political tactic, and when "civil disobedience" is a topic hotly debated on every side, it is impossible for a Task Force on Law and Law Enforcement to file a report that does not discuss this age-old subject, however briefly.

---

*This section reproduces Chapter 2 of the Report of our staff Task Force on Law and Law Enforcement, *Law and Order Reconsidered* (U.S. Government Printing Office: Washington, D.C., 1969). The chapter was prepared by the Directors of the Task Force, based in part on contributions by Francis A. Allen, Dean of the Law School, University of Michigan; Charles Monson, Associate Academic Vice President, University of Utah; and Eugene V. Rostow, Professor of Law, Yale University.

In a democratic society, dissent is the catalyst of progress. The ultimate viability of the system depends upon its ability to accommodate dissent; to provide an orderly process by which disagreements can be adjudicated, wrongs righted, and the structure of the system modified in the face of changing conditions. No society meets all these needs perfectly. Moreover, political and social organizations are, by their nature, resistant to change. This is as it should be, because stability—order—is a fundamental aim of social organization. Yet stability must not become atrophy, and the problem is to strike the proper balance between amenability to change and social stability.

Every society represents a style of living. The style is represented by the way in which people relate to the social structure, the way in which social decisions are made, the procedures which govern the ways people in the society relate to each other. In a democratic society such as ours, the governing ideals are government by the rule of law, equality before the law, and ultimate control of the lawmaking process by the people. We depend upon these principles both to accommodate and to limit change, and to insure the style of living we prefer.

As Tocqueville observed, America is peculiarly a society of law. The law has played a greater part among us than is the case in any other social system—in our restless and jealous insistence on the utmost range of freedom for the individual; in our zeal to confine the authority of the state within constitutional dikes; and in our use of law as a major instrument of social change. The practice of judicial review in the United States has had an extraordinary development, with no real parallels elsewhere. It has kept the law a powerful and persistent influence in every aspect of our public life.

We believe with Jefferson that the just powers of government are derived—and can only be derived—from the consent of the governed. We are an independent, stiff-necked people, suspicious of power, and hardly docile before authority. We never hesitate to challenge the justness and the constitutional propriety of the powers our

79

governments and other social institutions assert. In the robust and sinewy debates of our democracy, law is never taken for granted simply because it has been properly enacted.

Our public life is organized under the explicit social compact of the Constitution, ratified directly by the people, not the states, and designed to be enforced by the courts and by the political process as an instrument to establish and at the same time to limit the powers of government. As Justice Brandeis once observed, "[t]he doctrine of the separation of powers was adopted by the Convention of 1787, not to promote efficiency but to preclude the exercise of arbitrary power. The purpose was, not to avoid friction, but, by means of the inevitable friction incident to the distribution of the governmental powers among three departments, to save the people from autocracy. . . . And protection of the individual . . . from the arbitrary or capricious exercise of power . . . was believed to be an essential of free government."

The social contract of our Constitution goes beyond the idea of the separation of powers, and of enforceable limits on the competence of government. The governments established by the national and state constitutions of the United States are not omnipotent. A basic feature of the Constitution, made explicit in the Ninth and Tenth Amendments, is that right not delegated to governments are reserved to the people. The Amendments may not be directly enforceable in the courts, but the idea they represent animates many judicial decisions, and influences the course of legislation and other public action.

In a multitude of ways, the Constitution assures the individual a wide zone of privacy and of freedom. It protects him when accused of crime. It asserts his political rights—his right to speak, to vote, and to assemble peaceably with his fellows to petition the government for a redress of his grievances. Freedom of speech and of the press are guaranteed. Religious liberty is proclaimed, and an official establishment of religion proscribed. And the Constitution seeks assurance that society will remain open and diverse, hospitable to freedom, and organized around many centers of power and influence, by making the rules of federalism and of liberty enforceable in the courts.

80

The unwritten constitution of our habits is dominated by the same concern for preserving individual freedom against encroachment by the state or by social groups. The anti-trust laws; the rights of labor; the growing modern use of state power to assure the equality of the Negro; the wide dispersal of power, authority, and opportunity in the hands of autonomous institutions of business, labor, and education—all bespeak a characteristic insistence that our social arrangements protect liberty, and rest on the legitimacy of consent, either through the Constitution itself, made by the people, and capable of change only by their will, or through legislation and other established methods of social action.

In broad outline, such is the pluralist social compact which has evolved out of our shared experience as a people. It has its roots in our history. And it grows and changes, in accordance with its own rules and aspirations, as every generation reassesses its meaning and its deals.

Our Contemporary Discontents

Today there are many who maintain that these ideals, and the institutions established to maintain them, no longer operate properly. In recent years, increasing numbers of Americans have taken to the streets to express their views on basic issues. Some come to exercise their right to dissent by parades and picketing. Some dramatize their causes by violating laws they feel to be wrong. Some use the issues being protested as drums to beat in a larger parade. For example, the Vietnam war has been used on one side as a dramatic moment in the ubiquitous, always-evil Communist conspiracy; on the other as an exemplar of the fundamental diabolism of western capitalist nations. Some take to the streets in the belief that the public, if made aware of their grievances, will institute the necessary processes to correct them. Others come in anger; not hopeful, but insistent; serving notice, not seeking audience. Finally, there are even a few who take to the streets to tear at the fabric of society; to confront, to commit acts of violence, to create conditions under which the present system can be swept away.

Out of the widening protest, one disturbing theme has repeatedly appeared. Increasingly, those who protest speak

81

of civil disobedience or even revolution as necessary instruments of effecting needed social change, charging that the processes of lawful change built into the system are inadequate to the task.

The American response to this disobedience to law—to events which are contrary to our fundamental beliefs about the mode of social and political change—has been ambivalent. The reason lies in the fact that the American people are going through a crisis of conscience. The issues in whose name violence has been committed have deeply disturbed and divided the American people. The tactics of the demonstrators have encountered angry opposition, but many Americans continue to sympathize with some or all of the goals sought by the demonstrators. After all, although one might argue that the Negro has advanced in the last ten years, few would maintain he has attained full first-class citizenship. And who would say the ghettos are not an agonizing disgrace? Similarly, Vietnam is hardly an open-and-shut case. The only point of view from which it is clearly praiseworthy is the self-interest of ourselves and our allies. The draft, another key issue, is at best a regrettable and clumsily administered system. Finally, when the young charge that our system—political and social—is shot through with hypocrisy, only the most fanatic feels no twinge.

We must, of course, realize that civil rights demonstrations arise from great suffering, disappointment and yearning. We must recognize the importance to the democratic process, and to the ultimate well-being of our nation, of young people combatting hypocrisy and indifference. But when these emotions become a basis for action and when that action creates social disorder, even the most sympathetic are forced to judge whether and to what extent the ends sought justify the means that are being used.

The difficult problem in this endeavor is to maintain perspective. The issues have reached a stage of polarization. Partisans on each side constantly escalate the rhetorical savagery of their positions, adding nothing but volume and abuse. There is a great temptation to take sides without thoughtful inquiry—if for no other reason than because it is simpler. What are some of the considerations which should guide us in this inquiry?

Moral Justifications for Disobedience to Law:
The Needs of the Individual

The idea that men have the right to violate the law under certain circumstances is not new. The oldest justification for such action seems to have been through appeal to a higher "natural law" which is the only proper basis of human law. This theory, which dates at least as far back as Plato, and which is in our own Declaration of Independence,[5] has recently found expression in the thought of Martin Luther King:

A just law is a man-made law of God. An unjust law is a code that is out of harmony with the moral law. To put it in the terms of Saint Thomas Aquinas, an unjust law is a human law that is not rooted in eternal and natural law.[6]

For St. Thomas political authority was derived from God and hence binding in conscience, but where authority was defective in title or exercise, there was no obligation of conscience.[7] Such a condition arose in the case of a ruler who had either usurped power or who, though legitimate, was abusing his authority by ruling unjustly. Indeed, when the ruler contravened the very purpose of his authority by ordering a sinful action, the subject was under an obligation *not* to obey. In the case of abuse of authority, St. Thomas apparently endorsed nothing more than passive resistance by the citizen; but where the ruler illegitimately possessed himself of power through violence, and there was no other recourse for the citizen, then St. Thomas allowed active resistance and even tyrannicide.

Later Catholic thinkers, such as the Jesuit, Francis Suarez, denied the divine right of kings, holding that the ruler derives his authority immediately from the people and only ultimately from God. These doctrines led logically to the conclusion that in any circumstances in which a ruler turns into a tyrant, whether originally a legitimate ruler or not, he may be deposed by the people, by force if necessary. This conclusion became, of course, the generally accepted view in the secular world, with the theories of Locke and Jefferson and the American and French Revolutions in the eighteenth century and the rise of liberal democracy in the nineteenth.

The notion of a "social compact" was always closely bound up with the emerging ideas of popular sovereignty.[8] This theory, especially prominent in John Locke, expresses the view that governments evolve by the consent of the governed and that the constitution establishing a government is a contract or agreement which, once it is established, is binding upon all men, both those opposed to it and those who favor it. When government's laws are consistent with terms of the covenant, then the people must obey them. But the people "are absolved from obedience when illegal attempts are made upon their liberties or properties, and may oppose the unlawful violence of those who were their magistrates when they invade their properties contrary to the trust put in them. . . ."[9]

Most of the unlawful opposition today to the Vietnam war is justified on the ground that the war is itself immoral and "unlawful" in various respects. Since it is immoral, the argument goes, there is no moral duty to obey those laws which are in the aid of the conduct of the war. Indeed, the argument continues, one's true moral duty is to resist the war and to take affirmative action to impede its prosecution. On theories of this kind, Americans have refused to be drafted; they have disrupted Selective Service facilities and destroyed Selective Service records; they have vilified the President, the Secretary of State and the Secretary of Defense and attempted to disrupt their public speeches; they have attempted to bar companies and governmental agencies participating in the war effort from university campuses and to disrupt the universities that refused to accede to that demand.

At the level of individual morality, the problem of disobedience to law is wholly intractable. One is tempted to suggest that even if the war is immoral, the general level of morality of the country is not much improved by the conduct described above. Moreover, if we allow individual conscience to guide obedience to the law, we must take all consciences. The law cannot distinguish between the consciences of saints and sinners. As Burke Marshall has said:

If the decision to break the law really turned on individual conscience, it is hard to see in law how Dr. King is better off than Governor Ross Barnett of Mississippi, who also believed deeply in his cause and was willing to go to jail.[10]

Where issues are framed in purely moral terms, they are usually incapable of resolution by substantially unanimous agreement. Moral decisions are reached by "individual prudential application of principle, with the principles so general as to be only of minimal assistance and with almost the whole field thus left to prudence."[11] This fact is illustrated by the story of the exchange that occurred between Emerson and Thoreau, the latter of whom had in 1845 personally seceded from the United States in protest against slavery. As part of his anti-slavery campaign, Thoreau was spending a night in jail. Emerson paid him a visit, greeting him by saying, "What are you doing in there, Henry?" Thoreau looked at him through the bars and replied, "What are you doing out there, Ralph?"[12]

But the issue raised by conscientious disobedience to law also has some more tractable social dimensions. What is the effect upon our society of this kind of conduct? For instance, how does it affect the people who engage in the disobedience? Does it have an effect upon other people? What does it do to our system of laws?

The Problem of Contagion: The Needs of Society

Although there are some who argue that tolerating any form of law violation serves as an encouragement of other forms of anti-social or criminal behavior by the violators, some research in this area suggests precisely the opposite. A series of studies of approximately 300 young black people who engaged in a series of acts of civil disobedience were undertaken in a western city. On the basis of their observations, the authors concluded: "[T]here have been virtually no manifestations of delinquency or anti-social behavior, no school drop-outs, and no known illegitimate pragnancies. This is a remarkable record for any group of teen-age children of any color in any community in 1965." [13]

In any event, the evidence is insufficient to demonstrate that acts of civil disobedience of the more limited kind inevitably lead to an increased disrespect for law or propensity toward crime. In fact, some experts have argued that engaging in disciplined civil disobedience allows people to

85

channel resentment into constructive paths, thereby reducing the propensity for engaging in antisocial behavior.

But the fact that disobedience to law does not appear adversely to affect the attitudes of the people who engage in it is only one small part of the problem. For such conduct does have a serious adverse effect both upon other people in the society, and, most importantly of all, upon the system of laws upon which society must inevitably depend.

The effect of civil disobedience upon others in the community is clear. Except in the case of those acts designed solely to appeal to the conscience of the community, the purpose of much contemporary disobedience to law is to influence community action by harassing or intimidating the members of the community into making concessions to a particular point of view. In the case of the opposition to the Vietnam war, for example, those engaged in acts of disobedience are largely bent upon making miserable the lives of public officials who support the war, upon bringing economic pressure to bear on commercial enterprises participating in the war effort, and upon generally inconveniencing the public to dramatize a disaffection for war and convince others that the war is not worth the trouble it is causing. To the extent that these efforts succeed, others are obviously adversely affected.[14] But the most serious effect of all is suggested in the following question:

[W]hat lesson is being taught to the wider community by the precept and example of civil disobedience? It is tutelage in nonviolence or in defiance of authority, in rational confrontation of social ills or in undisciplined activism?" [15]

There is every reason to believe that the lesson taught by much of the current disobedience to law is disastrous from the standpoint of the maintenance of a democratic society.

The experience of India in this regard is instructive because that country has had such a long and widespread familiarity with the practice of civil disobedience:

The fact is that the effect of protest behavior on the functioning of the political system has been palpable. We have already seen that Indians compel official attention and constrain decision-making by deliberately engaging in activities that threaten public order. Violence or the threat of violence has become an important instrument in Indian politics. Public protests involving a threat to public order and nonviolent civil disobedience have become habitual responses to alleged failures by government to do what a group of people want. While it is true that political accommodation is real in India, it is achieved at a higher level of political disorder than in any other of the world's democracies.[16]

The experience of India seems to indicate that civil disobedience has a strong tendency to become a pattern of conduct which soon replaces normal legal processes as the usual way in which society functions. Put in American terms, this would mean, once the pattern is established, that the accepted method of getting a new traffic light might be to disrupt traffic by blocking intersections, that complaints against businessmen might result in massive sit-ins, that improper garbage service might result in a campaign of simply dumping garbage into the street, and so on. Of course, these kinds of actions are not unknown in America today, but in India they have become a necessary part of the political system. Without a massive demonstration to support it, a grievance simply is not taken seriously because everyone knows that if the grievance were serious, there would be a demonstration to support it.

The adverse effect upon normal democratic processes is obvious. Though not intended to destroy democratic processes, civil disobedience tends plainly to impair their operation. This is a fact to which those who engage in civil disobedience should give consideration lest, in seeking to improve society, they may well seriously injure it.

This observation, however, will not answer the arguments of those who believe that the urgency of their message is so strong that illegal tactics are weapons that must be used—whatever the risks that such use may entail. But even urgent messages too frequently repeated lose their appeal. Where once people at least listened patiently, now only deaf ears are turned. Moreover, as Martin Luther King recognized, violence against an oppressor only tends in the long run to justify the oppression. Repeatedly putting one's body "on the line" does not enhance, but diminishes, the worth of that body to the dominant society. Those militants who now advocate revolution as the only alternative have recognized this truth.

The belief that a violent revolution is necessary to

achieve social justice depends on the assumption that certain injustices are intrinsic to our system and therefore not amenable to change within the system. For revolution is justified only as a last resort, when justice is achievable by no other means.

We agree with the overwhelming majority of the people in this country that our problems, serious as they are, are not of the kind that make revolution even thinkable, let alone justifiable. We believe that political and social mechanisms do exist and have produced significant change in recent years. The remedy for the discontented, we believe, is to seek change through lawful mechanisms, changes of the kind that other chapters of the Task Force report suggest.

But our beliefs and our words are really beside the point. What is important is rather the beliefs of those diverse, alienated groups in our society for whom the political and social mechanisms do not seem to work. We can only hope that the majority will respond convincingly to the needs of the discontented, and that the discontented will remain open to the possibility of achieving this response through peaceful means.

Conclusion

Official lawlessness—by some southern governors, by some policemen, by corrupt individuals in positions of public trust—is widely recognized as intolerable in a society of law, even if this recognition is too infrequently translated into the effective action to do something about the problem. We believe that the time has also come for those participating today in the various protest movements, on and off the college campuses, to subject their disobedience to law to realistic appraisal. The question that needs to be put to young people of generous impulses all over the country is whether tactics relying on deliberate, symbolic, and sometimes violent lawbreaking are in fact contributing to the emergency of a society that will show enhanced regard for human values—for equality, decency, and individual volition.

For some in the protest movement, this is not a relevant inquiry; their motivations are essentially illiberal and destructive. But this is not descriptive of most of those engaged today in social protest, including most who have violated the law in the course of their protest; their intention is to recall America to the ideals upon which she is founded.

We believe, however, that candid examination of what is occurring in the United States today will lead to the conclusion that disobedience to valid law as a tactic of protest by discontented groups is *not* contributing to the emergence of a more liberal and humane society, but is, on the contrary, producing an opposite tendency. The fears and resentments created by symbolic law violation have strengthened the political power of some of the most destructive elements in American society. Only naive and willful blindness can obscure the strength of these dark forces, which, but for the loosening of the bonds of law, might otherwise lie quiescent beneath the surface of our national life. An almost Newtonian process of action and reaction is at work, and fanaticism even for laudable goals breeds fanaticism in opposition. Just as "extremism in defense of liberty" does not promote liberty, so extremism in the cause of justice will extinguish hopes for a just society.

THREE ● A. ADDITIONAL STATEMENT OF CARDINAL COOKE

Our democratic society is based on the concept and common agreement that civil law deserves the respect and obedience of every citizen. Civil disobedience as an act of conscience expressed by public acts of defiance is permissible only as a last resort to obtain justice when all the other remedies available in our system of representation and checks and balances have been exhausted. Civil disobedience can only be justified when a civil law is conscientiously regarded as being clearly in conflict with a higher law—namely our Constitution, the natural law, or divine law. In this extreme case, non-violent forms of civil disobedience, accompanied by willing acceptance of any penalty the law provides, are the only means that can be justified in our democratic society. These principles are not only the foundation of an ordered society under law,

89

but they guarantee our freedom and our social progress as well.

● B. ADDITIONAL STATEMENT OF AMBASSADOR HARRIS

I must take exception to Section I of this chapter. No data developed by or presented to this Commission show a significant relationship between civil disobedience based upon conscience and violence, as the statement itself admits when it says that most civil disobedience does not involve acts of violence *per se*. Furthermore, governmental commissions should tread very lightly, if at all, in fields where individuals make claims of conscience. Those who have urged civil disobedience, from Gandhi to Martin Luther King, and including those who supported the trials of Nazi leaders at Nuremberg, have asserted that there are some laws so repugnant to the dignity of man that regardless of the concurrence of the majority, the law must not be obeyed. A nation whose history enshrines the civil disobedience of the Boston Tea Party cannot fail to recognize at least the symbolic merit of demonstrated hostility to unjust laws.

I am not nearly so certain as are the supporters of Section I that the legal process will always respond effectively to those who resort only to petition and lawsuit. Perhaps my uncertainty is due to the fact that I see a relationship between the civil disobedience of anti-segregation sit-ins and the eventual elimination of laws requiring segregation of the races. Certainly, black Americans had used legal process at least as early as the Dred Scott case. Yet, despite a Civil War, constitutional amendments, and court decisions, black Americans at the beginning of this decade were still faced with laws and practices treating them as second-class citizens. Section I condemns acts such as the sit-ins if they were not for the purpose of instituting a specific test case.

Section I lumps together refusals to obey a law because of the fundamental demands of conscience, on the one hand, and the simple refusal to obey a law because one disagrees with a particular law, on the other. Although I agree that both law violators are to be punished, I believe there is a difference in incidental willful violation of the law, and

90

carefully considered violation based upon clearly stated objections that have been brought to the attention of government through traditional legislative-legal process and have nonetheless been ignored.

It should be clear that extensive acts of civil disobedience based upon the demands of conscience are a symptom, and not a cause of societal ills. When otherwise law-abiding citizens claim that conscience will not permit them to obey laws supported by the majority, that majority must, if the society is to remain healthy, examine the laws to ascertain whether they are fair and just, and change them if they are not. This is the process followed in reacting to the civil disobedience of black Americans, and it is a process no less necessary in dealing with others who resort to civil disobedience because of a claim that their conscience will not permit obedience of the law.

I believe, as stated in Chapter VI, that "every society, including our own, must have effective means of enforcing its laws, whatever may be the claims of conscience of individuals." But law enforcement, without continuing review and modification of law, is not the hallmark of a democratic society.

Those who adopted Section I have never belonged to a group required to sit in the back of the bus, or excluded from restaurants because of race, with the approval of legislatures, courts and administrators. I am a member of such a group, and I refused to obey those segregation laws, even though I knew they had been approved by the Supreme Court in *Plessy* v. *Ferguson* and affirmed by decades of acceptance by the majority. It seems unlikely that the segregation law would have been changed had only one person or a small group indicated opposition to it.

It is not inconceivable to me that other persons may feel as deeply about other subjects as I did about racial segregation, and with equal justification. Such well-founded opposition, even if expressed through the ultimate recourse to civil disobedience, is a reflection of the highest respect and hope for a democratic society. It manifests a faith that if the majority understand the real consequences of its intransigence, the majority will change.

Willingness to incur the wrath and punishment of government can represent the highest loyalty and respect for

91

a democratic society. Such respect and self-sacrifice may well prevent, rather than cause, violence.[17]

• C. ADDITIONAL STATEMENT OF SENATOR HART

Despite the compelling logic of the majority opinion on civil disobedience, I feel that history will continue to note circumstances when it is not immoral to be illegal.

Certainly, it is risky for a society to tolerate the concept of civil disobedience, however non-violent it may be. The British governors of India will testify to that. But my faith in the flexibility of the American democratic system just will not allow me to get terribly "up tight" about the prospect of massive disobedience.

We all revere the rule of law. Yet, legal absolutism is as hard to swallow as straight whisky. A drop of water not only improves the flavor of the grain but diminishes the strain on the system that must absorb it.

Perhaps unfortunately, this issue of unquestioning respect for law arises at a moment of history when the civil rights movement has proven the social efficacy of occasional, selective civil disobedience.

As Ambassador Harris points out in her views, legal absolutism would have had an equally difficult time achieving full consensus after the Boston Tea Party.

If an American citizen honestly feels his conscience to be offended by a law, I would have difficulty disputing his right to dramatize his dissent through disobedience provided that:

a. His disobedience is absent violence on his part, and
b. He is willing to submit to the sanctions that disobedience may visit upon him.

Understand, any tolerance that I might feel toward the disobeyer is dependent on his willingness to accept whatever punishment the law may impose. This willingness provides the test of moral conviction and is the safeguard against capricious lawlessness.

If the dramatic act attracts no sympathy from the public that is its audience, if it raises no issue that evokes mass response, if it makes no constitutional point that the courts can agree with, then little harm is done to the fabric of society.

And if the act illuminates a wrong, some good could come of it. My experience in Congress tells me that remedial legislation is not always enacted in response to the cool logic and moral concepts of the legislators.

Reputable scholars tell us that there are indeed occasions when public "heat" has prodded leadership bodies into actions they may otherwise have avoided—a theory I find difficult to dispute.

My faith in the Constitution is great. And our constitutional system will certainly admit of fewer Joans of Arc than less enlightened structures.

Still, a close scrutiny of my own failings—at the risk of unfairly projecting a generalization from a single specific case—leads me to have some doubts about the infallibility of Congress.

It is even conceivable that I might concur in a bill that history comes to regard as an immoral measure. And if one or several citizens truly feel their consciences so offended by that law that they are willing to accept punishment rather than obey it, then I find it difficult to condemn them in advance.

• D. ADDITIONAL STATEMENT OF JUDGE HIGGINBOTHAM

1

When this Commission has been unanimous on so many matters of fundamental importance, it is indeed unfortunate that a majority of seven has caused a minority of six to get involved in an extended debate on the tangential issue of non-violent civil disobedience.[18] The Task Force chapter on "Disobedience To Law,"[19] which apparently all of the Commissioners today adopt, clearly states: "In any event the evidence is insufficient to demonstrate that acts of civil disobedience of the more limited kind lead to an increased disrespect for law or propensity toward crime."

Of course, it is always easier to blame the failures of our society on those who protest than it is to accept our responsibility to create a just society.

93

Is non-violent civil disobedience, as the majority suggests, the major factor to single out as leading inevitably to the erosion of law and the onset of violence? It was not non-violent civil disobedience which caused the death of the Kennedys and Dr. King. It is not non-violent civil disobedience which causes millions to go to bed ill-housed, ill-fed, and too often with too little hope.

Only last month in their superb report on *Poverty Amid Plenty: The American Paradox,* the President's Commission on Income Maintenance Programs found that in 1968, twenty-five million Americans were living in poverty as measured by the federal government's own poverty index. The Commission further found:

". . . severe poverty and its effects throughout the nation and among all ethnic groups. This poverty is not only relative to rising American living standards, but is often stark and absolute. There are too many American families with inadequate shelter, inadequate clothing, absolute hunger, and unhealthy living conditions. Millions of persons in our society do not have a sufficient share of America's affluence to live decently. They eke out a bare existence under deplorable conditions." [20]

The major problem in our country thus is not non-violent civil disobedience, rather, as the National Advisory Commission on Civil Disorders (the Kerner Commission) noted, it has been our failure to have "a realization of common opportunities for all within a single society," and the failure to have a "commitment to national action" which is ". . . compassionate, massive and sustained, backed by the resources of the most powerful and the richest nation on this earth. From every American it will require new attitudes, new understandings and, above all, new will."[21]

2

During the early 1960s, John Fitzgerald Kennedy, Martin Luther King, Robert Francis Kennedy and Lyndon Baines Johnson gave great hope to many who were weak, or poor, and particularly to those who were non-white.

As I read one portion of Section I, there appears to be an implicit call for a retreat from the spirit of the early 1960s when our country was finally starting to face up to its obligation to right the wrongs which had been imposed

94

on black Americans for more than three centuries. Nowhere is that retreat more evident than in the majority statement that:

We suggest that if in good faith the constitutionality of a statute, ordinance or a court decree is to be challenged, it could be done effectively by *one* individual or a small group. While the judicial test is in progress, all other dissenters should abide by the law involved until it is declared unconstitutional.

Is it the majority's position that while Rosa Parks litigated her refusal to take a back seat in 1955 on the Montgomery, Alabama bus, all other Negroes were obligated to continue to accept the degradation of the rear seats assigned them?

Is the majority suggesting that when the first Negroes sat in at a lunch counter in Greensboro, North Carolina, all other Negroes were forbidden to seek an integrated lunch until the issue reached the Supreme Court? Does the majority suggest that there is no correlation between the march in Selma, Alabama, and the ultimate passage of the 1965 Civil Rights Act?

So that no one will misunderstand me, let me make clear my concern about the outbreak of riots and other violent public disorders. I do not urge, I do not sanction, I do not suggest violence—spontaneous or planned—as a way to correct injustices in our system. Moreover, I believe that all those adjudicated guilty under constitutionally valid laws, whether for conscientious civil disobedience or for some other violation of law, must bear the penalties.

Of course, a willingness to accept such penalties was an outstanding characteristic of the leaders of the civil rights movement during the last two decades (particularly Dr. King)—unlike many of those who unlawfully sought to frustrate the goals of the civil rights movement. The majority statement ignores the many critical distinctions—of which this is just one—between the actions of the civil rights leaders and their powerful opponents in the South who often used violence or who persistently violated their oath of office to uphold the law of the land.

If the majority's doctrine of "everyone wait until the outcome of the one individual test case" had been applied by black Americans in the 1960s, probably not one present major civil rights statute would have been enacted. I fear that the majority's position ignores the sad actual history of some of the most tragic "legal" repression of the civil rights of Negroes in this country.

Burke Marshall, "one of the late President Kennedy's most valued advisors,"[22] set a standard of commitment to human rights which should be a model for our country during its present troubled times. In 1964, in his illuminating book, *Federalism and Civil Rights,* Mr. Marshall, then Assistant Attorney General of the Civil Rights Division, discussed the Mississippi experience on the right to vote:

For significant portions of a few states, and for most of Mississippi, Negro disenfranchisement is still a current practice, almost ninety-five years after the enactment of the Fifteenth Amendment. This has been true since the removal of direct (meaning, in this case, military) federal control over the voting and registration processes, and the return of those processes to the states.

This year [in 1964] we have seen the Governor of one state interfere with a local registration board because too many Negroes were being registered. It was only two years ago that another state passed a whole new set of laws aimed at restricting Negro registration, and last year that a third issued new instructions for the strict use of the registration form as a kind of aptitude test.

When the will to keep Negro registration to a minimum is strong, and the routine of determining whose applications are acceptable is within the discretion of local officials, the latitude for discrimination is almost endless. The practices that can be used are virtually infinite.

In Mississippi then, the statistics alone are illuminating. In 1899, twenty-five years after the armed maneuvering of 1874 and nine years after the 1890 convention, the number of Negroes of voting age who were registered was down to 9 percent. By 1955, the gap had widened. In only eleven counties were over 10 percent registered (and in one of those counties the figure was to fall to less than 2 percent the following year); in eight counties, the figure was between 5 and 10 percent; in twenties counties it was from 1 to 5 percent; and in forty-three counties less than 1 percent of Negroes of voting age were registered. The total Negro registration in the state was slightly over 4 percent. These figures are approximately accurate today.

After the invalidation of the white primary, Negroes were prevented, until 1955, from registering by repeated uses of

96

devices so absurd as to be drearily cynical. They were asked to define, for county registrars themselves without training or education, terms such as ex post facto, habeas corpus, due process of law, impeachment, and to interpret the preamble to the Mississippi Constitution. Some were told that they could not register until they could repeat the entire Mississippi Constitution by heart. In one county, Negro applicants were invariably informed that the registrar was not in. In another they were simply refused permission to apply at all.

The pattern of such practices had its inevitable effect. Except in a handful of counties, Negroes could not register to vote, and they did not try.

Following the school decisions of 1954, Mississippi changed its voting laws to meet the expected onslaught of federal law. These became effective on March 24, 1955. As of March, 1964, . . . data . . . taken from records analysis in seventy-two of the eighty-two counties in the state, describe individual incidents and designs of behavior that resulted in continued Negro disenfranchisement under the new laws.

The records show . . . a wide variation in the comprehensibility of the sections of the Mississippi Constitution chosen to test applicants, a matter within the complete discretion of the registrar. For example, the simplest section used is the one stating that there shall be no imprisonment for debt. In one county, this was given often to whites, but never to Negroes. On the other hand, Negroes have been given most complex sections to explain, such as Section 236, describing in detail the levee taxes for the state.

Where the same section is used to test members of both races, the results are not fairly judged. The records disclosed repeated examples where Negroes were turned down for having given inadequate answers even though their answers were better than those given by whites who were accepted.

There were many instances, throughout the counties, of assistance being given to whites, but not to Negroes. In some counties, application forms filled out by whites consistently showed, beyond any possibility of coincidence, almost identical answers on the constitutional interpretation test. In addition, on many occasions, illiterate whites who could not read or answer the questions on the application form without help were registered after being coached by the registrar. At the same time, well-educated Negroes were turned down.[23]

I have cited the Mississippi voting experience in some detail because it demonstrates the tenacity with which injustice can cling to an oppressed group for more than one hundred years when legislative and judicial branches lack the will to destroy injustice.

Recent advances in the field of civil rights have not come about—and could never have come about—solely through judicial tests made "by one individual" while all others in the silent black majority waited for the ultimate constitutional determination.

Rather, the major impetus for the Civil Rights Acts of 1957, 1960, 1964 and 1965, which promised more equal access to the opportunities or our society, resulted from the determination, the spirit, and the non-violent commitment of the many who continually challenged the constitutionality of racial discrimination and awakened the national conscience.[24]

3

A debate on civil disobedience is inexpensive and undemanding. It requires no regeneration of our political and social institutions, no effort to open the doors of opportunity to the disadvantaged, no acts of courage and compassion by dedicated individuals seeking to heal the divisions in our society. It requires neither a reordering of national priorities, nor a reallocation of our immense financial resources.

A debate on civil disobedience can be costly in one sense, however: it can distract attention from the real work and the real contributions of this Commission. When legislators and future historians appraise the work of our commission, I hope that they will remember, not this minor skirmish over a secondary issue, but rather the important recommendations we have made under the unending dedication and great leadership of Dr. Eisenhower.[25] Most fervently of all, I further hope that our nation will find the resolve to support, with decisive action, some of the significant programs which we and other national commissions have recommended, and particularly those of sufficient scope and importance to require a reordering of our nation's priorities and a reallocation of our financial resources.

Despite significant contributions which I think this Commission has made, I must confess to a personal sense of increasing "commission frustration." From having served

98

on three previous national fact-finding commissions, I fear that as some of the conditions in America get worse and worse, our reports about these conditions get better and better. There is too little implementation of the rational solutions proposed, and too often the follow-up is only additional studies.

In the last 25 years our country has been deluged with significant Presidential and national fact-finding commissions, starting with President Truman's Commission to Secure These Rights in 1947. Some of the other great commissions have included the Crime Commission (President's Commission on Law Enforcement and Administration of Justice), The Council to the White House Conference to Fulfill These Rights, the Kerner Commission (National Advisory Commission on Civil Disorders), the Kaiser Commission (President's Committee on Urban Housing), and the Douglas Commission (National Commission on Urban Problems). Thus the problems of poverty, racism and crime have been emphasized and re-emphasized, studied and re-studied, probed and re-probed.

Surveying this landscape, littered with the unimplemented recommendations of so many previous commissions, I am compelled to propose a national moratorium on any additional temporary study commissions to probe the causes of racism, or poverty, or crime, or the urban crisis. The rational response to the work of the great commissions of recent years is not the appointment of still more commissions to study the same problems—but rather the prompt implementation of their many valuable recommendations.

The Kerner Commission concluded its report as follows:

One of the first witnesses to be invited to appear before this commission was Dr. Kenneth B. Clark, a distinguished and perceptive scholar. Referring to the reports of earlier riot commissions, he said:

"I read that report . . . of the 1919 riot in Chicago, and it is as if I were reading the report of the investigating committee on the Harlem riot of '35, the report of the investigating committee on the Harlem riot of '43, the report of the McCone Commission on the Watts riot.

"I must again in candor say to you members of this commission—it is a kind of Alice in Wonderland—with the same moving picture re-shown over and over again, the same analysis, the same recommendations, the same inaction.[26]

And I must also conclude my comments with the perceptive statement of a distinguished psychiatrist, Price M. Cobbs, who testified before our Commission. In a foreword to one of the Task Force reports submitted to us, Dr. Cobbs and his colleague, Dr. Grier, note:

The National Commission on the Causes and Prevention of Violence has a grave task. If violence continues at its present pace, we may well witness the end of the grand experiment of democracy. The unheeded report of the Kerner Commission pinpointed the cause of our urban violence, and this report presents the tragic consequences when those in power fail to act on behalf of the weak as well as the powerful.

This country can no longer tolerate the divisions of black and white, haves and have-nots. The pace of events has quickened and dissatisfactions no longer wait for a remedy.

There are fewer great men among us to counsel patience. Their voices have been stilled by the very violence they sought to prevent. Martin Luther King, Jr., the noble advocate of nonviolence, may have been the last great voice warning the country to cancel its rendezvous with violence before it is too late.

The truth is plain to see. If the racial situation remains inflammatory and the conditions perpetuating poverty remain unchanged, and if vast numbers of our young see small hope for improvement in the quality of their lives, then this country will remain in danger. Violence will not go away because we will it and any superficial whitewash will sooner or later be recognized.[27]

---

1. Incorporated herein as Section II.
2. Norman Dorsen, Professor of Law and Director of the Arthur Garfield Hays Liberties Program, New York University School of Law.
3. Francis A. Allen, Dean of the Law School and Professor of Law, University of Michigan.
4. *Walker* v. *City of Birmingham,* U.S. 307, 320-321.
5. "We hold these truths to be self-evident, that all men are created equal, that they are endowed by their Creator with certain unalienable Rights, that among these are Life, Liberty and the pursuit of Happiness."
6. King, "Letter from the Birmingham Jail" (1963).
7. See generally the illuminating article by MacGuigan, "Civil Disobedience and Natural Law, " 11 *Catholic Lawyer* 118 (1965).
8. See Copleston, *History of Philosophy,* vol. 3 (Westminster, Md., 1953), pp. 348-49.
9. Locke, *Second Treatise on Civil Government,* ch. 19, "Of the Dissolution of Government," sec. 228.
10. Burke Marshall, "The Protest Movement and the Law," 51 U. Va. L. Rev. 785, 800 (1965).
11. MacGuigan, *op. cit.,* p. 125.

12. *Ibid.*

13. Pierce and West, "Six Years of Sit-Ins: Psychodynamics Causes and Effects," 12 *International Journal of Social Psychiatry* 30 (Winter 1966).

14. Even in the narrowly defined situation of acts designed solely to appeal to the conscience of the community, adverse effects frequently flow to others. Thus a refusal to accept induction into the armed services means that someone else must serve.

15. Allen, "Civil Disobedience and the Legal Order," Part 1, 36 *University of Cincinnati Law Review* 1, 30 (1967).

16. Bayley, *Non-violent Civil Disobedience and the Police: Lesson to be Learned from India* (consultant paper submitted to the Task Force), p. 15.

17. "In fact, some experts have argued that engaging in disciplined civil disobedience allows people to channel resentment into constructive paths, thereby reducing the propensity for engaging in antisocial behavior." *Law and Order Reconsidered,* Chapter 2, "Disobedience to Law," p. 19 (incorporated as Section II of this chapter).

18. There is no disagreement among any of the Commissioners in our unanimous condemnation of civil disobedience accompanied by violence. I sincerely regret that due to the pressure of our adjournment time, we were not able to have an additional Commission meeting wherein my present separate statement could be presented and considered. For I know that by their *deeds,* some members of this Commission's majority, such as Congressman William M. McCulloch, have been great profiles in courage to all men interested in equal justice under the law. Congressman McCulloch, one of the most distinguished members of the United States House of Representatives was a member of the Kerner Commission, and for decades he has been a champion for the human rights of all.

19. This chapter is a portion of the extraordinarily excellent and well-balanced report of the Task Force on Law and Law Enforcement under the superb leadership of James S. Campbell, Esquire.

20. Report of the President's Commission on Income Maintenance Programs, *Poverty Amid Plenty: The American Paradox,* (Prelim, Ed. November 12, 1969), p. 1.

21. *Report of the National Advisory Commission on Civil Disorders* (U.S. Government Printing Office: Washington, D.C., 1968), p. 1.

22. Foreword by the then Attorney General Robert F. Kennedy, July 15, 1964, to Marshall, *Federalism and Civil Rights,* (New York: Columbia University Press, 1964), p. x.

23. *Ibid.,* pp. 15-19. See also the perceptive statement of Stephen J. Pollak, the able Assistant Attorney General in charge of the Civil Rights Division in 1968, in his Emancipation Day speech at Mobile, Alabama, Jan. 5, 1969.

24. I do not, of course, suggest that such protests alone produced the important civil rights legislation of the recent decade, for the support was multi-faceted.

25. Dr. Milton S. Eisenhower has been the president of three great American universities. He has been the perfect model of an effective and impartial chairman. He has devoted hundreds of hours to the Commission's task, and, in addition, he has the extraordinary virtue of being able to listen both intently and patiently.

26. *Report of the National Advisory Commission on Civil Disorders, op. cit.,* p. 265.

27. *The Politics of Protest* (New York: Simon and Schuster, 1969), pp. ix-x. Drs. Cobbs and Grier are the authors of *Black Rage.*

V ● ASSASSINATION*

This Commission was established in the dark hours following the assassination of Senator Robert F. Kennedy as he campaigned for the presidential nomination of his party.

*An edited version of statement issued November 2, 1969.

Just two months earlier, one of America's great spiritual and moral leaders, the Reverend Martin Luther King, had been slain by an assassin's bullet. Not quite five years before these terrible murders, President John F. Kennedy had been assassinated in the prime of his life.

As we Americans mourned the loss of these three young and vital men, we could not help but wonder if the slayings were grotesque symptoms of some awful disease infecting the nation. Had assassination become part of our political life? What did these assassinations signify for America and its future?

Assassination is only one of many topics within this Commission's purview, but an especially important one. Eight American Presidents—nearly one in four—have been the targets of assassins' bullets, and four died as a result.

Violence has been a recurring theme in American life, rising to a crescendo whenever social movements—agrarian reform, abolition, reconstruction, organized labor—have challenged the established order. Though presidential assassinations have not been typical of these periods of great stress, such periods have often produced assassinations of other prominent persons. Consistently they have subjected political leaders to vilification and threats to their safety.

The 1960s afford a grim example. The present decade, though by no means the worst in American history, has witnessed disturbingly high levels of assassination and political violence. No clear explanation emerges from a consideration of the men who have been slain; no ideological pattern fits murders as diverse as those of George Lincoln Rockwell and Medgar Evers or President Kennedy and Doctor King.

In comparison to the other nations of the world, the level of assassination in the United States is high. It is still high when the comparison is limited to other countries with large populations or other Western democracies.

Probably no other form of domestic violence—save civil war—causes more anguish and universal dismay among citizens than the murder of a respected national leader. Assassination, especially when the victim is a President, strikes at the heart of the democratic process. It enables one man to nullify the will of the people in a single,

102

savage act. It touches the lives of all the people of the nation.

The reaction to the slaying of a President lives in the public memory and is recorded in national surveys. Americans were shocked by the killing of President Kennedy. Most described themselves "at a loss" or "sad" or "hopeless." Many adult Americans wept, were dazed and numb or felt very nervous; others had trouble sleeping and eating. Many were ashamed of their country and felt a burden of collective guilt for the assassination. Some escaped the feeling by insisting that the act had been committed by a foreign agent.

The other side of the public reaction was an outpouring of rage and vindictiveness against the assassin. Only one out of three Americans felt Lee Harvey Oswald deserved a trial; one in five was pleased that Oswald had been murdered. (Vindictiveness attended earlier presidential assassinations: John Wilkes Booth, for example, probably shot himself, but a Union sergeant claimed to have killed him as an agent of God and was widely acclaimed for the alleged killing. Garfield's assassin, Charles Guiteau, though not killed was shot at twice—also with widespread approval. The trial of Leon Czolgosz for the assassination of McKinley took less than eight and a half hours, including the time spent impaneling the jury.)

Deeply affected by President Kennedy's assassination, many chose conspiracy as the only possible explanation of the dreadful and otherwise senseless act. Although three out of four persons believed Oswald was the assassin, 62 percent believed others were involved. When asked who or what was to blame, apart from the man who pulled the trigger, only 20 percent could specify a group: 15 percent said Communists or leftists and 5 percent said right-wingers or segregationists.

Suspicions of conspiracy are rooted in the history of American presidential assassinations. When a deranged house painter tried to kill Andrew Jackson in 1835, rumor spread that the man was an agent of a Whig conspiracy against Jackson. Charles Guiteau's sister and others argued that President Garfield was killed by a member of the conservative faction of the Republican party. When Giuseppe

Zangara shot at President-elect Roosevelt in 1933 but killed the mayor of Chicago instead, some claimed the killing was not a mistake but the intent of a gangland conspiracy. Technically a conspiracy existed in the murder of Abraham Lincoln, though the conspirators were a motley few with no backing from powerful groups; still the suspicion survives in folklore that Booth and his crew were associated with prominent government officials. Suspicions about Oswald as conspirator may survive as long, despite the exhaustive investigation and contrary findings of the Warren Commission.

Considering the high visibility, the substantial power, and the symbolic (as well as actual) importance of the American presidency, it is not surprising that Presidents are prime victims of assassination, or that conspiracy theories attend the event. The presidency is the fulcrum of power, the focus of hopes, and the center of controversy in American politics. What better target for those who wish to punish a nation, strike out at a symbol of great power, or simply draw the attention of the world and history to themselves? John Wilkes Booth remarked that the person who pulled down the Colossus of Rhodes would be famous throughout history.

ONE • PRESIDENTIAL ASSASSINS

The evidence for American history is overwhelming: no presidential assassination, with the exception of an abortive attempt on the life of President Truman, has been demonstrated to have sprung from a decision of an organized group whose goal was to change the policy or the structure of the United States government. With that single exception, no United States presidential assassin has ever been linked to such a group, either as a policy maker or as a member or hireling carrying out its directives.

The occasions on which American Presidents have been assassination targets have in common this absence of an organized conspiracy. But they have little else in common. The type of President, his party affiliation, his public policies, the length of time he was in office, his personal characteristics, his political strength—all of these provide no

104

clue to the likelihood of his assassination. The men who have been targets differ greatly. For example, Lincoln was the President of a divided nation during a civil war, Garfield a compromise candidate of a faction-torn party, and McKinley a popular President of a relatively unified and stable society.

To the extent that a pattern exists at all, it exists in the personalities of those who have been presidential assassins. In the biographies of these lonely, demented men we may discern common elements that help to explain their actions. From those common elements we may begin to draw a picture of the archetypal assassin.

Richard Lawrence, the house painter who attempted to kill President Jackson in 1835, was a man of grand delusions. At times he claimed to be Richard III of England; he believed the United States owed him large sums of money and, further, that Jackson was responsible for blocking his claim. As later assassins would do, Lawrence focused his mind on a particular political issue. Jackson had vetoed the bill to recharter the Bank of the United States; if Jackson were killed, Lawrence believed, the bank would be rechartered and all working men would benefit.

Other assassins were self-appointed saviors. John Wilkes Booth apparently believed that Lincoln had achieved the presidency through voting fraud and intended to make himself king. Booth claimed that he had acted as an agent of God in killing the President. Charles Guiteau thought it was his God-appointed task to kill James A. Garfield. After killing President McKinley, Leon Czolgosz claimed that he had removed "an enemy of the good working people." John Schrank, who attempted to kill Theodore Roosevelt, saw McKinley's ghost in a dream and heard it accuse Roosevelt of the McKinley assassination; Schrank also regarded himself as an agent of God. Giuseppe Zangara apparently believed himself a savior of the poor; he bore no personal malice toward Franklin D. Roosevelt, but attempted to kill him just because he was the chief of state (though he had not yet taken office).

Alone among assassins, Oscar Collazo and Griselio Torresola were members of a recognized political movement. Both were ardent Puerto Rican nationalists, and their attempt to storm Blair House, the temporary residence of

President Truman, appears to have been part of a plot to dramatize the cause of an independent Puerto Rico. Yet the plot was inept, not only because Blair House was well-secured, but because Truman was an inappropriate target. As President he had initiated important steps toward self-determination for Puerto Rico. After the attempted assassination, Puerto Ricans quickly denounced Collazo and Torresola.

Presidential assassins typically have been white, male, and slightly built. Nearly all were loners and had difficulty making friends of either sex and especially in forming lasting normal relationships with women. Lawrence, Schrank, and Zangara were foreign-born; the parents of all but Guiteau and Oswald were foreign-born. Normal family relationships were absent or disrupted. Booth was an illegitimate child; Guiteau's mother died when he was seven; Czolgosz lost his mother when he was twelve; Schrank's father died when Schrank was a child; Zangara's mother died when he was two; Oswald's father died before he was born and his mother's subsequent marriage lasted only three years. All of the assassins were unable to work steadily during a period of one to three years before the assassination. All of the assassins tended to link themselves to a cause or a movement and to relate their crime to some political issue or philosophy. All but Oswald used a handgun. At great risk to themselves, nearly all chose the occasion of an appearance of the President amid crowds for the assassination attempt.

Thus it might have been hypothesized in 1968 that the next assassin to strike at a President—or presidential candidate, as it turned out—would have most of the following attributes:

- from a broken home, with the father absent or unresponsive to the child;
- withdrawn, a loner, no girl friends, either unmarried or a failure at marriage;
- unable to work steadily in the last year or so before the assassination;
- white, male, foreign-born or with parents foreign-born; short, slight build;
- a zealot for a political, religious, or other cause, but not a member of an organized movement;

106

- assassinates in the name of a specific issue which is related to the principles or philosophy of his cause;
- chooses a handgun as his weapon;
- selects a moment when the President is appearing amid crowds.

We do not know with any degree of certainty why these characteristics appear in the presidential assassin. (Certainly the personal attributes can be found in many valuable, trustworthy citizens.) Nor do we know why the assassin politicizes his private miseries or why he chooses to express himself through such a terrible crime. Perhaps he comes to blame his own failures on others. Maybe because he does not live in a true community of men and has no rewarding relationships with others, he relates instead to an abstraction: "the poor" or "mankind." Once his own inner misery becomes identified with the misery of those whom he champions, he places the blame for both on the nation's foremost political figure. Incapable of sustained devotion toward a long-range goal, the assassin is capable of short bursts of frenzied activity which are doomed to failure. Each failure seems to reinforce the self-loathing and the need to accomplish—in one burst of directed energy— something of great worth to end his misery and assert his value as a human being.

TWO • PATTERNS OF ASSASSINATION

Deranged, self-appointed saviors have been the murderers of American Presidents. They have also been responsible for many of the assassinations of other national leaders and public officials. This Commission's Task Force on Assassination studied 81 assaults, fatal and non-fatal, on American Presidents, members of Congress, governors, mayors, and other officeholders. In case after case, their study reveals, the attacks were prompted by fanatic allegiance to a political cause or revenge for some petty slight or imagined evil. Only in the years immediately following the Civil War were assassinations typically undertaken by organized groups to alter or terrorize government.

While non-conspiratorial assassination has been the American pattern, it surely has not been typical for the rest

107

of the world. Throughout most of the world assassination has been used as an instrument of calculated political change, as a means of seizing power or terrorizing a government until it falls. Thus, for example, assassinations were a major part of the strategy of mass revolution in Russia and Eastern Europe beginning late in the nineteenth century. In Latin America assassinations have been committed less by fanatics or unstable persons than by daring political adventurers bent on seizing power for themselves or their supporters. And in the Middle East, assassination continues to be used as a deliberate political weapon by one political group against another. Where conspiratorial assassination is common, many besides the chief of state are apt to be targets.

Because assassination typically serves a political function, it is possible to predict with a fair degree of accuracy, using characteristics that are crudely measurable, what countries will experience high rates of assassination at particular moments in their history. For example, high rates of assassination tend to occur in countries experiencing political instability, in countries undergoing rapid economic development, under regimes that are coercive but not wholly totalitarian, in nations with high rates of homicide but low suicide rates.

By several of these measurements, the United States should be a nation with a low rate of murders of political figures—contrary to the actuality of its high rate. Thus, for example, almost alone among the nations with the highest level of economic development and greatest degree of political freedom the United States has a high assassination rate. Countries with high suicide rates tend to have low assassination rates; the United States is among a handful of exceptions.

During only one period of its history did the United States experience the turmoil and instability classically associated with high assassination rates: in the Reconstruction era immediately following the Civil War. During that decade, America experienced close to half of all the assassinations in its history. In the defeated South, still occupied by Union troops, many officeholders were not regarded as "legitimate" incumbents by the population. Many white Southerners resented the continuing presence of the mili-

108

tary, the systematic disenfranchisement of former Confederates, and the new political power of former slaves and Northern "carpetbaggers." Some took violent action: two governors of Louisiana and a host of other state and local political figures became victims of assassination plots.

A century later the assassination rate in the United States is only a small fraction of the rate during Reconstruction, but still it is comparatively high and remains to be accounted for. A number of explanations have been offered: our frontier culture, the ready availability of guns, tensions among diverse groups, a low standard of political decorum.

It may be that persistent low-level turbulence and non-conspiratorial assassination are associated, just as conspiratorial assassination usually occurs amid other intense forms of political violence. Consistent with its principles of freedom, the United States tolerates a fair amount of political tumult—not enough to inspire political assassination, but perhaps sufficient to provide the condition under which the twisted mind of the assassin decides that an imagined evil must be set right through violence. Dissidents in the United States have often been very vocal and very abusive; they sometimes have heaped scorn on a President, even vilified him. Americans demonstrate boisterously, stage emotion-charged strikes and sit-ins, hurl stones and filth and foul language at authorities who, in turn, have not always been restrained and fair in their use of power. Though an assassin is mentally deranged, the violent rhetoric of our politics and our constant flirtation with actual violence may be factors that bring him at least halfway to his distorted perception of what actions are right and legitimate.

Although the United States has differed significantly from the rest of the world in the kind of assassination it has experienced, there are indications that the future may bring more similarities than distinctions. Many of the conditions associated with conspiratorial assassination in other countries appear to be developing in this country:

• Political violence in the United States today is probably more intense than it has been since the turn of the century. If civil strife continues to become more violent, political assassinations may well occur.

• There is much talk today of revolution and urban guer-

109

rilla warfare by extremists, and there have been outbreaks of violence with aspects of guerrilla warfare, as in the Cleveland shoot-out of July, 1968. If extremists carry out their threats, we can expect political assassinations.

• Even if the rhetoric of revolution and vilification of governmental authority is never translated into deed, the constant excoriation of America's institutions and leaders may destroy their legitimacy in the eyes of other segments of society. The assassinations during the Reconstruction era arose in just such a context.

• Throughout the tragic history of race relations in this country, Negroes have been the victims of white terrorist murderers. To this recurring threat is added a new one: plots and murders from within the radical wing of the black protest movement. The increasing number of Negroes holding public office and positions of political prominence will thus be running risks of assassination from two opposing extremist groups. From whichever direction, such attacks would appropriately be regarded as political assassinations.

• Racial tensions have been at a high level in this country during the 1960s. If violent racial confrontations increase, the level of political violence in the United States could approach that of countries in which political assassinations typically occur.

• Finally, the United States may in the next few years undergo even more rapid socio-economic change than it has in the recent past. Rapid change is another characteristic that correlates with high levels of conspiratorial assassination.

Present trends warn of an escalating risk of assassination, not only for Presidents, but for other officeholders at every level of government, as well as leaders of civil rights and political-interest groups. Accordingly, this Commission suggests:

1. *that the Secret Service be empowered to extend its protective services to that limited number of federal officeholders and candidates for office whose lives are deemed imperiled as a result of threat, vilification, deep controversy, or other hazarding circumstances.* A Joint Resolution of the Ninetieth Congress, in June of 1968, authorized the Secret Service to protect "major" presidential and vice-presidential candidates, the eligibility of persons to be determined by the Secretary of the Treasury after consultation with a special advisory committee consisting of the Congressional leadership. Specifically, we recommend that the Secretary and the special advisory committee be empowered to designate, without publicity, a lim-

110

ited number of persons (federal officeholders or candidates) as temporary assassination risks and to assign them Secret Service protection wherever and whenever needed.

2. *that state and local governments carefully review the adequacy of the protection accorded to candidates and office-holders, especially governors and mayors, and that the protection be strengthened where it is deficient.* The responsibility for protection should be clearly delineated, and new avenues of cooperation should be opened between those with state or local protective responsibilities and the Secret Service and the Federal Bureau of Investigation, to include a sharing both of technological information and of information about dangerous persons and potential assassins.

In Chapter VII, "Firearms and Violence," we make recommendations that, if adopted, would greatly curtail the risk of assassination to all who might be targets. We have recommended drastically limiting the availability of handguns through restrictive licensing. We have further recommended intensified research to develop mechanisms that would assist law enforcement officers in detecting concealed firearms and ammunition on a person. Handguns are the weapons favored by assassins (by all but one presidential assassin, for example); effective detection devices would minimize the risk of assassination in meeting halls and other enclosed gathering places.

The precautions we are urging are worthwhile whether or not this nation faces a new outbreak of political assassinations. We do not predict that such an outbreak will occur. But we feel compelled to note that some of the conditions for such an outbreak are present or may be developing. These conditions add urgency to the need to develop effective protection against assassination.

We can only hope, along with all Americans, that the conditions which have kept our society free of the scourge of conspiratorial assassination will prevail—conditions such as the ability of the American people to absorb radical challenge, to respond to the need for reform, to keep their basic democratic values intact even in periods of bewildering and buffeting social change.

111

THREE • PRESIDENTIAL PROTECTION

Whatever the future holds for the United States, it is clear that, among all public figures, Presidents will continue to run the greatest risks of assassination. It is in the nature of their office; it is in the nature of the distorted logic by which assassins choose their targets.

The death of President Kennedy poignantly demonstrated the resilience of the American people in the face of tragedy and of their institutions of government at a time of abrupt transition. With skill and grace President Johnson exercised a calming influence on the nation, and the nation rallied in support of the new administration. That has been the pattern in the American past. We cannot safely assume, however, that our republic will always fare so well. An assassination of a President occurring during an edgy, critical moment in history could have disastrous consequences. Moreover, even when an assassination does not impair the strength of the nation or the continuity of its policies, the murder of a President is a tragedy of unrivaled proportions.

In the years since President Kennedy's death, and as urged by the Warren Commission, the policies and procedures for guarding Presidents have been thoroughly studied and imaginatively reconsidered, and many improvements have been made. A detailed discussion here of new procedures would lessen their effectiveness. We simply state that the Secret Service has reported to this Commission improvements in equipment and the various procedures of intelligence work. The Secret Service is confident that, had its new intelligence system been in effect in 1963, the activities of Lee Harvey Oswald would have brought him to the attention of the Secret Service before the fatal attack on President Kennedy. As we have pointed out, more research is needed, especially in the technology of concealed weapons detection.

There can be no perfect system for guarding the President short of isolating him, confining him to the White House and limiting his communication with the American public to television broadcasts and other media. This extreme solution is neither practicable nor desirable. For

112

political reasons and for the sake of ceremonial traditions of the office, the American people expect the President to get out and "mingle with the people." (Among the eight Presidents who have been assassination targets, all but Garfield and Truman were engaged in either ceremonial or political activities when they were attacked.)

Still, a President can minimize the risk by carefully choosing speaking opportunities, public appearances, his means of travel to engagements, and the extent to which he gives advance notice of his movements. He can limit his public appearances to meeting places to which access is carefully controlled, especially by the use of electronic arms-detection equipment. Effective security can exist if a President permits. Moreover, during the past twenty years television has proven an accepted and effective vehicle for presidential communication with the American public, and its continued and possibly expanded use by the President is to be encouraged.

During election campaigns there are extraordinary pressures both on the incumbent President and the contenders for his office that serve to maximize their risks as targets of assassination. Rightly or wrongly, presidential candidates judge that they must be personally seen by audiences throughout the country, through such rituals as motorcades, shopping-center rallies, and whistle-stop campaigns. Whether the long grind of personal-appearance campaigning is really the most effective investment of a candidate's time is debatable, since even the most strenuous travel schedule will expose him to only a small percentage of the American people. It has been argued that the grueling pace is itself a test of the candidate. It is more difficult to argue that political rallies test the candidate's reasoned consideration of the issues, since the speeches usually are brief, superficial, and suited to the carnival atmosphere of rallies. While campaign rallies involve the public in the electoral process by bringing that process close to them, they cannot be said to involve the public deeply in the pressing, complex issues of the nation.

A more reasonable defense of personal-appearance campaigning is that it provides important "feedback" for the candidate: he can sense the public mood through audience response to his speeches, learn of their problems and feel-

113

ings through the questions they raise and comments they make, and observe firsthand—as Kennedy is remembered to have done in his West Virginia campaign—the conditions that will demand his attention if he is elected. Yet this function can be better served in the quieter atmosphere of an enclosed meeting place where, we note, the risk of assassination can be significantly reduced.

But the most promising vehicle for campaigns effective in reaching large audiences and safe to the candidates is *television*. The intimacy with which television projects events and personalities has been amply demonstrated, and it is doubtful whether heavier reliance on television appearances need sacrifice any of the intimate contact with American people which candidates now associate with personal appearances. It has also been demonstrated that the American people have come to rely heavily on television in forming their opinions of presidential candidates. In a poll conducted for the Television Information Office in November, 1968, 65 percent of the respondents said television was their best source for becoming acquainted with candidates for national office.

The fuller potentiality of television for presidential campaigning has not been explored primarily because of the high cost of television time. Yet the value of television in reaching large audiences has been recognized, and more and more campaign funds are being invested in its use. Indeed, as campaign costs continue to soar, some fear that presidential politics will eventually become a contest where only millionaires need apply.

Out of concern for the safety of Presidents and presidential candidates, this Commission recommends that the Congress enact a law that would grant free television time to presidential candidates during the final weeks preceding the national election. The amount of television time allocated to the candidates should be adequate to establish a new pattern in presidential campaigning and to reduce significantly the pressure toward personal appearances in all parts of the country.

To ensure that candidates used their time for responsible, informative presentation of themselves and their views, the free time might be allocated only in half-hour blocks. Within his allotted time, however, a candidate would be free to choose the format best suited for his presentation.

114

It has long been recognized that broadcasters have a public-service commitment to the American people in exchange for their licensed use of the airwaves.[1] To ensure an equitable sharing of that commitment, consideration would have to be given to the question of whether all networks should be required to carry each program or only one network at a time, with the burden shared in rotation. Moreover, a formula would have to be devised for allotting time in a way that would give fair expression to important minor parties. Consideration should also be given to expanding greatly federal support of public television facilities for the express purpose of having these facilities share the political education function with the commercial networks.[2]

Though this proposal is put forth out of a desire to lessen the risk of assassination to Presidents and presidential candidates, other considerations lend merit to the proposal. The superiority of television as a forum for serious consideration of modern complex issues has already been noted. Moreover, political rallies attract the curious and the party faithful. Many of the marginally motivated; stay home. On the premise that it is easier to flick a dial in the living room than to drive across town to a rally, we note that television programs could widen the base of political participation in America.

FOUR ● POLITICAL VIOLENCE IN AMERICA

Broader participation in American politics might be an antidote to the political violence that has been a recurring feature of American life and which has recently been on the upswing. Our concern is not simply that the future may bring to America the alien phenomenon of conspiratorial assassination. Irrational, non-political killings of national leaders will also be a continuing risk as long as political violence, in rhetoric or act, is present to inspire the assassin. For while such assassins are mentally unbalanced, their beliefs are not wholly antithetical to what other Americans believe but simply distortions thereof.

Thus, assassins are not alone in believing in the efficacy of political violence. Nor are they alone in their simplistic,

115

exaggerated view of the power of the American President. Ever since George Washington's day, we Americans have mythologized our Presidents. We have attributed to them powers beyond human limitation and far beyond the realities of our constitutional system. Through the nation's press we follow every move, public and private, of the President —sometimes in adulation, sometimes in malicious anticipation of some sign that the man is only human.

Political violence often arises when a group feels the government has been unresponsive to legitimate demands. This Commission recognizes, as do many Americans, that the political institutions in our democracy need to be made more sensitive and responsive to the interests they are intended to represent. It is not difficult to understand the impatience and alienation of those who believe that the government has been consistently neglectful of their welfare. It is noteworthy that many are organizing new political groups to press for reforms. They are demonstrating a basic truth of American politics: groups that appreciate the complexities of American government, and that can organize to promote their ends through persuasion at the right times and places, benefit the most from policy decisions. The counter-trend—shortcutting to violence before the peaceful means of redressing grievances have been exhausted—can only be deplored. That counter-trend has been alive in this decade but not unique to it. Except for those to whom the complexities of government are workaday business Americans have not typically been patient with the subtleties of political issues. In part this stems from the natural preference for simplicities; in part it reflects the glossing over of subtleties by politicians, journalists, and the educators of our nation's children.

A significant decrease in the level of political violence in our country requires a new level of participation in the increasingly complex processes of local, state, and federal government and a new level of communication between government and the people it serves. Those responsible for the institutions of government must serve both needs—by clarifying their functions and purposes, and by responding to the needs and legitimate grievances of all they are intended to represent.

Thus legislators and administrators must creatively use

116

the political processes to ensure the prompt amelioration of wrongs. Thus legislators, administrators, and private citizens must share with the President the responsibility for realistic demonstration that the society is in fact acting in behalf of all citizens.

The nation's press must respond to these needs—by clearly representing the complexities of the institutions of government, by fully and fairly reporting the issues these institutions face, and by delving into the issues deserving governmental attention. By lessening its attention to the personal lives of the President and his family, with correspondingly greater attention to the working nature and limitations of the presidency, the nation's press may achieve the additional effect of discouraging a simplistic notion of the presidency that assassins are not alone in holding.

The nation's schools must also respond to these needs: by emphasizing in American history and social studies the complexities and subtleties of the democratic process; by shunning the myths by which we have traditionally made supermen of Presidents, "founding fathers," and other prominent persons; by restoring to history books a full and frank picture of violence and unrest in America's past, in the hope that children can be educated to repudiate violence and recognize its futility.

There are themes in American culture that have served us for good and ill. American folklore has always emphasized—and continues to emphasize in television heroes—direct action and individual initiative. Equally compelling within the American experience has been the emphasis placed on freedom of conscience. Many of the authentic heroes of American history have been individuals willing to suffer ostracism and to employ unconventional (and even violent) means to realize goals unpopular to a majority of citizens. While these qualities have been a source of strength and a goad to progress for our nation, it is not difficult to see their perverse relationship to the act of a demented assassin.

Perhaps a new generation of Americans, trained to these subtleties of American life, shamed by its violence as they are proud of its achievements, determined to achieve a better record for their time and sophisticated in the ways to achieve it, will guarantee a more peaceable America.

117

FIVE • CONCLUSION

These are long-range hopes, and responsible citizens must give serious attention to how we can best realize them. For the short range, this nation is not powerless to prevent the tragedy of assassination. We conclude with a reiteration of the steps that can be taken to minimize greatly the risk of assassination:

- selective expansion of the functions of the Secret Service to include protection of any federal officeholder or candidate who is deemed a temporary but serious assassination risk;
- improved protection of state and local officeholders and candidates, and strengthened ties between those holding this responsibility and the appropriate federal agencies;
- restrictive licensing of handguns to curtail greatly their availability;
- development and implementation of devices to detect concealed weapons and ammunition on persons entering public meeting places;
- a significant reduction of risky public appearances by the President and by presidential candidates;
- a corresponding increase in the use of public and commercial television both as a vehicle of communication by the President and as a campaign tool by presidential candidates.

---

1. Given television's superiority, a shift toward its greater use by presidential candidates appears inevitable. But other campaign reforms, such as the increased use of enclosed meeting places, may require strong endorsement by the major political parties if they are to be effected. It is unrealistic to expect individual candidates, acting upon their own initiative, to alter significantly the traditional pattern of campaigning.

2. A Twentieth Century Fund Commission on Campaign Costs in the Electronic Era has just issued its report, suggesting among other things that the federal government pay for television time for presidential candidates at one-half the normal commercial rate. The Commission has also recommended a formula for the allocation of such time, called "voters' time," between major and minor candidates. Though the recommendations of the Twentieth Century Fund Commission are somewhat different from ours, we hope they will be given consideration by the President and the Congress, along with those we submit in this statement. We also note that Great Britain, with more than twenty years experience in allocating broadcast time to a number of political parties, offers proof that this knotty problem may be equitably solved.

VIOLENCE IN AMERICAN HISTORY:
A PICTORIAL SAMPLING

Pictorial Selection Staff
JUDITH HARKISON
ANTHONY E. NEVILLE
JAMES S. CAMPBELL

Boston Massacre of 1770 in which
five defiant Americans were
killed by British troops. This
engraving is by Paul Revere.
LIBRARY OF CONGRESS

At the Boston Tea Party, 1773, a mob
dumped 342 chests of English
tea in the harbor and tarred and
feathered a tax collector.
THE JOHN CARTER BROWN LIBRARY

Whiskey Rebellion, 1794. Farmers
in western Pennsylvania
rose in rebellion over an excise
tax on distilleries.

Nat Turner led a slave rebellion in
1831, killing more than 50
whites during a six-week rampage. He
and 16 others were hanged.

Entered according to Act of Congress in the year 1844 by James Baillie in the Clerks office of the dis.ᵗ Court of the South.ᵗ dis.ᵗ

RIOT IN P

JU

Lithography & Print-Coloring on reasonable terms by James Baillie N⁰ 33 Spruce S⁺ N.Y.

ΟELPHIA

Ethnic and religious strife between
immigrants and native Americans
made the mid-1800's a time of sustained
urban riots and violence.

In 1859 John Brown and his band captured the
federal arsenal at Harpers Ferry, but
lost it to the U.S. Marines on the next day.
FRANK LESLIE'S ILLUSTRATED WEEKLY

A mob broke into an Illinois jail in 1844
and killed Morman leaders Joseph and Hiram
Smith because of their new religious beliefs.
LIBRARY OF CONGRESS

The Civil War still stands as the
largest military bloodletting
in American history. Here a band
of guerrillas, sympathetic to
the South, pillage Lawrence, Kansas.
KANSAS STATE HISTORICAL SOCIETY

The most notorious 19th-century "bad-
men" were Frank and Jesse James,
seated left to right. Cole and Bob
Younger stand behind them.

At the end of a frontier gun-fight,
two men lie shot to death on
the sidewalk in front of a saloon in
Hayes, Kansas. (Date unknown.)
KANSAS STATE HISTORICAL SOCIETY

Wild Bill Hickok gained fame
for shooting a harmless
man to death and acquitting
himself on a plea of self-
defense. He went on to
be a U.S. marshal in the West

William F. Bonney, or Billy
the Kid, was idolized by
poor villagers of the South-
west. He supposedly killed
22 men before he was
shot at age 21 by a sheriff.

Bonnie Parker and Clyde Barrow, "public enemies" of the 1930's. With the demise of them, John Dillinger and Pretty Boy Floyd, the tradition of the social bandit died.
UNITED PRESS INTERNATIONAL

The Hatfield family, 1899. "Devil Anse" Hatfield, patriarch
of the family that feuded with the McCoys, sits amid kin-
folk at Welch, West Virginia.
LIBRARY OF CONGRESS

Geronimo, whose raiders killed many
U.S. soldiers, settlers and
reservation Indians in American territory during the Indian wars.
NATIONAL ARCHIVES

A white hunter scalped by Indians.
The photograph was taken
shortly after the incident near
Dodge City, Kansas, in 1868.
SMITHSONIAN INSTITUTION

Racism was a part of the American frontier. Here an anti-Chinese riot in Denver, in 1880.

Racially arrogant Judge Roy Bean,
seated on the keg, holds
court and tries a horse thief at
Langtry, Texas, in 1900.
NATIONAL ARCHIVES

A western vigilante court in session.
Nowhere was lynch justice
more swift, certain, or flourishing
than on the Western frontier.
HARPER'S WEEKLY

In 1881 Charles Guiteau shot President
Garfield in the Washington railroad station.
The President survived the wound
for more than two months, but finally died.
Guiteau was convicted of murder and
hanged, but, while a prisoner, an attempt was
made on his life (right), and he
nearly suffered the fate of Lee Harvey Oswald.
LIBRARY OF CONGRESS

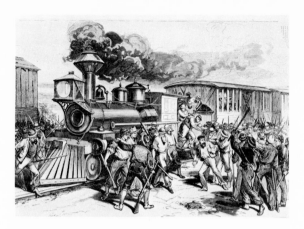

Labor violence broke out in
West Virginia in 1877, when Baltimore and Ohio workmen left
their trains, angered over wage cuts.
FRANK LESLIE'S ILLUSTRATED WEEKLY

Soon after the B & O incident,
railroad strikes spread across the
nation. Here federal troops
were called in to restore order.

Seven police were killed when
they moved in on an anarchist who
was addressing a crowd of
1,000 in Chicago's Haymarket Square.
LIBRARY OF CONGRESS

During the Ludlow Massacre, 1914,
National Guardsmen killed striking coal-
miners and set fire to their tents.
Hundreds of families were left homeless.

1937 was a bloody year of labor
violence. One dispute, the Little Steel
strike, accounted for sixteen
deaths and many others badly injured.

An 1874 caricature of Cincinnati
police who arrested women peacefully
demonstrating, but allegedly
ignored important vices in the town.
HARPER'S WEEKLY

This anti-war protest in New
York, June 16, 1917, resulted in a
number of skirmishes between
the police and the demonstrators
NATIONAL ARCHIVES

In 1874, in Choctaw County,
Alabama, a company of whites ambushed
Negroes returning from church,
killing ten and wounding thirteen.
HARPER'S WEEKLY

Ku Klux Klan members in 1868.
With the end of slavery, white men
of the South developed the
Klan to deal violently with Negroes.
RUTHERFORD B. HAYES LIBRARY

Lynch-mob violence was common throughout the country, but it was especially used with Southern Negroes. This Negro was lynched and burned in Waco, Texas, in the year 1916.

Between 1915 and 1919, twenty-two racial
disturbances occurred in American cities. One of
the worst, in Chicago in 1919, resulted
in the deaths of fifteen whites and twenty-three
Negroes. The riot was preceded by two
years of frequent bombing of Negro residences.

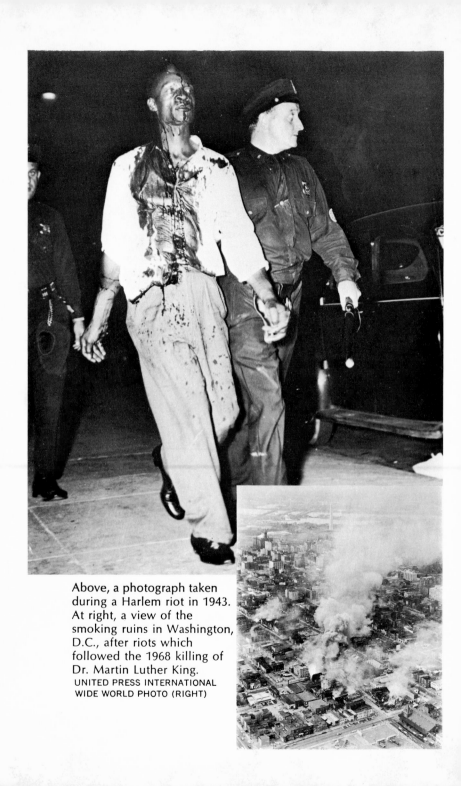

Above, a photograph taken
during a Harlem riot in 1943.
At right, a view of the
smoking ruins in Washington,
D.C., after riots which
followed the 1968 killing of
Dr. Martin Luther King.
UNITED PRESS INTERNATIONAL
WIDE WORLD PHOTO (RIGHT)

VI ● VIOLENCE AND LAW ENFORCEMENT*

Order is a prerequisite of society, a mainstay of civilized existence. We arise every workday with unspoken expectations of order in our lives: that the earth will be spinning on its axis, that the office or factory will be functioning as before, that the mail will be delivered, that our friends will still be friends, that no one will attack us on the way to work.

Our expectations are not always met. The technological creations on which modern life depends do not always function with the predictability of the physical laws of the universe. Human behavior is even less predictable. To ensure reasonable predictability to human behavior, to minimize disorder, to promote justice in human relations, and to protect human rights, societies establish rules of conduct for their members.

In a far earlier day—and still, to some extent, in small and traditional societies—the rules of conduct had only to be passed from one generation to the next by teaching and example. Universal acceptance and long tradition gave force to the rules, as did the knowledge that rule-breakers could be quickly identified by the tightly knit community, that culprits had nowhere to run, that the community would ostracize them for their misdeeds. Still, every society in history has produced deviant members. And as societies have grown larger and more complicated, so have the problems of maintaining the social order.

In modern societies many of the rules of social conduct have come to be codified as laws. The intricacies of life in the twentieth century require laws. The act of driving an automobile from one place to another requires a book full of regulations concerning speed, traffic lanes, signals, safety devices of the vehicle, and the skill of the driver. Many other realms of social interaction also require legal

*An edited version of statement issued November 1, 1969.

119

regulation for the sake of justice, safety, and preservation of the social order.

Law furnishes the guidelines for socially acceptable conduct and legitimizes the use of force to ensure it. If utopian conditions prevailed—if all citizens shared a deep commitment to the same set of moral values, if all parents instilled these values in their children and kept close watch over them until adulthood, if all lived in stable and friendly neighborhoods where deviants would face community disapproval—then perhaps we would seldom need recourse to the negative sanctions of the law. But these are not the conditions of today's pluralistic society, and the law is needed to reinforce what the other institutions for social control can only do imperfectly.

This function of the law requires that it be backed by coercive power—that it be enforced. Agents of the legitimate authority must function effectively to deter lawbreaking and apprehend lawbreakers, and the laws must provide sanctions to be applied against wrongdoers. When law is not effectively enforced, the odds become more enticing for the potential offender, crime increases, and the legal system—government itself—becomes discredited in the eyes of the public. As respect for law declines, crime increases still more.

To acknowledge these basic truths is not, of course, to argue in favor of oppressive conduct by police or retributive treatment of offenders. On the contrary, police lawlessness, degrading prison conditions, and other deficiencies in criminal justice damage the goal of an orderly society by making the law seem unworthy of obedience. That, too, breeds crime and disorder.

Likewise, to say that the law requires force as a condition of effectiveness is not to argue that law enforcement must be total. The surveillance that would be required to deal swiftly with every offense, major or minor, would be astronomically costly and an insufferable intrusion upon the lives of a free people that would not be long endured. Indeed, as *Law and Order Reconsidered,* the Report of our staff Task Force on Law and Law Enforcement, suggests, some offenses like minor traffic infractions and intoxication now command a disproportionate share of our criminal justice resources, and many of these offenses would better

120

be handled by various means outside of the criminal justice process.

Devotion to the principle of law is one of the great strengths of the American society, a source of the nation's greatness. As Theodore Roosevelt remarked, "No nation ever yet retained its freedom for any length of time after losing its respect for the law, after losing the law-abiding spirit, the spirit that really makes orderly liberty." Today, however, respect for law in America is weakened by abuses and deficiencies within our legal system, and it is these which are the basis of our concern.

Respect for law is also threatened by some types of civil disobedience, notably the activities of normally law-abiding citizens, regrettably including even some leaders in public life, in deliberately violating duly enacted, constitutionally valid laws and court orders. Moreover, those who violate such laws often claim they should not be punished because in their view the law or policy they are protesting against is unjust or immoral. Civil disobedience is an important and complex subject, and we shall examine the dangers to society of deliberate law-breaking as a political tactic in Chapter IV, "Civil Disobedience." Every society, including our own, must have effective means of enforcing its laws, whatever may be the claims of conscience of individuals. Our present statement is concerned with the fairness and efficiency of our law enforcement system, which must apply, without fear or favor, to all who violate the law.

As a preface to our discussion, then, we offer these two reminders:

1. Order is indispensable to society, law is indispensable to order, enforcement is indispensable to law.

2. The justice and decency of the law and its enforcement are not simply desirable embellishments, but rather the indispensable condition of respect for law and civil peace in a free society.

ONE • GOVERNMENT AND THE POOR

The American system of government has been one of the most successful in modern history. But despite the reservoir of citizen trust and deference toward the government which has been a stabilizing feature of our democracy, there has always been in our history a competing attitude of insistence on results, on government's achievement of the aims supported by the citizen, as a precondition of his consent to the exercise of governmental power.

In American political theory, governments are humanly created institutions to serve human ends. The principles are stated in the Declaration of Independence: first, that the purpose of democratic government is to secure the rights of life, liberty, and the pursuit of happiness for all citizens; second, that the powers of government are derived from the consent of the governed.

Governments in the United States—local, state, and federal—must therefore be cognizant of the needs of citizens and take appropriate action if they are to command continuing respect and if their laws are to be obeyed. Disenchantment with governmental institutions and disrespect for law are most prevalent among those who feel they have gained the least from the social order and from the actions of government.

A catalog of the features of American life that push people toward alienation and lawlessness usually emphasizes evils in the private sector: landlords who charge exorbitant rents for substandard housing, the practice of "blockbusting" that feeds on racial antagonism to buy cheap and sell dear under inequitable purchase contracts, merchants with unscrupulous credit-buying schemes, employers and unions who discriminate against minorities. But we need also to consider how the institutions of law and government, often inadvertently, contribute to the alienation.

There are few laws and few agencies to protect the consumer from unscrupulous merchants. There are laws for the protection of tenants defining what landlords must provide, but housing inspection agencies have little power and are understaffed; often they can act only in response to complaints and seldom can they force immediate repairs, no matter how desperately needed. Welfare agencies, designed to help the poor, operate under strictures that contribute to the degradation of the poor. As the President recently stated, our welfare system "breaks up families,

. . . perpetuates a vicious cycle of dependency . . . [and] strips human beings of their decency."

If welfare assistance is arbitrarily cut off, if a landlord flagrantly ignores housing codes, if a merchant demands payment under an unfair contract, the poor—like the rich —can go to court. Whether they find satisfaction there is another matter. The dockets of many lower courts are overcrowded, and cases are handled in assembly-line fashion, often by inexperienced or incompetent personnel. Too frequently courts have jurisdiction over landlord-tenant and small claims disputes serve the poor less well than their creditors; they tend to enforce printed-form contracts, without careful examination of the equity of the contracts or the good faith of the landlords and merchants who prepare them.

The poor are discouraged from initiating civil actions against their exploiters. Litigation is expensive; so are experienced lawyers. Private legal aid societies have long struggled to provide legal assistance to the poor, but their resources have been miniscule in comparison to the vast need for their services.

Some of this is changing. The President has recently proposed reforms in the welfare system designed to preserve family structures, sustain personal dignity, eliminate unfairness and preserve incentives to work. Private groups and new government programs are beginning to respond to the legal needs of the poor. In 1968 the Legal Services Program of the Office of Economic Opportunity handled almost 800,000 cases for the poor and won a majority of the trials and appeals. In test cases the OEO lawyers won new standards of fair treatment of the poor from welfare agencies, landlords, inspectors, urban renewal authorities, and others. They were assisted in their work by VISTA volunteers with legal training and Reginald Heber Smith Fellows, law school graduates with one year fellowships who are assigned to OEO Legal Services offices. But the 1,800 OEO Legal Services Program lawyers, 700 VISTA lawyers, and 250 Smith Fellows, together with 2,000 legal aid attorneys, are still only a small beginning in the long-range task of assuring justice for the poor. Many more attorneys are needed. Indeed, the entire bar must also assume a larger share of the responsibility, as many younger lawyers and law firms are now beginning to do.

In recent years the legal profession has contributed an increasing portion of its time to aiding the poor and this trend will undoubtedly continue despite the financial problems involved.

We recommend that federal and state governments take additional steps to encourage lawyers to devote professional services to meeting the legal needs of the poor.

Specifically, we recommend that:

1. The Legal Services Program of the Office of Economic Opportunity, which already has won the strong support of the organized bar and the enthusiasm of graduating law students across the country, should be continued and expanded. The more recently started VISTA lawyers program and the Smith fellowships program should also be enlarged. Experiments should be encouraged with new programs to provide trained attorneys to deal with particular types of legal problems faced by the poor, such as welfare rights and consumer protection. The independence of all government-supported programs providing legal services to the poor should be safeguarded against governmental intrusion into the selection of the types of cases government-financed lawyers can bring on behalf of their indigent clients. The relationship between lawyer and client is as private as that between doctor and patient, and the fact of poverty must not be the basis for destroying this privacy.

2. All states should provide compensation to attorneys appointed to represent indigent criminal defendants in the state and local courts. A state may wish to provide such compensated legal assistance through the use of paid Public Defender staff lawyers, or it may choose to compensate private court-appointed attorneys at a specific rate, on the model of the Federal Criminal Justice Act.

3. The federal government and the states should provide adequate compensation for lawyers who act in behalf of the poor in civil cases. Payment—either full or partial depending on the client's ability to pay—could be made on the basis of certificates issued by the court as to the need of the client and (in suits for plaintiffs) the good faith

of the action. Other appropriate safeguards could be introduced to be administered by the courts with the assistance of the local bar associations. Some federal funding for the state court programs might also be required.

The institution of government that is the most constant presence in the life of the poor is the police department. Crime rates are high in the urban slums and ghettos, and the police are needed continually. As they do their job, the police carry not only the burden of the law but also the symbolic burden of all government; it is regrettable, yet not surprising, that particularly the tensions and frustrations of the poor and the black come to focus on the police. The antagonism is frequently mutual. Racial prejudice in police departments of major cities has been noted by reliable observers.[1] Prejudice compromises police performance. Policemen who systematically ignore many crimes committed in the ghetto, who handle ghetto citizens roughly,[2] who abuse the rights of these citizens, contribute substantially to disaffection with government and disrespect for law.

Our laws provide for civil and criminal sanctions against illegal police conduct, but these are rarely effective. The so-called exclusionary rule also has some deterrent effect; it prevents use of illegally obtained evidence in trials, but this does not affect unlawful searches and seizures or other police activities that do not result in arrest and trial. A citizen can take his complaint of misconduct directly to the police department. Every major police department has formal machinery for handling citizen complaints and for disciplining misbehaving officers. But for a variety of reasons, including inadequate investigative and hearing procedures and light punishments for offenses, this internal process of review is largely unsatisfactory.

Even if all the compromising practices were eliminated, however, it is doubtful whether internal review boards could engender widespread trust—simply because they are internally administered. New York, Philadelphia, Washington and Rochester are among the few large American cities to have experimented with an external review board composed primarily of civilians. In the four months that New York City had a civilian review board, more than twice as many complaints were processed than during the

125

preceding twelve months by the police department's own board. These experiments have fallen victim to organized opposition, however, most vocally from the police themselves. The police argue that civilian review lowers police morale, undermines respect of lower echelon officers for their superiors, and inhibits proper police discretion by inducing fear of retaliatory action by the board. The police also resent being singled out among all local governmental officials for civilian review.

The resentment is understandable. The police are not the only public servants who sometimes fall short of their duties or overstep their powers, who act arbitrarily or unjustly. If an independent agency is to exist for handling citizen grievances, it should be open to complaints concerning every governmental office: the welfare agency, the health department, the housing bureau, the sanitation department, as well as the police.

Independent citizens' grievance agencies would be a useful innovation. They could investigate and, where justified, support individual complaints against public servants. They could also perform a broader function—recommend policy changes to governmental institutions that will make them more responsive to public needs. By encouraging and goading governmental institutions to greater responsiveness, and by vindicating them against unfounded complaints, these grievance agencies could strengthen public respect for the institutions of government and thus strengthen the social order.

Both the President's Commission on Law Enforcement and Administration of Justice (Crime Commission) and the National Advisory Commission on Civil Disorders (Kerner Commission) recommended that local jurisdictions establish adequate mechanisms for processing citizen grievances about the conduct of public officials. That recommendation has not received the attention or the response it deserves.

To increase the responsiveness of local governments to the needs and rights of their citizens, we recommend that the federal government allocate seed money to a limited number of state and local jurisdictions demonstrating an interest in establishing citizens' grievance agencies.

Because of the novelty of this function in American government, the allocating federal agency should encourage diversity in the arrangements and powers of the grievance agencies in the experimenting states and cities, should provide for continuing evaluation of the effectiveness of the differing schemes, and should publicize these evaluations among all state and local jurisdictions so that each can decide the arrangement best suited for itself. Consideration should also be given to the creation of a federal citizens' grievance agency to act on complaints against federal employees and departments. The federal agency could also serve as an experimental model for similar agencies in the cities.

We have supported this recommendation upon evidence that the poor experience special frustrations in their relationships with the government and that these frustrations breed disrespect for law. To undergird that support we add the obvious notation that the poor are not the only ones who feel that government is unresponsive to their needs. The alienation of "the forgotten American," living above the poverty line but below affluence, is also genuine and a matter for compassionate concern.

Law-abiding, patriotic, a firm believer in traditional American values, "the forgotten American" is angered and distrustful about the same institutions of government—except for the police—that alienate the poor. Some extremists prey upon his frustration and alienation by promising simplistic solutions and pointing at scapegoats—usually Negroes. The festering and sometimes violent antagonisms between lower-middle-class whites and poor blacks have their ironic side, for the two groups share many needs: better jobs, better schools, better police protection, better recreation facilities, better public services. Together they could accomplish more than they can apart. Citizens' grievance agencies could provide a modest but important start toward the reconciliation of antagonisms and the restoration of respect for the institutions of government among all citizens.

While we strongly urge innovative devices such as citizens' grievance agencies, we must not ignore the strengthening of such time-honored mechanisms of popular government as the right and the duty to vote. Extension

127

and vigorous enforcement of the 1965 Voting Rights Act, and intensified efforts to persuade all qualified citizens to vote, remain the most direct method for citizens to shape the quality and direction of their government. Equally important as creating new citizens' grievance agencies is the continuing effort to develop more effective voter education and registration programs.

TWO • THE CRIMINAL JUSTICE PROCESS

Our society has commissioned its police to patrol the streets, prevent crime, and arrest suspected criminals. It has established courts to conduct trials of accused offenders and sentence those who are found guilty. It has created a correctional process consisting of prisons to punish convicted persons and programs to rehabilitate and supervise them so that they can become useful citizens. It is commonly assumed that these three components—law enforcement (police, sheriffs, marshals), the judicial process (judges, prosecutors, defense lawyers) and corrections (prison officials, probation and parole officers)—add up to a "system" of criminal justice.

A system implies some unity of purpose and organized interrelationship among component parts. In the typical American city and state, and under federal jurisdiction as well, no such relationship exists. There is, instead, a reasonably well-defined criminal *process,* a continuum through which each accused offender may pass: from the hands of the police, to the jurisdiction of the courts, behind the walls of a prison, then back onto the street. The inefficiency, fall-out and failure of purpose during this process is notorious.

According to the 1967 report of the President's Crime Commission, half of all major crimes are never reported to the police.[3] Of those which are, fewer than one-quarter are "cleared" by arrest. Nearly half of these arrests result in the dismissal of charges. Of the balance, well over 90 percent are resolved by a plea of guilty. The proportion of cases which actually go to trial is thus very small, representing less than one percent of all crimes committed. About one quarter of those convicted are confined in penal

128

institutions; the balance are released under probation supervision. Nearly everyone who goes to prison is eventually released, often under parole supervision. Between one-half and two-thirds of all those released are sooner or later arrested and convicted again, thereby joining the population of repeater criminals we call recidivists.

Nearly every official and agency participating in the criminal process is frustrated by some aspect of its ineffectiveness, its unfairness or both. At the same time, nearly every participant group itself is the target of criticism by others in the process.

Upon reflection, this is not surprising. Each participant sees the commission of crime and the procedures of justice from a different perspective. His daily experience and his set of values as to what effectiveness and fairness require are therefore likely to be different. As a result, the mission and priorities of a system of criminal justice are defined differently by a policeman, a prosecutor, a defense attorney, a trial judge, a correctional administrator, an appellate tribunal, a slum dweller and a resident of the suburbs.

For example: The police see crime in the raw. They are exposed firsthand to the agony of victims, the danger of streets, the violence of lawbreakers. A major task of the police officer is to track down and arrest persons who have committed serious crimes. It is discouraging indeed for such an officer to see courts promptly release defendants on bail and permit them to remain free for extended periods before trial, or prosecutors reduce charges in order to induce pleas of guilty to lesser offenses, or judges exclude incriminating evidence, or parole officers accept supervision of released prisoners but check on them only a few minutes each month.

Yet the police themselves are often seen by others as contributing to the failure of the system. They are charged with ineptness, discourtesy, dishonesty, brutality, sleeping on duty, illegal searches. They are attacked by large segments of the community as being insensitive to the feelings and needs of the citizens they are employed to serve.

Trial judges tend to see crime from a more objective position. They see facts in dispute and two sides to each issue. They may sit long hours on the bench in an effort to adjudicate cases with dignity and dispatch, only to find counsel unprepared, or weak cases presented, or witnesses missing, or warrants unserved, or bail restrictions unenforced, or occasional juries bringing in arbitrary verdicts. They find sentencing to be the most difficult of their tasks, yet presentence information is scanty and dispositional alternatives are all too often thwarted by the unavailability of adequate facilities.

Yet criminal courts themselves are often poorly managed and severely criticized. They are seriously backlogged; in many of our major cities the average delay between arrest and trial is close to a year. All too many judges are perceived as being inconsiderate of waiting parties, police officers and citizen witnesses. Too often lower criminal courts tend to be operated more like turnstiles than tribunals. In some jurisdictions, many able jurists complain that some of their most senior colleagues refuse to consider or adopt new administrative and managerial systems which could improve significantly the quality of justice and the efficiency of the court and which would also shorten the time from arrest to trial.

Corrections officials enter the crime picture long after the offense and deal only with convicted persons. Their job is to maintain secure custody and design programs which prepare individual prisoners for a successful return to society. They are discouraged when they encounter convicted persons whose sentences are either inadequate or excessive. They are frustrated by legislatures which curtail the flexibility of sentences and which fail to appropriate necessary funds. They are dismayed at police officers who harrass parolees, or at a community which fails to provide jobs or halfway houses for ex-offenders.

Yet, with a few significant exceptions, the prisons and correctional facilities operate in isolation and reject public scrutiny. Programs of rehabilitation are shallow and dominated by greater concern for punishment and custody than for correction. Prison inmate work assignments usually bear little relationship to employment opportunities outside. Internal supervision is often inadequate, and placed in the hands of inmates. Thus correctional administrators are often said to be presiding over schools in crime.

While speaking of prisons, it should be noted that jails

130

—institutions for detaining accused persons before and during trial and for short misdemeanor sentences—are often the most appalling shame in the criminal justice system. Many are notoriously ill-managed and poorly staffed. Scandalous conditions have been repeatedly reported in jails in major metropolitan areas. Even more than the prisons, the jails have been indicted as crime breeding institutions. Cities are full of people who have been arrested but not convicted, and who nevertheless serve time in facilities worse, in terms of overcrowding and deterioration, than the prisons to which convicted offenders are sentenced. Accused first offenders are mixed indiscriminately with hardened recidivists. In most cases, the opportunities for recreation, job training or treatment of a nonpunitive character are almost nil. These deficiencies of jails might be less significant if arrested persons were detained for only a day or two, but many unable to post bail or meet other conditions of release are held in jail for many months because the other components of the legal system do not provide for speedy trials.

In the mosaic of discontent which pervades the criminal process, public officials and institutions, bound together with private persons in the cause of reducing crime, each sees his own special mission being undercut by the cross-purposes, frailties or malfunctions of others. As they find their places along the spectrum between the intense concern with victims at one end, and total preoccupation with reforming convicted lawbreakers at the other, so do they find their daily perceptions of justice varying or in conflict.

These conflicts in turn are intensified by the fact that each part of the criminal process in most cities is overloaded and undermanned, and most of its personnel underpaid and inadequately trained. Too little attention has been paid to the Crime Commission's finding that the entire criminal justice system—federal, state and local, including all police, all courts and all corrections—is underfinanced, receiving less than two percent of all government expenditures. On this entire system, we spend less each year than we do on federal agricultural programs and little more than we do on the space program.

Under such circumstances it is hardly surprising to find in most cities not a smooth functioning "system" of

131

criminal justice but a fragmented and often hostile amalgamation of criminal justice agencies. Obvious mechanisms for introducing some sense of harmony into the system are not utilized. Judges, police administrators and prison officials hardly ever confer on common problems. Sentencing institutes and familiarization prison visits for judges are the exception rather than the rule. Usually neither prosecutors nor defense attorneys receive training in corrections upon which to base intelligent sentencing recommendations.

Nearly every part of the criminal process is run with public funds by persons employed as officers of justice to serve the same community. Yet every agency in the criminal process in a sense competes with every other in the quest for tax dollars. Isolation or antagonism rather than mutual support tends to characterize their intertwined operations. And even when cooperative efforts develop, the press usually features the friction and often aggravates it.

One might expect the field to be flooded with systems analysts, management consultants and publicly-imposed measures of organization and administration in order to introduce order and coordination into this criminal justice chaos. It is not. A recognized profession of criminal justice system administrators does not exist today.

In fact, most of the criminal justice subsystems are also poorly run. For example, court administrators are rare, and court management by trained professionals is a concept that is taking hold very slowly. The bail "system," which should involve coordination among at least a half dozen agencies, is presided over by no one. Few cities have neutral bail agencies to furnish bail-setting magistrates with reliable background data on defendants. In making their bail recommendations prosecutors usually ignore community ties and factors other than the criminal charge and the accused's criminal record. Defense lawyers infrequently explore nonmonetary release conditions in cases involving impecunious clients. Detention reports on persons held long periods in jail prior to trial are rarely acted on by courts, and bail review for detainees is seldom requested. Enforcement of bail restrictions and forfeitures of bond for bail-jumpers are unusual. Bail bondsmen go unregulated.[4]

Effective police administration is hard to find. The great majority of police agencies are headed by chiefs who started as patrolmen and whose training in modern management techniques, finance, personnel, communications and community relations is limited. Lateral entry of police administrators from other departments or outside sources such as military veterans is usually prohibited by antiquated Civil Service concepts.

Apart from lack of leadership, the process of crime control in most cities lacks any central collection and analysis of criminal justice information. It has no focal point for formulating a cohesive crime budget based on system needs rather than individual agency requests. It has no mechanism for planning, initiating or evaluating systemwide programs, or for setting priorities. It has no specialized staff to keep the mayor or other head of government regularly informed of the problems and progress of public safety and justice. Crime receives high-level attention only as a short-term reaction to crisis.

Nor does the criminal justice process function in coordination with the more affirmative social programs for improving individual lives. For example, a major goal of an offender's contact with the criminal process is said to be corrective—rehabilitation followed by reintegration into the community, with enhanced respect for law. Yet the opposite is often true: the typical prison experience is degrading, conviction records create a lasting stigma, decent job opportunities upon release are rare, voting rights are abridged, military service options are curtailed, family life disruptions are likely to be serious, and the outlook of most ex-convicts is bleak. The hope of the community that released offenders have been "corrected" is defeated by outdated laws and community responses.

Experienced judges have resorted increasingly in recent years to various forms of post-conviction probation. They have done so after weighing the possibilities for rehabilitation if the offender is so released against the usually disastrous prognosis which would accompany his incarceration. It is a painful choice, little understood by the public. But the decision to seek correction of an offender in the community reflects not a compassionate attitude towards law-breakers, but a hardheaded recognition, based on data, that long term public safety has a better chance of being protected thereby.

133

The bleak picture of criminal justice we have painted is not without its bright spots. Within the past few years, scattered about the country, innovations have been introduced, new leadership has emerged, modern facilities have appeared, and systems analysis has been undertaken.[5] The impact has to date been small, but hopes have been raised. States here and cities there have demonstrated that something can be done to improve crime control with justice. The question is whether these incidents will initiate a national trend or will disappear as isolated sparks doused by the rain.

THREE • TOWARD A CRIMINAL JUSTICE SYSTEM

The administration of criminal justice is primarily a state and local responsibility. The grave deficiencies we have noted reflect the fact that our states and cities lack both the resources to make a substantial investment in physical improvements, personnel, and research, and the management techniques to operate the system efficiently. Acting on the findings and recommendations of the Crime Commission, the federal government in recent years has sought to make additional resources available.

In the Omnibus Crime Control and Safe Street Act of 1968, the Congress created the Law Enforcement Assistance Administration, for the purpose of making grants for law enforcement planning and operation to the states, and its subsidiary, the National Institute of Law Enforcement and Criminal Justice, to encourage research and development in the field of law enforcement. In another 1968 enactment, Congress also authorized the Department of Health, Education, and Welfare to carry on comparable activities in the field of juvenile delinquency and youth opportunity. Both of these programs, however, have only a modest degree of funding; fiscal 1970 appropriation requests for law enforcement are less than $300 million—a sum which, together with matching state funds, would increase the nation's expenditures in that field by less than 10 percent. About $15 million is being requested for the youth programs.

The nation is justifiably concerned about the increased rate of crime and about the conditions that give rise to crime, including our inadequate system of criminal justice.

In this Commission's judgment, we should give concrete expression to our concern about crime by a solemn national commitment to double our investment in the administration of justice and the prevention of crime, as rapidly as such an investment can be wisely planned and utilized.

When the doubling point is reached, this investment would cost the nation an additional five billion dollars per year—less than three-quarters of one percent of our national income and less than two percent of our tax revenues. Our total expenditure would still be less than 15 percent of what we spend on our armed forces. Surely this is a modest price to pay to "establish justice" and "insure domestic tranquility" in this complex and volatile age.

Given the realities of state and local financial resources, the federal government will have to take the lead in making this commitment, and in providing most of the required funds under the matching grant formulas already contained in the 1968 statutes. The federal commitment should be made in a manner that will convince the states, cities and the public that they can rely on the seriousness and continuity of the undertaking, and that they can invest matching funds of their own without fear that the federal portion may be curtailed midway in the program.

Congress has available a variety of tested methods for making meaningful long-term commitments along these lines. These include:

(a) Amending the 1968 statutes to authorize the Law Enforcement Assistance Administration and the Department of Health, Education, and Welfare to enter into long-term contracts with state and local agencies, committing the federal government to expenditures for the capital and operating costs of specified projects over a period of up to 10 years. Actual disbursements would be subject to annual appropriation measures.

(b) Amending the 1968 statutes to authorize the issuance of federal guarantees of long-term bonds issued by state and local agencies to cover capital costs of the construction of new facilities and obtaining major items of new equipment (*e.g.*, communications systems), with an underlying contract under which annual contributions in a predetermined amount would be made by the federal government toward payment of interest and amortization of principal on the bonds. Actual expenditures would be subject to annual appropriation measures, but the credit of the United States would stand behind the bonds. The Public Housing program is financed in this manner.

(c) Multi-year appropriation measures, such as those that have been made for urban renewal, federal construction projects, defense contracting and similar purposes.

Money alone will not secure crime reduction, however. Wealthy states and localities which have limited their activity merely to expending more funds have become no more noticeably crime-free than jurisdictions which have not. Similarly, a substantial portion of the Crime Commission's proposals in 1967 are remarkably similar to those urged by the Wickersham Commission established by President Hoover 37 years earlier—yet despite that Commission's equally impressive documentation, conservatism and presidential prestige, little follow-through occurred. Experience with crime commissions at the state and local levels shows similar results.

This pattern suggests the existence of substantial built-in obstacles to change. It suggests that unless much more attention is given to the inability and unwillingness of present crime control systems to effectuate reform, new money may go down old drains. Vexing problems of politics, organization and leadership underlie the maintenance of the status quo and need to be faced directly.

In the search for more effective ways of carrying out Crime Commission recommendations, we have noted two promising but comparatively untried strategies based on recent experiments on the frontiers of criminal justice; these are:

(a) a program to coordinate criminal justice and related agencies more effectively by establishing central criminal justice offices in major metropolitan areas; and

(b) a program to develop private citizen participation as an integral operating component, rather than a conversational adjunct, of criminal reform.

The two innovations complement one another; the success of citizen participation will in many ways be dependent on

136

the establishment of a central criminal justice office, and vice versa.

The Criminal Justice Office

The pervasive fragmentation of police, court and correctional agencies suggests that some catalyst is needed to bring them together. An assumption that parallel and overlapping public agencies will cooperate efficiently can no longer suffice as a substitute for deliberate action to make it happen in real life.

Periodic crime commissions—which study these agencies, file reports and then disappear—are valuable, but they are much too transient and non-operational for this coordinating role. A law enforcement council—consisting of chief judges and agency heads who meet periodically—is usually little more than another committee of overcommitted officials.

A full-time criminal justice office is basic to the formation of a criminal justice system. Its optimum form, *i.e.*, line or staff, and its location in the bureaucracy, need to be developed through experimentation.

The function could be vested in a criminal justice assistant to the mayor or county executive, with staff relationships to executive agencies, and liaison with the courts and the community. Alternately, it could operate as a ministry of justice and be given line authority under the direction of a high ranking official of local government (*e.g.*, Director of Public Safety or Criminal Justice Administrator), to whom local police, prosecutor, defender and correctional agencies would be responsive. (Special kinds of administrative ties to the courts would be evolved to avoid undermining the essential independence of the judiciary.) A third alternative might take the form of a well-staffed secretariat to a council composed of heads of public agencies, courts and private interests concerned with crime. To avoid the ineffectiveness of committees, however, either the chairman of the council or its executive director would have to be given a good measure of operating authority.

Whatever its form, the basic purposes of the criminal

137

justice office would be to do continuing planning, to assure effective processing of cases, and to develop better functioning relationships among the criminal justice subsystems and with public and private agencies outside the criminal justice system. For example:

- It would develop a system of budgeting for crime control which takes account of the interrelated needs and imbalances among individual agencies and jurisdictions.
- It would initiate a criminal justice information system which would include not simply crime reports (as is typical today), but arrests, reduction of charges, convictions, sentences, recidivism, court backlogs, detention populations, crime prevention measures, and other data essential to an informed process.
- It would perform or sponsor systems analysis and periodic evaluation of agency programs and encourage innovations and pilot projects which might not otherwise have a chance in a tradition-oriented system.
- It would perform a mediating and liaison role in respect to the many functions of the criminal process involving more than one element of the system, *e.g.,* to develop programs for the reduction of police waiting time in court, to improve pretrial release information and control, to enlist prosecutors and defense attorneys in cooperative efforts to expedite trials, to bring correctional inputs to bear on initial decisions whether to prosecute, to improve relations between criminal justice agencies and the community.
- It would also perform the vital but neglected function of coordinating the criminal justice agencies with programs and organizations devoted to improving individual lives—*e.g.,* hospitals, mental health organizations, welfare and vocational rehabilitation agencies, youth organizations and other public and private groups.
- It would develop minimum standards of performance, new incentives and exchange programs for police, court attaches and correctional personnel.

The comprehensive grasp of the system by an experienced criminal justice staff would facilitate informed executive, judicial and legislative judgments on priorities. It would help decide, for example, whether the new budget should cover:

- A modern diagnostic and detention center to replace the jail, or an increase of comparable cost in the size of the police force;

138

- Additional judges and prosecutors, or a prior management survey of the courts;
- A computerized information system or a new faculty for juveniles;
- New courtrooms or new halfway houses.

For a full-time well-staffed criminal justice office to be successful, it must achieve a balanced perspective within its own ranks on the problems of public safety and justice. Practical experience in law enforcement, in the protection of individual rights, and in the efficiency and effectiveness of programs must be represented, as must the interests of the community. Such representation can be provided through an advisory board to the criminal justice office and through involvement of relevant persons in task force efforts to attack particular problems. Broadbased support of the office is quite important.

The transition from today's condition to a well-run system will not be easy. Especially troublesome is the fact that the criminal justice process does not operate within neat political boundaries. Police departments are usually part of the city government; but county and state police and sheriffs usually operate in the same or adjacent areas. Judges are sometimes appointed, sometimes elected, and different courts are answerable to local, county and state constituencies. Correctional functions are a conglomerate of local and county jails, and county and state prisons. Prosecutors may be appointed or elected from all three levels of government. Defense lawyers usually come from the private sector but are increasingly being augmented by public defender agencies. Probation system are sometimes administered by the courts, sometimes by an executive agency.

If this confusing pattern makes the creation, location, staffing and political viability of a criminal justice office difficult, it also symbolizes why little semblance of a system exists today and why criminal justice offices are so badly needed in our major metropolitan areas.

To encourage the development of criminal justice offices, we recommend that the Law Enforcement Assistance Administration and the state planning agencies created pursuant to the Omnibus Crime Control and Safe Streets Act take the lead in initiating plans for the creation and staffing of offices of criminal justice in the nation's major metropolitan areas.

The creation of criminal justice offices will require the active participation and cooperation of all the various agencies in the criminal justice process and of officials at many levels of state and local government. Helpful insights in establishing the first such offices may be derived from the experiences of some of the state law enforcement planning agencies (e.g., Massachusetts) now making efforts in this direction, from the criminal justice coordinating role developed by the Mayor's office in New York over the past two years, and from the experience of the Office of Criminal Justice established in the Department of Justice in 1964.

Private Citizen Involvement

Government programs for the control of crime will be most effective if informed private citizens, playing a variety of roles, participate in the prevention, detection and prosecution of crime, the fair administration of justice, and the restoration of offenders to the community. New citizen-based mechanisms are needed at the local and national levels to spearhead greater participation by individuals and groups.

In recent years, an increasing number of citizen volunteer programs have become allied with one or another phase of the criminal justice process. These are in addition to long-standing efforts of organizations like the Big Brother movement and Boys' Clubs. Remarkable have been certain programs utilizing citizen volunteers for probation supervision and guidance of juvenile and misdemeanant offenders.[6]

Perhaps the most successful of private organizations in attacking the broad range of crime control problems through a public-private partnership is New York City's Vera Institute of Justice.[7] Its unique role in cooperation with the system has developed over eight years. Its non-bureaucratic approach has permitted it to test new programs, through experiments and pilot projects, in a way no public agency would likely find successful. Its core funding is entirely private; its individual project financing comes from federal, state, and private sources.

Vera has achieved a number of concrete successes. Its Manhattan Bail Project resulted in bail reforms so successful in New York City that they became the basis of the federal Bail Reform Act of 1966. Its summons project proved the practicability of permitting the police to issue station house citations for minor offenses, sparing both police and citizens the time-consuming process of arraignment and similar pre-trial court procedures.

There are a number of reasons why private organizations such as Vera can be successful where a public agency cannot. Because municipal agencies are chronically understaffed and underfinanced, they are unable to divert resources for experimental purposes except in the most limited manner. Private organizations do not pose threats to existing agencies and carry no residue of past misunderstandings. They can intercede with a city's power structure without being bound by chains of command. They can test programs through a pilot project carried out on a small scale, which can be easily dismantled if it proves unsuccessful. If it proves effective, it can be taken over as a permanent operation by the public agency and the private group can move on to a new area.

In the broader field of improving urban society, citizens' organizations have launched programs in a number of major cities to stimulate both public and private efforts to improve housing, schools, and job opportunities for the urban poor, to identify and treat the juvenile offender, and to improve relations between the police and residents of the inner city.[8] These efforts are of vital importance, because improvements in the criminal justice machinery, isolated from improvements in the quality of life, *e.g.,* education, housing, employment, health, environment, will merely return convicted offenders to the hopelessness from which they came.

The successes of such groups have demonstrated that public institutions are receptive to changes proposed by private organizations. Organizations such as these should receive maximum encouragement and every effort should be made to extend their influence on the broadest scale. Of particular importance is the potential supporting role

141

which private groups can have in relation to the new offices of criminal justice we have recommended.

We urge the creation and continued support—including private and public funding—of private citizens' organizations to work as counterparts of the proposed offices of criminal justice in every major city in the nation.

A catalyst is needed at the national level to help in the formation of such local citizen groups.

We therefore recommend that the President call upon leading private citizens to create a National Citizens Justice Center.

A similar presidential initiative led to the formation in 1963 of the Lawyers Committee for Civil Rights Under Law, a private group which has enlisted the organized Bar in the effort to make civil rights into a working reality.

The membership of the Center could be drawn from many sources, such as the National Council on Crime and Delinquency, the American Bar Association, and the members, staffs and consultants of the four federal commissions which have recently studied the problems of crime, violence, and social disorder—the President's Commission on Crime in the District of Columbia, the President's Commission on Law Enforcement and Administration of Justice, the National Advisory Commission on Civil Disorders, and this Commission.

The Center would supplement rather than duplicate the promising and important work of existing private entities. Following the successful precedent of Vera, the Center would concentrate on the various aspects of the criminal justice system, from crime prevention and arrest to trial and correction, including the specialized treatment of actual and potential juvenile offenders. We would expect it to receive financial support from foundations, business and labor sources, as well as from the legal profession.

The Center would help to form and support local private counterparts of Vera in our major urban areas, to work alongside local government agencies on specific operating and administrative problems. It would act as a clearing house for transmitting news of successful innovative procedures developed in one city to the attention of agencies faced with similar problems in another. It would cross-fertilize new approaches, and provide continuing public education about the complexity of crime prevention and the treatment of offenders. It would offer workable answers to the persistent citizen question—what can I do to help? Not least important, it might lessen the future need for *ad hoc* presidential commissions in this field, by assuring greater use of the findings and recommendations of the many commisssions that have gone before.

FOUR • CONCLUSION

The levels of funding and the various public and private mechanisms we have suggested could go a long way toward organizing our criminal justice agencies into an effective system; our recommendations of additional legal services for the poor and new citizens' grievance agencies could do much to strengthen respect for legal processes and for the institutions of government.

The injection of federal funds into state crime control programs in 1968 was an important step, and the Law Enforcement Assistance Administration is doing a commendable job with limited resources. Much more money must be provided, and must be injected into research, development, and pilot projects, if the outdated techniques of yesterday are to be converted into an effective criminal justice system tomorrow.

Until more funds are committed, and until staffed organizations—public and private—are developed to assure wise investment and monitoring of new funds, the control of violent crime will be a campaign fought with bold words and symbolic gestures, but no real hope of success. The mobilization of private and public resources toward an ordered society—one in which the rights of all citizens to life, to liberty, to the pursuit of happiness are safeguarded by our governing institutions—deserves a high priority for the decade of the 1970s.

SEPARATE STATEMENT

Commissioner Ernest W. McFarland notes that many of the findings and recommendations of the Commission Chapter on Violence and Law Enforcement were addressed largely to the problems and needs of the larger cities. He does not believe that all the recommended changes are needed or are applicable to Arizona and some of the other less urbanized states even though definite change and improvement are required in the larger cities. Upon this basis, he stated he was willing to vote for the recommendations, hoping they would be carefully studied by all the communities and states to determine whether, even if not wholly applicable, some part might be helpful in meeting their needs.

1. *E. g.*, Donald J. Black and Albert J. Reiss, Jr., "Patterns of Behavior in Police and Citizen Transactions," *Studies in Crime and Law Enforcement in Major Metropolitan Areas,* Field Survey III, Vol. 1, a Report of a Research Study Submitted to the President's Commission on Law Enforcement and Administration of Justice (Washington, D.C.: Government Printing Office, 1967).
2. In a survey conducted by this Commission most white Americans disagreed with the statement: "The police frequently use more force than they need to when carrying out their duties." But a majority of Negro respondents agreed with the statement, as did a third of the lower-income people and 40 percent of the metropolitan city dwellers. In many of our recent urban disturbances, the triggering event was an arrest or other police encounter that appeared to bystanders to be unfair.
3. President's Commission on Law Enforcement and Administration of Justice, *The Challenge of Crime in a Free Society* (Washington, D.C.: Government Printing Office, 1967), pp. 20-22. Major crimes are homicide, rape, robbery, aggravated assault, burglary, larceny over $50 and auto theft.
4. The Report of the Commission's Task Force on Law and Law Enforcement contains a study of our bail system and recent proposals for "preventive detention" of persons arrested for serious crimes who, in the judgment of the court on a preliminary hearing, are deemed likely to commit a serious crime if released on bail while awaiting trial. The Commission agrees with the conclusion of the American Bar Association in approving the Report of the Special Committee on Minimum Standards for the Administration of Criminal Justice that "because of the drastic effects of preventive detention, the difficulties inherent in predicting future criminality and the unresolved constitutional issues," preventive detention should not be adopted. While there is a very real public interest in preventing criminal activity by released persons awaiting trial this interest would be better served by reforming the criminal justice system to expedite trials than by adding the additional burden of a preliminary trial to predict the likelihood of future criminality. (It should be noted that even at present some crimes, such as first degree murder, are not bailable.)
5. For example, the new Federal Judicial Center under the leadership of retired Supreme Court Justice Tom Clark has initiated several innovative administrative and managerial projects which offer great promise for reduction of court backlogs and the shortening of time periods to trial. It is reported that one project in the U.S. District Court for the District of Columbia resulted in the judges reducing the criminal docket in a recent two-week period more than they had in the entire prior year. Another example of important work being done is the course of instruction for District Attorneys being given by the National College of District Attorneys.
6. Example programs in this area include those outlined by Volunteers in Probation, Inc. (formerly Project Misdemeanant Foundation), Royal Oak, Michigan, and the Juvenile Court of Boulder, Colorado.
7. The Vera Institute was founded in 1961 by industrialist Louis Schweitzer and named for his mother. Until 1966, it was funded entirely by the Schweitzer family. In 1966, in order to expand and start special projects, Vera was given a 5-year grant from the Ford Foundation, and since then it has also received other federal, state and private grants earmarked for special projects. Herbert Sturz has been the Director of the Institute since 1961.
8. Among the leading national organizations working in these fields are the League of Women Voters, the Urban League, the American Friends Service

144

VII ● FIREARMS AND VIOLENCE*

Whether guns cause violence, contribute to it, or are merely coincidental to it has long been debated. After extensive study we find that the availability of guns contributes substantially to violence in American society. Firearms, particularly handguns, facilitate the commission and increase the danger of the most violent crimes—assassination, murder, robbery and assault. The widespread availability of guns can also increase the level of violence associated with civil disorder. Firearms accidents, while they account for only a small percentage of all accidents, cause thousands of deaths and injuries each year.

This relationship between firearms and violence tends to obscure two other important facts bearing on the firearms question. First, the vast majority of gun owners do not misuse firearms. Millions of Americans are hunters, target shooters, and collectors, who use their guns safely and responsibly and who, perhaps more than many of their fellow citizens, deplore the criminal use of firearms. Second, in attending to the firearms problem, we must not forget that the root causes of American violence go much deeper than widespread gun ownership. Firearms generally facilitate, rather than cause, violence.

The challenge for this Commission—and for the nation as a whole—is to find ways to cope with illegitimate uses of guns without at the same time placing undue restrictions on legitimate uses. We believe this is possible if both the advocates and the opponents of gun control legislation will put aside their suspicions and preconceptions, accept the fact of a common danger without exaggerating its dimensions and act for the common good.

---

*An edited version of statement issued July 28, 1969.

145

ONE • THE DOMESTIC ARMS BUILDUP

Our Task Force on Firearms estimates that there are now about ninety million firearms in the United States. Half of the nation's sixty million households possess at least one gun, and the number of guns owned by private citizens is rising rapidly.

During the first half of this century, about ten million firearms on the average were added to the civilian firearms supply in each decade. In the decade since 1958, however, nearly thirty million guns have been added to the civilian stockpile. Moreover, the sharpest increases have occurred in the last five years—a period of urban riots and sharply rising crime rates. Annual rifle and shotgun sales have doubled since 1963. Annual handgun sales have quadrupled.

Some of the increased gun sales in recent years have resulted from an increase in hunting and sport shooting, a fact consistent with the rising amount of money being spent on leisure time activities. But these predictable increases in sales of sporting arms cannot explain the much larger increases in the sales of handguns. With a few scattered exceptions, handguns are not sporting guns.

A substantial part of the rapidly increasing gun sales, particularly handgun sales, must be attributed to the rising fear of violence that the United States has recently experienced. Studies by our Task Force on Firearms, as well as by the Stanford Research Institute and the Senate Subcommittee on Juvenile Delinquency, show that gun sales in a particular area tend to increase sharply during and after a period of disorder. After the 1967 Detroit riot, for example, gun sales skyrocketed; Detroit issued four times as many handgun permits in 1968 as it did in 1965, and a nearby, predominantly white suburb issued five times as many permits.

Lending impetus to the arms buildup are the exhortations of extremist groups, both black and white. In their speeches and publications, leaders of these groups urge their members to buy firearms and be prepared to use them against "the enemy." Neighborhood protective associations have proliferated and have sometimes come to share the

146

fears of the right-wing paramilitary groups, with the result that firearms are now being stockpiled in homes as well as "in the hills." A new wave of American vigilantism could result from these activities. Further, black extremist organizations urge their members to obtain firearms for neighborhood and home defense, and sometimes for guerrilla warfare and terrorist activities as well. Ironically, extremist groups, regardless of race, are remarkably alike in their attitudes toward firearms and their opposition to firearms control.[1]

Quite apart from civil disorders, the urban arms buildup has increased the role of firearms in accidents and violent crime. Our Task Force has found that in Detroit accidental firearms deaths were three times greater in 1968, the year after the riot, than in 1966, the year before the riot. Between 1965 and 1968, homicides in Detroit committed with firearms increased 400 percent while homicides committed with other weapons increased only 30 percent; firearms robberies increased twice as fast as robberies committed without firearms. (These rates of increase are much higher than for the nation as a whole.)

Other studies confirm our finding that the proportion of gun use in violence rises and falls with gun ownership. The urban arms buildup threatens not only to escalate future civil disorders, but also to bring with it greater misuse of firearms in crimes and accidents.

TWO • FIREARMS AND VIOLENT CRIME

Many Americans are alarmed by the rise of violent crime in the United States, and not without reason. Personal injury and death from crime occur more often in the United States than in any other industrial nation of the world.

Firearms are a primary instrument of injury and death in American crime. Two out of every three homicides are committed with guns. Since 1963 the number of homicides involving firearms has increased 48 percent in the United States while the number of homicides committed with other weapons has risen only 10 percent.

The circumstances of most homicides suggest that a person without ready access to a gun would not inevitably kill

147

with another weapon. Studies show that most persons who commit homicide are not relentless, determined killers, but rather are persons likely to act on impulse in a moment of rage or passion and without a plan or determined intent to kill. There is no hard evidence to prove or disprove the thesis that lacking a gun, an enraged person will resort to a knife or other weapon. But there is evidence demonstrating that the fatality rate of firearms attacks is more than four times greater than the fatality rate of knife attacks (knives being the next most frequent and lethal weapon used in homicides). Thus, even if the number of violent attacks did not go down, the number of fatalities resulting from violent attacks would be substantially reduced if the attackers did not have guns.

The deadliness of firearms is perhaps best illustrated by the fact that they are virtually the only weapons used in killing police officers. Policemen are armed. They are trained in the skills of self-defense. They expect trouble and are prepared for it. Yet, from 1960 through 1967, 411 police officers were killed in the course of their official duties—76 of them in 1967 alone. Guns were used in 96 percent of these fatal attacks on police.

In assassinations, guns play a crucial role because they extend the deadliness and the effectiveness of the assassin. Of the nine assassination attempts on American presidents or presidential candidates, all involved firearms. All, except the assassination of President Kennedy, involved handguns.

Guns also play an increasingly deadly role in aggravated assault and robbery. In 1968, 23 percent of all aggravated assaults were committed with guns, as opposed to only 13 percent in 1963. One out of every three robberies (two out of every three armed robberies) is committed with a gun, and the fatality rate for victims of firearms robberies is almost four times as great as for victims of other armed robberies.

In all these violent crimes, handguns are the weapon predominantly used. Although only slightly more than one-fourth (or 24 million) of the firearms in the nation are handguns, they account for about half of all homicides and three-fourths of all firearms homicides. When firearms are involved in aggravated assaults and robberies in large cities, the handgun is almost invariably the weapon used.

148

THREE • FIREARMS AND SELF-DEFENSE

It may seem incongruous that in our advanced and civilized society individual citizens should feel the need to keep a gun for self-protection. Yet a 1966 public opinion survey, conducted for the President's Commission on Law Enforcement and Administration of Justice, disclosed that more than 22 million households (37 percent of the total and 66 percent of the households with guns) included self-defense as one reason, among others, for owning a firearm. Since many owners keep their guns in the home for protection against intruders, it is important to assess, to the extent possible, the nature of the threat from intruders and the chances of gun owners to defend themselves successfully with their weapons.

What is the nature of the threat in the home? The number of killings in the home by burglars and robbers[2] is not large relative to the total number of homicides. Burglars usually try to avoid contact with the homeowner: they rely on stealth and are more likely to flee than fight when discovered. The robber poses a much greater threat to the personal safety of the occupant of the house, but robberies occur in the home far less often than in other places.[3] Because of these factors, studies in several cities indicate that killings in the home by robbers and burglars account for no more than 2 percent or 3 percent of all criminal homicides.[4]

What are the householder's chances of successfully defending himself with a gun? In only a relatively small number of instances do home robberies or burglaries result in the death of the victim. Examination shows that in the great majority of the cases, the householder had no warning and thus no chance to arm himself with a gun. Studies in Los Angeles and Detroit indicate that only about two percent of home robberies, and two-tenths of one percent of home burglaries, result in the firearms death or injury of the intruder at the hands of the householder.[5] Moreover, in considering the value of handguns, or firearms generally, for self-defense in the home, one must also take into account the risks associated with home possession of a gun. A substantial number of the 23,000 annual firearms accidents occur in the home. Of the 8,000 annual firearms homicides, a large percentage occur among family members or acquaintances, and many of these also occur in the home.

From the standpoint of the individual householder, then, the self-defense firearm appears to be a dangerous investment. The existence of guns in one-half of America's homes may deter intruders. One may assume a robber is reluctant to ply his trade in homes rather than on the street because of the possibility that he may encounter an alert, armed householder. Our Task Force made an effort to study the extent of this deterrence, but was unable to arrive at any firm conclusion. The evidence is convincing, however, that the home robber most often has the advantage of surprise, and the armed segment of our population is paying a heavy price in accidents and in the shooting of family members, friends and acquaintances for whatever deterrent effect their possession of self-defense firearms may be providing. In a more rational world, home intrusion would be deterred by other means—such as non-lethal weapons, alarm systems, and other security arrangements —that are less dangerous to the occupants of the home.

Burglars and robbers also threaten businesses, and firearms are frequently kept in places of business for protection. Such firearms are useful primarily against robbers, since burglars usually break and enter after the business has closed. Research to date does not permit us to draw firm conclusions as to the net usefulness of self-defense firearms possessed by storeowners and other businessmen. We do know, however, that business self-defence firearms do not cause the great number of accidents caused by home firearms or involve the same risk of homicide to family members and friends. Thus, the home and the business establishment must be clearly distinguished from each other when considering the usefulness of firearms for self-defense.

FOUR • FIREARMS CONTROL IN THE UNITED STATES

The United States still does not have an effective national firearms policy. Federal gun laws have been passed largely in response to sensational episodes of gun violence. In general the approach of these laws has been to use federal power merely to curtail interstate movements of firearms, leaving each of the states free to adopt the degree and kind of internal control it wished. Moreover, even this limited policy objective was not effectively implemented. It was perfectly legal, until the passage of the Gun Control Act of 1968, to sell or ship weapons from a state which had little or no firearms control to persons in a state with a stricter system. Since attempts to establish uniform state and local firearms laws never succeeded, the few serious efforts at state and local regulation (as in Massachusetts and New York) have been consistently frustrated by the flow of firearms from jurisdictions with looser or no controls.

Under this patchwork statutory regime, our firearms population has grown to the point where guns are readily available to everyone—legally in most cases, illegally in the rest. The Gun Control Act of 1968 does curtail imports of cheap foreign firearms; it significantly restricts mail order and interstate gun shipment to individuals, and it forbids the possession of handguns by convicted felons and other dangerous classes. But the 1968 Act is not designed to affect either the overall size of the tremendous United States gun population which is the legacy of past firearms policies, or the hand-to-hand or "street" sales of second-hand guns. Yet such sales appear to be the major source of the firearms used in crime. We have learned that almost half of all rifles and shotguns and more than half of all handguns are acquired second-hand—usually from a friend or other private party.

Our lack of an effective national firearms policy is primarily the result of our culture's casual attitude toward firearms and its heritage of the armed, self-reliant citizen. These are the factors that have prevented passage of effective gun regulation legislation in the United States. Guns are routinely carried in pockets and left in closets, corners, and bureau drawers. In many parts of the country, they are standard equipment in pickup trucks and small business. Nearly 15 million licensed hunters make extensive use of firearms for sporting purposes. The hero of American movies and television is the man with a gun—the soldier,

151

cowboy, spy, sheriff, or criminal—and our children accumulate an arsenal of toy guns. Accustomed to firearms, convinced that they are household necessities, entertained by fiction and drama that portray the gun as a glamorous instrument of personal justice, many Americans underestimate the consequences of widespread firearms availability.

Despite the acceptance of guns as a common part of everyday American life, there is also a growing realization in the United States of the social costs of ineffective gun control. On the one hand, firearms manufacturers are on record favoring the requirement of an identification card for firearms owners and denying gun ownership to felons and mental and physical incompetents. On the other hand, advocates of strict gun control are increasingly inclined to acknowledge the legitimate use of guns by sportsmen. Both the President's Commission on Law Enforcement and Administration of Justice in 1967 and the National Advisory Commission on Civil Disorders in 1968 recommended that the federal government and the states should act to strengthen the presently inadequate firearms control laws.

In determining what our national firearms policy should be, it is necessary to keep clearly in mind that just as the term "firearms" includes different kinds of weapons which contribute unequally to violence, so also does the phrase "gun control" comprise a number of quite separate ideas. For different strategies of gun control can be identified, though in legislative measures the strategies are often found in various combinations.

(1) *Registration of firearms.* Registration is designed to provide a record of all persons who own firearms as well as the firearms they own. Proponents point out that registration would help police trace weapons and thus deter a registered owner from criminal use or illegal transfer of his firearm. Opponents of registration reply that criminals will not register firearms and that the registration process is costly.

(2) *Prohibition of gun ownership by certain classes of persons (felons, addicts, etc.).* This type of control is put forward as making it more difficult for poor gun risks to obtain firearms from legitimate sources. Licensing and investigation of applicants are often utilized as part of this strategy. Opponents argue that the prohibited class can

152

still obtain guns by theft or in the hand-to-hand market, while legitimate users are caused added inconvenience.

(3) *Increased criminal penalties for the use of guns in crime.* Increased penalties are urged as a means to deter criminals from using firearms. Opponents point out that existing penalties for violent crime are already severe and that an extra measure of punishment will have little additional deterrent effect.

(4) *Restrictive licensing.* This method requires all persons seeking to buy a particular type of firearm, typically a handgun, to demonstrate to the authorities an affirmative need to own the firearm. Its proponents urge that alone among the four control strategies, restrictive licensing is designed to reduce substantially the number of handguns in circulation. Its opponents note that restrictive licensing systems require the surrender of many previously lawful firearms, and amount to "confiscation."

Can any of these systems of firearms control be expected to reduce firearms violence? Some argue that with 90 million firearms in our country, no system of control will prevent persons from obtaining guns and using them illegally. The criminal, they declare, can always get a gun. The argument is not without merit, for it points the way to the steps which must be taken.

Our studies have convinced us that the heart of any effective national firearms policy for the United States must be to reduce the availability of the firearm that contributes the most violence. *This means restrictive licensing of the handgun.* We believe, on the basis of all the evidence before us, that reducing the availability of the handgun *will* reduce firearms violence.

Although no other nation in history has ever attempted to institute firearms control with so many guns already dispersed throughout all segments of the population, foreign crime statistics provide some encouraging insights into the possible results of stricter control of the handgun in the United States. Thus in England and Wales, with restrictive licensing systems and with much lower rates of violent crime than the United States, only 18 percent of homicides in 1967 were committed with firearms weapons compared to 64 percent in the United States. Only six percent of all robberies in England and Wales in 1967 involved

153

guns, as compared to 36 percent in the United States. These lower rates of homicides and armed robberies and more importantly of firearms usage in such crimes suggest that a system which makes it substantially more difficult to obtain firearms can reduce the use of firearms in violent behavior and consequently can reduce both the frequency and the dangerousness of such behavior. In England and Wales the criminal cannot—or at least does not—always get a gun, and the public safety is much improved as a result.[6]

FIVE • RECOMMENDATIONS FOR A NATIONAL FIREARMS POLICY

The Commission offers the following recommendations to reduce the role which firearms play in violence in the United States.

We urge a public education campaign, aided by the National Rifle Association and other private organizations devoted to hunting and sport shooting, to stress the duties and responsibilities of firearms ownership so that a new awareness of the proper role of firearms in American life can prevail in the more than 30 million homes which possess firearms. In particular, we urge the nation's gun manufacturers to issue safety booklets with each gun that they sell and to administer safety tests by mail to purchasers based upon these booklets.

We urge individual citizens—particularly on the basis of the statistics on firearms accidents—to reflect carefully before deciding that loaded firearms are necessary or desirable for self-defense in their homes.

Research

We urge that further research be undertaken on the relationships between firearms and violence and on the measures that can reduce firearms violence. Further work should especially be done on how firearms accidents occur and can be prevented and on the psychological impact of guns on criminals.

Further research is also needed as part of the effort to design firearm control systems that are no more restrictive than necessary and which minimize costs to firearms users and to the community as a whole.

Scientific research should be intensified on devices to assist

154

law enforcement personnel in detecting the presence of concealed firearms on the person.

The federal government should join with private industry to speed the development of an effective non-lethal weapon. We consider this recommendation to be of the utmost importance. So long as crime rates mount in this nation and civil disorders threaten, law-abiding Americans understandably fear for their safety. An effective non-leathal weapon could serve defensive needs without risk to human life.

Legislation

We conclude that the rising tide of firearms violence in this country merits further legislative action at the present time.

It is the ready availability of the handgun, so often a weapon of crime and so infrequently a sporting arm, that is the most serious part of the current firearms problem in this country. The time has come to bring the handgun under reasonable control.

A restrictive licensing system for handguns is needed. State governments should be given the first opportunity to establish such systems in conformity with minimum federal standards that afford considerable discretion to each state to adopt a system suitable to its own needs. Accordingly—

We recommend federal legislation to encourage the establishment of state licensing systems for handguns. The federal legislation would introduce a federal system of handgun licensing, applicable only to those states which within a four-year period fail to enact a state law that (1) established a standard for determining an individual's need for a handgun and for the licensing of an individual who shows such a need and (2) prohibits all others from possessing handguns or buying handgun ammunition.

We propose that the states be permitted to determine for themselves what constitutes "need" to own a handgun. For the federal system applicable to states which fail to enact their own licensing systems, we recommend that determinations of need be limited to police officers and security guards, small businesses in high crime areas, and others with a special need for self-protection. At least in major metropolitan areas, the federal system should not

155

consider normal household protection a sufficient showing of need to have a handgun.

We also recommend that a system of federal administrative or judicial review be established to assure that each state system is administered fairly and does not discriminate on the basis of race, religion, national origin, or other unconstitutional grounds.

We note that it will be necessary to compensate those handgun owners who are required to give up previously lawful firearms; this cost, which should be borne by the federal government, could amount to $500 million.

Finally, we emphasize that laws controlling handguns should provide serious penalties for the possession of such guns by unlicensed persons. The apprehension of such persons should in time greatly reduce the rate of violent crime in the United States.

Shotguns and rifles are far less of a threat than handguns, particularly in the area of violent crime. At the same time, legitimate use of the long gun is widespread. The significant differences between handguns and long guns call for substantially different control strategies. We can make substantial inroads on firearms violence without imposing major inconveniences on hunters and skeet and trap shooters, and without impeding other legitimate activities of millions of long gun owners. Accordingly—

We recommend federal legislation to establish minimum standards for state regulation of long guns under which (1) an identification card would be required for long gun owners and purchasers of long gun ammunition (a system similar to that recommended by gun manufacturers) and (2) any person 18 and over would be entitled to such a card, except certain classes of criminals and adjudicated incompetents. For states which do not adopt such regulations within four years, a federal regulatory system would be established.

We do not recommend federal legislation to require nationwide registration of existing long guns. Substantially the same benefits could be obtained from less costly and burdensome control strategies.

We do recommend that persons who transfer long guns be required to fill out a single card giving the serial number, type, make, and model of the weapon, the transferee's social security and firearms identification card numbers, the transferor's name and social security number, and the date of the transaction.

156

Restrictive licensing of handguns and the simple identification card system for long guns represent the key legislative recommendations of this Commission in the area of gun control. There are, however, a number of other important goals which uniform and effective gun control legislation should accomplish. We urge the nation's lawmakers to consider them.

First, the Gun Control Act of 1968, which is intended to curtail the import of firearms unsuitable for sporting use, should be extended to prohibit domestic production and sale of "junk guns." Second, a federal firearms information center should be established to accumulate and store information on firearms and owners received from state agencies; this information would be available to state and federal law enforcement agencies. Third, licensed gun dealers should be required by federal statute to adopt and maintain security procedures to minimize theft of firearms.

SIX • CONCLUSION

An effective national firearms policy would help to reduce gun violence in the United States. It would also have a significance beyond the question of firearms. In comparison with most of the causes of violence in America, the firearms problem is concrete and manageable. But it is also complex and emotion-laden. For the United States to move effectively toward its solution would signify a new ability to transcend our violent past.

SEPARATE STATEMENT

Four members of the Commission (Senator Roman L. Hruska, Judge Ernest W. McFarland, Congressman Hale Boggs, and Leon Jaworski) state that there is a great deal with which they agree in this chapter on "Firearms and Violence." They feel, however, that the needs are not the same in the various states, or, for that matter, in all parts of a state. It is their opinion that each state should be

157

permitted to determine for itself without additional restrictions from the federal government the system which best meets its needs to control the use of both the handguns and the long guns. They are unable, therefore, to concur fully with the Commission's recommendations.

STATISTICAL APPENDIX

1. Total number of firearms in civilian hands (U.S., 1968):

rifles:	35 million.
shotguns:	31 million.
handguns:	24 million.
TOTAL:	90 million.

2. Annual increase in number of firearms in civilian hands (U.S., 1962 vs. 1968):

rifles:	1962, 0.7 million	1968, 1.4 million.
shotguns:	1962, 0.7 million	1968, 1.4 million.
handguns:	1962, 0.6 million	1968, 2.5 million.
TOTAL:	1962, 2.1 million	1968, 5.3 million.

3. Mode of acquisition of firearms (U.S., 1968):

rifles:	New, 56%	Used, 44%.
shotguns:	New, 54%	Used, 46%.
handguns:	New, 46%	Used, 54%.

Note: More than 50% of all acquisitions of used firearms are from private parties, rather than from stores.

4. Accidental deaths of civilians from firearms and other causes (U.S., 1967):

motor vehicles:	53,100
falls:	19,800
fires:	7,700
drowning:	6,800
firearms:	2,800
poisons:	2,400
machinery:	2,100

5. Total number of major violent offenses (U.S., 1964 vs. 1967):

homicides:	1964, 9,250	1967, 12,100.
aggravated assaults:	1964, 200,000	1967, 253,300.
robberies:	1964, 129,830	1967, 202,050.

6. Criminal uses of firearms (U.S., 1964 vs. 1967):

homicides:	1964, 55% with firearms	1967, 63% with firearms.
aggravated assaults:	1964, 15% with firearms	1967, 21% with firearms.
robberies:	1964, not available	1967, 37% with firearms.

7. Deadliness of firearms vs. knife attacks (U.S., 1967):

    Percentage of firearms attacks resulting in death: 12.8
    Percentage of knife attacks resulting in death: 2.9

(Firearms attacks are thus 4.4 times as deadly as knife attacks.)

8. Type of gun used in crimes committed with firearms (large U.S. cities, 1967):

homicide:	Long guns, 8%	Handguns, 92%.
aggravated assault:	Long guns, 14%	Handguns, 86%.
robbery:	Long guns, 4%	Handguns, 96%.

Note: Handguns were used in 76% of gun homicides throughout the United States in 1967.

Source: Task Force on Firearms to this Commission, *Firearms and Violence in American Life,* (Washington, D.C.: Government Printing Office, 1969).

---

1. This is not to imply that all persons who oppose additional controls are extremists.

2. Robbery involves taking property by force; burglary involves illegal entry without force against the person.

3. The 17-city victim-offender survey conducted by our Task Force on Individual Acts of Violence shows an average of 6 percent of armed robberies occurring in the home.

4. Home intrustions resulting in sexual attacks are also a threat, but they occur much less frequently than commonly believed. Our victim-offender survey suggests that substantially less than one fourth of the 27,000 rapes or rape attempts reported in the United States each year are committed by intruding strangers in the home. Since about 20,000 robberies (armed and unarmed) and 800,000 burglaries occur annually in the home, not more than three-quarters of one percent of home intrusions result in an attempted rape.

5. No data are available on how frequently robberies and burglaries are foiled by the householder's display of a gun that is not fired. Nor are data available on the use of guns by women to prevent attempted rapes; presumably this occurs extremely infrequently.

6. Comparison of firearms crimes in cities within the United States, although complicated by the problem of "leakage" across state lines, also shows that rates of firearm use in violence are lowest in the Northeast where firearms possession rates are the lowest.

VIII ● VIOLENCE IN
TELEVISION ENTERTAINMENT PROGRAMS*

The mass media are an integral part of the daily life of virtually every American. Among these media the youngest, television, is the most pervasive. Ninety-five percent of American homes have at least one TV set, and on the average that set is in use for about 40 hours each week. The central place of television in American life makes this

---

*An edited version of statement issued September 23, 1969.

medium the focal point of a growing national concern over the effects of media portrayals of violence on the values, attitudes, and behavior of an ever-increasing audience.

Commercial television occasionally offers the American public some of the finest in classical and contemporary drama, music, and entertainment, excellent documentaries and panel discussions on subjects of cultural and social interest, and it regularly brings the nation together with its skilled coverage of major political events and such exploits as the Apollo space flights. But many of television's entertainment programs feature violence, and this Commission has received from the general public more suggestions, strong recommendations and often bitter complaints about violence on television than about any other single issue.

We approach this question with great care. In our concern about violence and its causes, it is easy to make television a scapegoat. But we reemphasize what we said in our Progress Report last January: there is no simple answer to the problem of violence—no single explanation of its causes, and no single prescription for its control. We urge that those who read this chapter do so carefully, without exaggeration of its findings, remembering that America also experienced high levels of crime and violence in periods before the advent of television.

The problems of balance, taste, and artistic merit in entertainment programs on television are complex. We cannot countenance government censorship of television. Nor would we seek to impose arbitrary limitations on programming which might jeopardize television's ability to deal in dramatic presentations with controversial social issues. Nonetheless, we are deeply troubled by the television's constant portrayal of violence, not in any genuine attempt to focus artistic expression on the human condition, but rather in pandering to a public preoccupation with violence that television itself has helped to generate.

Experience with pervasive mass communications—and particularly television—is so recent that at present there is much that is not fully understood and little that is proven beyond a reasonable doubt about the full social impact of the mass media. It is difficult to design studies linking human behavior or personality formation to media content, in view of the vast array of other variables in the

160

social environment that converge to shape a person's conduct and values. Television is but one powerful element in a complex nexus of social forces impinging on people's lives. Consequently, we have seen our principal task as being one of clarifying the issues surrounding the problem of television violence and its effects, weighing the evidence in light of the risks of continuing the recent volume and style of violence portrayed on television, and framing recommendations appropriate to a problem that is as yet imperfectly understood.

We do not and cannot answer all of the questions raised by television programs that contain violence. But we do believe that our findings are adequate to support the recommendations which we offer to the broadcasting industry, to the government, and to the public. Questions of social policy can rarely be resolved beyond a reasonable doubt—but when we know enough to act, there is no excuse for inaction.

ONE • WHO WATCHES TELEVISION AND WHAT DO THEY SEE?

Everyone knows that Americans spend a great deal of time before their television sets. A number of studies described in testimony[1] before this Commission suggest, however, that we are even heavier television users than we commonly realize.

A typical, middle-income, American male devotes a total of about five hours a day to the mass media. The most popular medium is television. His TV set is in use for six hours a day and he himself watches about two and one-half hours each weekday. He also listens to the radio about two hours each day, mostly outside his home, and he reads the newspaper for about 30 minutes each day. Movies and magazines are negligible consumers of his time: he has probably read or looked through a magazine in the last week, but he only goes to a movie every three or four months.

Low-income adults are even heavier viewers of television: one survey indicates that the adults in low income homes watch television on an average of more than five hours each day. The low-income adult reads the newspaper less frequently and less intensely than the average middle-class citizen, and for most low-income adults it has been six months or more since they saw a movie.

All surveys indicate that children and adolescents are the heaviest viewers of television. Depending on their particular social stratum, children and adolescents spend on an average anywhere from one-fourth to as much as one-half of their waking day before a television screen—as much or more than the time that they spend in school.

- One study of 15- to 17-year-olds found that on Sunday the middle-class youngsters watch television for four hours while the low-income youngsters watch it for upwards of five to six hours.
- Another study of fourth and fifth graders found that the lower income children watched television from five to seven hours *each weekday*.
- Moreover, some children watch television late into the evening hours: a Nielsen study showed many evening shows having a larger number of two- to five-year-olds watching than did any daytime show and over five million children under age twelve still watching between 10:30 and 11 p.m. one Monday night.[2]

The time spent by adults and children watching television today is greater than what it was a decade ago.[3] Adults, for example, report watching one-half hour more television each day in 1968 than they did in 1961, and studies of children's viewing time indicate a substantial increase in 1968 over the two to four hours per day reported in the late 1950s.

That there is a great deal of violence on television is clear to everyone. In an effort to specify how much and what kind, we have examined the results of the numerous analyses that have been made of the content of television programs.

Much relevant evidence is to be found in testimony presented in hearings before the Senate Subcommittee to Investigate Juvenile Delinquency in 1955, 1961, and 1964. Some of these studies counted the number and kinds of violent acts on television, finding, for example, in a week of television watching in New York City in 1953, an average of 6.2 acts or threats of violence per one-hour

162

program. Another study in 1962 compared the occurrence of "aggressive episodes" to the occurrence of "protective and affectionate" behavior, finding a four-to-one ratio of assault to affection. Other studies considered the proportion of total television fare represented by programs featuring violence. One such analysis suggested that the percentage of prime time "action and adventure" programs approximately tripled between 1954 and 1961, reaching the point where such programs constituted between one-half and two-thirds of all programs in the 7 to 10 p.m. time span. (Further analyses in 1964 showed no change in the offerings of television stations in several large cities, despite a substantial reduction of violent-format programs by CBS in the period between 1962 and 1964.)

More recent studies have tried to refine the analysis of television content by considering the extent to which violence is used as a means of problem-solving in television drama. Thus, in a study published in 1963 one group of researchers classified program goals and examined what methods were used to obtain these goals.[4] They found that violent means predominated: in children's shows, for example, violent means were 47% of the time, with "escape" and non-legal means short of violence adding another 15%. The researchers concluded that methods that are *not* socially approved seem to be portrayed in television content as having a better chance of achieving the desired goal than those methods which are socially approved.

Under the auspices of our Media Task Force, this Commission had an independent analysis made of all dramatic television programs presented by the three major commercial television networks during the prime children's and adults' viewing time (4 to 10 p.m.) on weekdays and Sunday and on Saturday mornings in the week of October 1 through 7, 1968 and in the same week in 1967.[5] This study attempted not only to measure in a number of different ways the amount of violence in network dramatic programs but also, and more importantly, to present a picture of the kind of world in which television violence occurs. Some of the findings of this study are here summarized:

163

• In both 1967 and 1968 approximately eight out of every ten dramatic programs contained some violence.[6] On the other hand, the total number of violent episodes in the study week declined by nearly one-fifth between the two years (from 478 to 394).[7] This decline somewhat exceeded the decline in the total number of hours of dramatic programs (from 64 to 58.5); accordingly, the rate of violent episodes per hour showed a decline from 7.5 in 1967 to 6.7 in 1968.

• Of the crime, western, and action-adventure programs comprising about two-thirds of the networks' dramatic programs in both 1967 and 1968, virtually all contained violence in both years. Similarly, in both years they averaged about nine episodes per hour.

• Cartoon programs comprised only about ten percent of the total hours of dramatic programs, but they were almost entirely concentrated in the children's programs on Saturday morning. Almost all the cartoon programs contained violence, and the rate of violent episodes was quite high in both years—more than twenty per hour.

• Three-fourths of all violent programs and nearly nine out of every ten violent episodes were found in the crime, western, action-adventure category. Analysis of *all* program categories showed that eight out of every ten violent episodes occured in a serious or sinister context. Overtly humorous intent (slapstick, sham, satirical) could be observed in only two out of every ten violent episodes in all program categories. Comparing the 1968 study week with that from 1967, however, there did appear to be a shift of perhaps one in every ten violent episodes out of the "serious" category into the "humorous" category.

• The programs of each of the three major commercial networks contributed in different ways to the overall level of violence on television, depending on the measure of violence which is used. ABC's dramatic programs, for example, contained the greatest number of violent episodes in 1967, but that network significantly reduced the number of such episodes and in the 1968 study week was lowest in total number. In both years, however, ABC led in the percentage of dramatic program hours containing violence. CBS was least violent by this measure; but it slightly increased that percentage in 1968. and it substantially increased the rate of violent episodes per program hour. In the 1968 study week, NBC had the greatest number of violent episodes, and taking the two study years together, NBC was the leader in the amount of time devoted to programs in the category of crime, western, action-adventure.

164

What these findings confirm is that, as of 1968, the viewing public was still being exposed to a high level of televised violence. What was the nature of this violence? What were the moral and social values explicit or implicit in the context within which the violence was portrayed?

• Violent encounters in televised drama, unlike violent encounters in real life, are rarely between intimates. They generally occur at close range between young to middle-aged single males who, half the time, are strangers to each other. Six times out of ten, the violent acts involve the use of weapons; equally often, the act evokes no counterviolence from the victim.

• More than half of all the leading characters in the programs (241 out of 455 identified in the two sample weeks) inflict violence in some form upon other persons. Most of these violent encounters (eight out of ten) are between clearly identified "good guys" and "bad guys." The violence is initiated about equally by each type, so that the distinction between "good" and "bad" is not determined by the use of violence.

• Those who commit acts of violence more often perceive them to be in their self-interest than in the service of some other cause. Nearly half of all the leading characters who kill (25 of 54) and more than half of all leading characters who are violent (126 of 241) achieve a clearly happy ending in the programs. To this extent, violence is portrayed as a successful means of attaining a desired end.

• Half of all violent episodes do not involve witnesses. When present, witnesses are usually passive and either do not or cannot intervene. In the rare instance in which a witness does intervene, it is as often to encourage or assist violence as it is to prevent it. To this extent, violence is not shown to be unacceptable in the immediate social context of the world of television drama.

• Lawful arrest and trial are indicated as a consequence of major acts of violence in only two out of every ten violent programs. But the question of legality seldom arises because in the world of television drama violence is usually presented outside of any relevant legal context.

• Physical pain—details of physical injury or death—is shown to be a consequence of violence in only one out of every four violent acts. In television drama violence does not hurt too much, nor are its consequences very bloody or messy, even though it may lead to injury or death.

165

In summary, then, television portrays a world in which "good guys" and "bad guys" alike use violence to solve problems and achieve goals. Violence is rarely presented as illegal or socially unacceptable. Indeed, as often as not, it is portrayed as a legitimate means for attaining desired ends. Moreover, the painful consequences of violence are underplayed and de-emphasized by the "sanitized" way in which much of it is presented.

The findings of this analysis are now a year old. Network officials testifying before this Commission last December told us that it takes about 18 months for programming decisions to be reflected in network schedules. Thus, the test of network intentions to reduce violence on television, as these were expressed in the spring and summer of 1968, can properly begin with this year's television season.

TWO • WHAT ARE THE EFFECTS OF TELEVISION VIOLENCE?

Each year advertisers spend $2.5 billion in the belief that television can influence human behavior. The television industry enthusiastically agrees with them, but nonetheless contends that its programs of violence do not have any such influence. The preponderance of the available research evidence strongly suggests, however, that violence in television programs can and does have adverse effects upon audiences—particularly child audiences.

Television enters powerfully into the learning process of children and teaches them a set of moral and social values about violence which are inconsistent with the standards of civilized society. As a child matures physically, he also undergoes a process of social preparation for adult roles. Much of this preparation ordinarily takes place through primary interaction with other people—in the family, in play groups, and in school. It goes on all the time the child is awake and active, even when neither he nor the persons with whom he interacts are consciously concerned with shaping his character. What he becomes is a result of his genetic endowment, his environment, what he has done, and what he has learned.

Reward and punishment, trial and error—*i.e.,* the re-

166

sponses that a child's behavior elicits—are significant sources of social learning in the early years of childhood. But as the child grows older, he learns increasingly more from what he observes in the behavior of others. His own behavior is shaped by observation of the successes and failures and the rewards and punishments meted out to those around him. In short, he learns by vicarious reinforcement.

Children turn to television primarily for entertainment, relaxation, or relief of boredom and loneliness. Despite the relative passivity of these motivations, a process of incidental "observational learning" takes place. A child's observational learning from television depends on a number of factors. One is the degree to which the child can identify with a TV character. Another is the extent to which he perceives utility for his own purpose in the behavioral or informational items portrayed. A third factor is his belief that learning and acting on the item will succeed in producing gratifications sought. Younger children, between the ages of three and eight, are particularly susceptible to observational learning when the material portrayed is new to them and therefore absorbs their attention. Because the life-experiences of younger children are narrow and limited, most of what they see on television is, of course, unfamiliar to them. Finally, the "reality" of the portrayal affects observatorial learning. What younger children see on television is peculiarly "real," for they are still in the process of learning to discriminate between fantasy and reality.

As they get older, children bring somewhat more purposeful motivations to their television viewing, even when they are primarily seeking entertainment. Many adolescents consciously rely on mass media models in learning to play real-life roles. In particular, they obtain ideas and advice about dating and behavior toward the opposite sex. This is especially true of those adolescents who are not well integrated into family and school life and who rely more heavily on the mass media for social learning because more conventional sources are not available. Television is a primary source of socialization for low-income teenagers. In the absence of family, peer, and school relationships, television becomes the most compatible substitute for real-life experiences.

167

One reason that children are inclined to learn from television is that it provides "the most accessible back door to the grown-up world."[8] It is never too busy to talk to them, and it never has to brush them aside while it does household chores. Unlike their preoccupied parents, television seems to want their attention at any time, and goes to considerable lengths to attract it. The image of the adult world which most children get from television drama is by and large an unwholesome one, but it is at least an image they find available when they may not have access to the guidance of parents. Indeed, parents too often use the television set as a baby-sitter, and for many this is an abdication of their parental responsibility to instill proper values in their children.

Moreover, as we have said, many young children are inclined to believe that the world they see portrayed on television is a reflection of the real world. The ability to differentiate between fact and fiction naturally increases with age and maturity, but it also appears to be a function of the child's particular social environment. Of teenagers asked whether they agreed or disagreed with such statements as: "The programs I see on television tell about life the way it really is" and "The people I see on TV programs are just like the people I meet in real life," 40 percent of the poor black adolescents and 30 percent of the poor whites strongly believed in the true-to-life nature of television content, as compared with only 15 percent of the middle class white youngsters. In short, young children and a large proportion of teenagers from low income families believe that people behave in the real world the way they do in the fictional world of television.

These findings are hardly surprising. Because of its apparent fidelity to reality, its vividness, its simultaneous appeal to both vision and hearing, television seems intrinsically authentic and credible, whether it presents fact or fancy. It requires some intellectual maturity or breadth of experience on the part of a youngster to discount what he sees and hears.

A large body of research on observational learning by preschool children (described in testimony before the Commission and in the staff report of our Mass Media Task Force) confirms that children can and do learn aggressive

168

behavior from what they see in a film or on a TV screen, and that they learn it equally from real life and fantasy (cartoon) models. They retain what they learn for several months if they practice the aggressive response at least once, and their re-enactment of such learned behavior is, in large part, determined by the perceived rewards and punishments meted out to the models they have observed.

Some defenders of violence on television, however, contend that viewers "drain off" aggressive tendencies by their vicarious participation in violent media programs. According to this reasoning, the mass media serve a socially useful "cathartic" function: by displaying violence they provide harmless outlets for the violent impulses of audience members and thereby prevent overt actions that would be socially undesirable.

Laboratory experiments on the reactions of adults and teenagers to violent film content provide little support for this theory. In fact, the vast majority of experimental studies on this question have found that observed violence stimulates aggressive behavior, rather than the opposite. Moreover, the stimulation of aggressive responses from exposure to filmed aggression is more likely to occur when the witnessed aggression occurs in a justified rather than in an unjustified context. Further experimental elaboration has shown that stimulation of aggression is most likely when the context of the film is similar to the viewer's perception of his own situation.

The psychiatric and psychological literature suggests other emotional effects that may be associated with exposure to media violence may have the effect not only of dulling the audience's emotional reactions to fictional violence, but may also desensitize viewers to violence in real life and, thus, make them more willing actually to engage in aggressive actions when provoking circumstances arise. On the other hand, exposure to particularly horrifying episodes focusing on the painful results of violence may possibly have just the opposite effect by sensitizing viewers to the potential harm that they themselves might inflict.

We believe it is reasonable to conclude that a constant diet of violent behavior on television has an adverse effect on human character and attitudes. Violence on television encourages violent forms of behavior, and fosters moral and social values about violence in daily life which are unacceptable in a civilized society.

We do not suggest that television is a principal cause of violence in society. We do suggest that it is a contributing factor. Television, of course, operates in a complex social setting and its effects are undoubtedly mitigated by other social influences. But it is a matter for grave concern that at a time when the values and the influence of traditional institutions such as family, church, and school are in question, television is emphasizing violent, antisocial styles of life.

Although the negative values imparted by television can be ameliorated by parental influence, our concern over television violence is not diminished by this fact. In the first place, surveys have found that while most parents wish to eliminate programs of crime, violence, and horror from their children's television diet, only a tiny fraction of these believe that they can actually keep their children from watching such programs. The practical problems of monitoring children's television habits are too great in the face of the pervasiveness of televised crime and violence. Further, television may reduce or even counteract parental influence. Children daily see acts committed on television for which they have been or would be punished, while the actors often appear to go unpunished and even to be rewarded.

Moreover, television is a particularly potent force in families where parental influences and primary group ties are weak or completely lacking, notably in low-income areas or where violent life-styles are common. In these instances, television does not displace parental influence: it fills a vacuum. The strong preference of low-income teenagers for crime, action, and adventure stories means that they are constantly exposed to the values of violent television programs without the ameliorating moral influence of their parents. This is a fact of considerable social importance, especially in light of the large amounts of time low-income youngsters spend with television and the high credence they place in what they watch. The television experience of these children and adolescents reinforces a distorted, pathological view of society.[9]

170

THREE • WHAT SHOULD BE DONE?

The television industry has consistently argued that its standards for the portrayal of violence and its machinery for enforcement of these standards are adequate to protect the public interest. We do not agree. The inadequacy of the standards and the enforcement machinery may be briefly stated.

The National Association of Broadcasters' Code, to which the three networks and some two-thirds of the nation's commercial television stations subscribe, sets overall industry standards for the portrayal of violence. These standards are aimed primarily at screening out material that might alarm audiences or offend their sensibilities. This deference to public taste, while better than nothing at all, results in an essentially cosmetic approach to the portrayal of violence which does not get to the heart of the problem.

The NAB Code's standards for children's programs— that portrayal of the "techniques of crime in such detail as to invite imitation" should be avoided and that violence should be portrayed only as "required by plot development or character delineation"—do not begin to meet the issues we have discussed. Despite the existence of some generalizations on the subject, the NAB Code notably omits any meaningful standards relating to the crucial issue of providing suitably balanced program fare—that is, reducing the number of programs which, because of their basic format, require the use of violence as the basic mode of conflict resolution.

In any event, although two of the three networks now submit programs in advance to the NAB for clearance under NAB standards, the primary responsibility for screening program content rests, as it properly should, upon the networks and individual stations themselves. ABC, CBS, and NBC: each has standards similar to the NAB Code; and each has a Program Standards and Practices Department with authority independent of other divisions to review scripts, roughcuts, and final films to assure adherence to NAB and network standards. As with the

171

NAB, however, the Program Standards and Practices Departments have no responsibility for determining program mix or format in the network schedule; they concern themselves only with the manner in which violence is portrayed in particular programs.

Although all of the networks say that they are keeping abreast of current research on the effects of violence on viewers, until recently none of them has conducted research on its own, and each has taken the position that the research others have done is wholly inconclusive. As one network official put it: "There are many conflicting points of view on the influence of the media on human behavior and there is no conclusive research on which appropriate guidelines can be based." We are informed that the networks are now beginning to conduct their own research on the effects of programs containing violence, but at present network standards on violence are based on essentially subjective interpretations of audience tastes and on what is considered appropriate to television's role as a "guest in the home."

We believe that the television networks, network affiliates, independent stations, and other members of the broadcasting industry should recognize the strong probability that a big incidence of violence in entertainment programs is contributing to undesirable attitudes and even to violence in American society. It is time for them to stop asserting "not proved" to charges of adverse effects from pervasive violence in television programming when they should instead be accepting the burden of proof that such programs are not harmful to the public interest. Much remains to be learned about media violence and its effects, but enough is known to require that constructive action be taken at once to reduce the amount and alter the kind of violent programs which have pervaded television.

We offer four recommendations to all the members of the television industry:

The broadcasting of children's cartoons containing serious, non-comic violence should be abandoned. The cartoons broadcast by the networks on Saturday morning during the 1967-68 and 1968-69 seasons were the most intensively violent programs on television, with perhaps the least amount of redeeming constructive value. We note that the networks have effected

172

substantial improvements in the cartoon programs offered this season. We urge that these improvements be maintained in coming seasons, and we urge affiliates and independent stations to refrain from broadcast of violent cartoons produced in prior years.

The amount of time devoted to the broadcast of crime, western and action-adventure programs containing violent episodes should be reduced. We include here full-length motion-pictures shown by both the networks and independent television stations. It is especially these kinds of programs in which the problems faced by the characters almost inevitably call for violent solutions, and thus it is these programs which most distort the nature of life in civilized society. In particular, we recommend that programs of this type be restricted to the late viewing hours when fewer very young children are watching television. (With respect to this recommendation, we note that the networks' 1969-70 program schedule seems to indicate the beginning of a favorable trend along the lines recommended here. We welcome this trend and urge its continuation.)

More effective efforts should be made to alter the basic context in which violence is presented in television dramas. When the resort to violence is depicted as an unusual and undesirable outcome, the context is sharply different from the world of contemporary television in which violence has been the routine method by which people solve problems. It may be simpler to write scripts and shoot film where confrontations are resolved by violence, but it is just these artistically and dramatically inferior programs that are probably doing the most damage.

The members of the television industry should become more actively and seriously involved in research on the effects of violent television programs, and their future policies, standards, and practices with regard to entertainment programs should be more responsive to the best evidence provided by social scientists, psychologists, and communications researchers. Although we believe in the desirability of further research and thus urge continuing cooperation with such valuable efforts as the current Surgeon General's study of television violence, we reemphasize our conclusion that enough is known to make inexcusable any delay in taking action along the lines we have recommended. In this regard, we especially urge the Surgeon General's committee and independent research groups to undertake regular analyses of television program content for the purpose of ascertaining whether a reduction in televised violence is being carried through, both by the networks and by the local stations.

We note that an effective response by the television industry to our recommendations may require some measure of joint action by the industry members. To the extent that cooperative action is necessary in the public interest, we are confident that appropriate antitrust clearances will be provided.

We offer one recommendation to the President and the Congress:

Adequate and permanent financing, in the form of a dedicated tax, should be provided for the Corporation for Public Broadcasting so that it may develop the kind of educational, cultural, and dramatic programming not presently provided in sufficient measure by commercial broadcasting.

We believe, as the Public Broadcasting Act of 1967 states, "that it furthers the general welfare to encourage noncommercial educational radio and television broadcast programming which will be responsive to the interests of people both in particular localities and throughout the United States, and which will constitute an expression of diversity and excellence," and "that it is necessary and appropriate for the federal government to complement, assist, and support a national policy that will most effectively make noncommercial radio and television available to all the citizens of the United States." We suggest financing by means of a dedicated tax because we believe that public television must be free from the political pressures that result from the need for annual federal appropriations.

Public broadcasts can be a much needed alternative to commercial programs. It is generally assumed that commercial television caters to the public taste. But television also creates the public taste. If a wide range of wholesome entertainment and public service programs is offered as an alternative to the current fare of entertainment violence, it is likely that this will effect changes in public tastes and ultimately make violent television programs less commercially attractive. But this longer-term possibility does not relieve commercial television of the responsibility to reduce now the volume and change the character of its violent programs.

We offer the following recommendations to the viewing public and especially to parents:

174

Parents should make every effort to supervise their children's television viewing and to assert their basic responsibility for the moral development of their children.

The viewing public should express to the networks and to the local stations both their disapproval of programs which they find objectionable and their support for programs they like. We believe that most families do not want large doses of violence on television, and thus we urge them to make the weight of their opinion felt.

Finally, we add a special word on motion pictures produced for initial showing in theaters. Movies have not been a focal point of this Commission's studies because children spend a far smaller part of their lives in motion picture theaters than before television sets. Motion pictures, however, often portray more extreme forms of violence, and we cannot ignore their potential for harm.

The motion picture industry has adopted a new voluntary film rating system whose primary objective is to identify, and to restrict access to, pictures which are inappropriate for children because of the treatment of "sex, violence, crime or profanity." The President of the Motion Picture Association of America stated to this Commission that the success of this system will depend on how fairly pictures are rated, how responsible is the attitude of filmmakers, and how well the ratings are enforced at the box office, as well as on how much the parents of the country want it to work. We agree with this judgment, and *we urge an evaluation of the effectiveness of the new movie-rating system with an emphasis on the question of the validity of the ratings as they relate to violence and the enforcement of the admission standards regarding minors.*[10]

Of course, the motion picture rating system can solve only part of the problem. Most motion pictures, after theater exhibition, are subsequently shown on television— where there is no possibility of restricting viewing of violent pictures to adults only. As with other kinds of programs, the responsibility for not showing unsuitably violent motion pictures lies with the networks and with the affiliated and independent stations.

FOUR • CONCLUSION

Television is one of our significant national resources, but our greatest resource is our children. Children begin to absorb the lessons of television before they can read or write. In a fundamental way, television helps to create what children expect of themselves and of others, and of what constitutes the standards of civilized society. Yet, as one witness before this Commission graphically stated it, we daily permit our children during their formative years to enter a world of police interrogations, of gangsters beating enemies, of spies performing fatal brain surgery, and of routine demonstrations of all kinds of killing and maiming.

The producers of television programs have access to the imagination and knowledge of the best talents of our time to display the full range of human behavior and to present prominently and regularly what is possible and laudable in the human spirit. They have time to think and experiment, and they have the entire history of man from which to draw. Television entertainment based on violence may be effective merchandising, but it is an appalling way to serve a civilization—an appalling way to fulfill the requirements of the law that broadcasting serve the "public interest, convenience and necessity." The recent favorable trend toward less violent programs is a hopeful sign that the nation's broadcasters share this view.[11]

SEPARATE STATEMENT

Judge McFarland, because of his interest in a television station, did not participate in the findings or approve them, but stated he recognized the television industry should continue to improve programming and help build character in the youth of our nation and voted to approve the recommendations of the Commission.

---

1. Testimony of Professor Bradley Greenberg, Department of Communications, Michigan State University, October 16, 1968.
2. Jack Lyle, "Contemporary Functions of the Mass Media," Appendix to *Media and Violence*, Report of the Media Task Force of the Commission.
3. Roper Research Associates, *A Ten-Year View of Public Attitudes Toward Television and Other Mass Media 1959–1968* (March 26, 1969); Schramm, Lyle & Parker, *Television in the Lives of Our Children* (1961).

4. Larsen, Gray & Fortis, "Achieving Goals Through Violence on Television," in *Violence and the Mass Media* (Larsen ed., 1968).

5. Dramatic programs—fictional stories of all kinds—accounted for two-thirds of the program hours offered by each network between 7 and 10 p.m. in 1968, as opposed to about three-fourths of such offerings in 1967. (The remaining programs—excluded from the study—include variety shows, game shows, and news or documentary presentations.) In both 1967 and 1968 virtually no dramatic programs were offered by the networks between 4 and 7 p.m., and our study made no attempt to determine whether and to what extent dramatic programs were transmitted by the local stations during this time period.

6. A program was defined for the purposes of this study as any discrete story unit, from a short cartoon to a full-length movie. Violence was defined as "the overt expression of force intended to hurt or kill."

7. A violent "episode" is a scene of whatever duration between the same violent parties—anything from a full-scale battle to a single violent encounter between two characters.

8. Robert Lewis Shayon, *Television and Our Children*, 1951, p. 37.

9. In Chapter 2, this Commission points out that in every major city the district which has the lowest level of education, the highest rate of unemployment, the poorest housing, and the highest degree of poverty is also the district with the highest rate of violent crime. These areas also have the most persistent television viewers. Here, the distinction between the use of violence on television and that in real life is less than it is in other areas.

10. We note that the Commission on Obscenity and Pornography has contracted for a study which will throw some light on these questions.

11. Current reviews of the programs carried since this statement was first issued in September, 1969, indicate that this favorable trend is continuing.

IX ● CAMPUS DISORDER*

The members of this Commission, along with most Americans, are deeply disturbed by the violence and disorder that have swept the nation's campuses. Our colleges and universities cannot perform their vital functions in an atmosphere that exalts the struggle for power over the search for truth, the rule of passion over the rule of reason, physical confrontation over rational discourse.

We are equally disturbed, however, by the direction of much public reaction to campus unrest. Those who would punish colleges and universities by reducing financial support, by passing restrictive legislation, or by political intervention in the affairs of educational institutions, may unwittingly be helping the very radical minority of students whose objective is to destroy our present institutions of higher education.

So threatening is the situation, so essential is the need for understanding and calm appraisal, that this Commis-

---

*An edited version of statement issued June 9, 1969.

sion felt compelled to speak during the past summer when students were home and campuses were closed rather than to remain silent until publication of its final report. We offered our comments then in the hope that they would contribute to constructive thought and action before the beginning of the new academic year last September.

The problem of campus unrest is more than a campus problem. Its roots lie deep in the larger society. There is no single cause, no single solution. We urge all Americans to reject hasty and simplistic answers. We urge them to distinguish between peaceful protest and violent disruption, between the non-conformity of youth and the terror tactics of the extremists. We counsel patience, understanding and support for those in the university community who are trying to preserve freedom and order on the campus. We do so in the conviction that our universities and colleges are beginning to learn how to achieve change without disorder or coercion.

ONE • STUDENT DISSATISFACTION

During the past year, many of America's universities and colleges have been seriously wounded. These wounds arise from multiple causes. One is the increasingly violent expression of widespread student discontent. Although much of this discontent often focuses on grievances within the campus environment, it is rooted in dissatisfactions with the larger society that the campus can do little about.

Students are unwilling to accept the gaps between professed ideals and actual performance. They see afresh the injustices that remain unremedied. They are not impressed by the dangers that previous generations have overcome and the problems they have solved. It means little to them that the present adult generation found the way out of a major depression to unparalleled heights of economic abundance, or that it defeated a massive wave of vicious totalitarianism and preserved the essential elements of freedom for the youth of today. To students, these triumphs over serious dangers serve primarily to emphasize other problems we are just beginning to solve.

Today's intelligent, idealistic students see a nation which

178

has achieved the physical ability to provide food, shelter and education for all, but has not yet devised social institutions that do so. They see a society, built on the principle that all men are created equal, that has not yet assured equal opportunity in life. They see a world of nation-states with the technical brilliance to harness the ultimate energy but without the common sense to agree on methods of preventing mutual destruction. With the fresh energy and idealism of the young, they are impatient with the progress that has been made but seems to them to be indefensibly slow.

At a time when students are eager to attack these and other key problems, they face the prospect of being compelled to fight in a war most of them believe is unjustified. This traumatic experience has precipitated an unprecedented mass tension and frustration.

In assessing the causes of student unrest, it would be a mistake to assume that all causes are external. There are undoubtedly internal emotional pressures and internal value conflicts in many students which contribute to their own dissatisfaction and thus to the tension and turmoil of campus life.

Students attribute the shortcomings they see to the smugness of their elders and the weaknesses of social institutions. They see the university, guardian of man's knowledge and source of his new ideas, as an engine for powering the reform of the larger society, and as the first institution they are in a position to reform.

We emphasize that most students, despite their view of society's failures, accept as valid the basic structure of our democratic system; their main desire is to improve its ability to live up to its stated values. Their efforts to do so are welcome when they take the form of petitions, demonstrations and protests that are peaceful and non-violent. Although many persons are unsettled by these activities (which are often of a bizarre nature), we must all remember that the peaceful expression of disturbing ideas and petitions for the redress of grievances are fundamental rights safeguarded by the First Amendment of our Constitution. Methods of dealing with "campus unrest" must not confuse peaceful protest and petition with violent disruption. To do so will aggravate rather than solve the problem.

A small but determined minority, however, aims not at reform but at the destruction of existing institutions. These are the nihilists. They resort to violent disruption as the means best suited to achieve their ends. By dramatic tactics of terror, they have focused widespread public attention upon themselves and have often induced university authorities either to surrender or to meet force with force. When they have managed on occasion to provoke counterforce to an excessive degree, they have succeeded in enlisting the sympathies of the more moderate campus majority.

They are the agent that converts constructive student concern into mindless mob hysteria. They are the chief danger to the university and its basic values.

There is also a minority of students who are not nihilists, but who feel that violence and disruption may be the only effective way of achieving societal and university reform.

TWO • THE CYCLE OF CAMPUS VIOLENCE

Forcible obstruction and violence are incompatible with the intellectual and personal freedom that lies at the core of campus values. In its recent *Declaration on Campus Unrest,* the American Council on Education noted that "there has developed among some of the young a cult of irrationality and incivility which severely strains attempts to maintain sensible and decent human communications. Within this cult is a minute group of destroyers who have abandoned hope in today's society, in today's university, and in the processes of orderly discussion to secure significant change." These "destroyers" seek to persuade more moderate students that verbal expressions of grievance go unheeded, while forcible tactics bring affirmative results.

Despite some eloquent and subtle rationalizations for violent methods of protest, the record of experience is incontrovertible. While violent protest is sometimes followed by the concessions sought, it more often produces a degree of counter-violence and public dismay that may gravely damage the cause for which violence is invoked.

180

Even when violence succeeds in achieving immediate social gains, it tends frequently to feed on itself, with one power group imposing its will on another until repressive elements succeed in reestablishing order. The violent cycles of the French and Russian revolutions and of the decade resulting in the Third Reich are stark summits of history to ponder. All history teaches that as a conscious method of seeking social reform, violence is a very dangerous weapon to employ.

That is why our nation has sought to avoid violent methods of effecting social change, and to foster instead the principles of peaceful advocacy proclaimed in the Bill of Rights and the rule of law. As the President has reminded us:

The purpose of these restraints is not to protect an "establishment," but to establish the protection of liberty; not to prevent change, but to insure that change reflects the public will and respects the rights of all.

The university is the citadel of man's learning and of his hope for further self-improvement, and is the special guardian of this heritage. Those who work and study on the campus should think long before they risk its destruction by resorting to force as the quick way of reaching some immediate goal.

Father Theodore Hesburgh of Notre Dame has observed that the university, precisely because it is an open community that lives by the power of reason, stands naked before those who would employ the power of force. It can survive only when the great majority of its members share its commitment to rational discourse, listen closely to those with conflicting views, and stand together against the few who would impose their will on everyone else.

Kingman Brewster of Yale has persuasively articulated this policy:

Proposition one is the encouragement of controversy, no matter how fundamental; and the protection of dissent, no matter how extreme. This is not just to permit the "letting off of steam" but because it will improve [the university] as a place to be educated. Proposition number two is a convincing intention to deal speedily and firmly with any forcible interference with student and faculty activities or the normal use of any [university] facilities. . . . I see no basis for compromise on

181

the basic proposition that forcible coercion and violent intimidation are unacceptable means of persuasion and unacceptable techniques of change in a university community, as long as channels of communication and the chance for reasoned argument are available.

Several attitudes held by members of the university community have often interfered with the application of these sensible standards. One is the belief of many that the civil law should not apply to internal campus affairs. They feel that the academy is an enclave, sheltered from the law, that the forces of civil authority may not enter the campus, save by invitation. This is a serious misconception—a residue of the time when the academy served in *loco parentis,* making and enforcing its own rules for students' behavior and protecting them from the law outside, save for such extreme crimes as murder and arson. Now that students themselves have firmly discarded school authority over their personal lives, they must logically accept the jurisdiction of civil authority. They cannot argue that of all Americans they are uniquely beyond the reach of the law.

At the same time, the university is ill equipped to control violent and obstructive conduct on its own. Most institutions have few campus police; most of these are not deputized and thus do not possess true police power. Few schools have explicit rules either defining the boundaries of permissible protest or stating the consequences if the boundaries are crossed. Some have very loose rules for disciplinary proceedings; others have diffused disciplinary power so widely among students, faculty and administration that effective discipline is difficult to impose and is seldom imposed quickly enough to meet an emergency. And in most institutions the ultimate internal disciplinary sanction of suspension or expulsion lies unused because the campus community shrinks from its probable consequence—exposure of dismissed students to the draft and what students call the "death sentence" of Vietnam.

THREE ● TO THE CAMPUS COMMUNITY

Out of many discussions with faculty members, students and administrators, and with full appreciation that no two institutions are the same, we offer the campus community the following specific suggestions:

(1) A broad consensus should be achieved among students, faculty and administration concerning the permissible methods of presenting ideas, proposals and grievances and the consequences of going beyond them. Excellent guidelines have been provided by the American Council on Education's recent *Declaration on Campus Protest*. These could usefully be supplemented by more detailed statements developed by representatives of the American Association of University Professors, the American Association of Universities, the American Council on Education, the Association of Land Grant Colleges and State Universities, the National Student Association, and possibly others. Where agreed-upon and explicit codes of student conduct and procedures for student discipline are lacking, they should be adopted; where they already exist they should be reviewed and, if necessary, improved.

Students have the right to due process and to participate in the making of decisions that directly affect them, but their right of participation should not be so extensive as to paralyze the disciplinary process itself. Codes for campus conduct should place primary reliance on the power of the institution to maintain order in its own house, and on its courage to apply its own punishment when deserved. These codes should also recognize the universal duty to obey the civil and criminal laws of the larger society, and the right of the civil authorities to act when laws are violated.

(2) Universities should prepare and currently review contingency plans for dealing with campus disorders. Advance plans should be made to determine, insofar as possible, the circumstances under which the university will use (i) campus disciplinary procedures, (ii) campus police, (iii) court injunctions, (iv) other court sanctions and (v) the civil police. A definite plan, flexibly employed at the moment of crisis, is essential. There have been enough violent and obstructive incidents on enough campuses to permit institutions to assess alternative courses of action and to anticipate both the varieties of disorder which might occur and the most appropriate response.

Most importantly, university authorities should make

183

known in advance that they will not hesitate to call on civil police when circumstances dictate, and should review in advance with police officials the degrees of force suitable for particular situations. It is a melancholy fact that even in cases where the need for calling the civil police has been generally recognized, the degree of force actually employed has frequently been perceived as excessive by the majority of the campus community, whose sympathies then turned against the university authorities. Indeed, there is reason to believe that a primary objective of campus revolutionaries is to provoke the calling of police and the kinds of police conduct that will bring the majority over to their side.

(3) Procedures for campus governance and constructive reform should be developed to permit more rapid and effective decision-making. There is a great misunderstanding and confusion as to where ultimate authority for campus decision-making lies. The fact is that the authority is shared among several elements.

By law, trustees are granted full authority over colleges and universities. But trustees cannot supervise the day-to-day affairs of a university; hence they delegate power to the president. The president, however, in addition to being the agent of the trustees, is the leader of the faculty. His effectiveness derives as much from campus consensus of faculty and students as it does from the power delegated to him by the trustees.

In the American system of higher education, the faculty plays the primary role in determining the educational program and all issues directly relevant to education and faculty research. Unlike the systems of some other countries, educational control in the American system is faculty-oriented; anything else is a deviation from the norm.

Faculty control of education and research is the best guarantee we have of academic freedom. It is a precious asset that must not under any circumstances be sacrificed. Most student demands for change pertain to educational and research matters, and too often their efforts have been directed toward administrative officers who usually do not have the power which students assume they possess. And often, too, some faculty members have mistakenly joined with students in using coercive force against administrative

184

officers when it is the faculty itself that should deal appropriately and effectively with the issues in question.

Most other powers in the university are diffused. For most purposes, shared power is an asset. But to prevent disorders, universities must be able to respond quickly. Campus protests are sometimes escalated to the level of force because legitimate grievances, peacefully urged, have been referred to university committees which were slow to respond. Scholars have the habit of examining any hypothesis, debating it exhaustively, deferring decision to await more evidence, and when something must be decided, shunning a consensus in favor of subtle shades of disagreement and dissent. For the process of education, these are admirable qualities. But for dealing with naked force, they can be a prescription for disaster. Faculties therefore have a special obligation to organize themselves more effectively, to create representative groups with power to act, and to maintain constant and systematic lines of communication with students. They should be ready to meet every challenge to the educational integrity of the institution. If this integrity is compromised, it will be the faculty that suffers the most.

Students should, of course, have a meaningful role in the governance of all non-educational, non-research functions. They should serve, too, on committees dealing with educational and related questions, exercising their right to be heard on these subjects, so long as the faculty remains paramount.

(4) Faculty leaders and administrative officers need to make greater efforts to improve communications both on the campus and with alumni and the general public. Campus difficulties are constantly aggravated by misinformation and misunderstanding. On campus, large numbers of faculty and students often act on the basis of rumor or incomplete information. Alumni and the general public receive incomplete, often distorted, accounts of campus developments. The communications media, on and off the campus, concentrate on controversy. Much of the peaceful progress of our colleges and universities is never communicated to the outside world. Campus authorities have the responsibility to see to it that a balanced picture is portrayed.

185

FOUR • TO THE LARGER SOCIETY

To the larger society, we make these suggestions:

(1) The majority of the American people are justifiably angry at students who engage in violent and obstructive tactics. While the public varies widely in its desire for social change, it shares a common belief in the value of social order. It also regards university students as among the most privileged in society—among those who should understand best the importance of freedom and the dangers of anarchy. One outlet for this public resentment has been the support of legislation withholding financial aid both from students who engage in disruption and from colleges and universities that fail to control them.

There has also been a steady weakening of public sentiment in favor of the additional public funding that higher education so badly needs. Current appropriations for new facilities and for annual operating costs have been insufficient. Some private universities have faced a reduction in individual and corporate gifts.

Existing laws already withdraw financial aid from students who engage in disruptive acts. Additional laws along the same lines would not accomplish any useful purpose. Such efforts are likely to spread, not reduce the difficulty. More than seven million young Americans are enrolled in the nation's colleges and universities; the vast majority neither participate in nor sympathize with campus violence. If aid is withdrawn from even a few students in a manner that the campus views as unjust, the result may be to radicalize a much larger number by convincing them that existing governmental institutions are as inhumane as the revolutionaries claim. If the law unjustly forces the university to cut off financial aid or to expel a student, the university as well may come under widespread campus condemnation.

(2) We believe that the urge to enact additional legislation should be turned into a channel that could assist the universities themselves to deal more effectively with the tactics of obstruction. State and municipal laws against trespass and disorderly conduct may not be wholly effective

186

means of dealing with some acts of physical obstruction. They were not written to deal with such conduct, and they do not cope with the central issue—forcible interference with the First Amendment rights of others. There is a need for statutes authorizing universities, along with other affected persons, to obtain court injunctions against willful private acts of physical obstruction that prevent other persons from exercising their First Amendment rights of speech, peaceable assembly, and petition for the redress of grievances. Such laws would not be aimed at students exclusively, but at any willful interference with First Amendment rights, on or off the campus, by students or by non-students. They would also be available to uphold the First Amendment rights of students as well as other citizens.[1]

(3) Finally, we urge the American people to recognize that the campus mirrors both the yearnings and weaknesses of the wider society. Erik Erikson, a renowned student of youth, has noted that young and old achieve mutual respect when "society recognizes the young individual as a bearer of fresh energy, and he recognizes society as a living process which inspires loyalty as it receives it, maintains allegiance as it extracts it, honors confidence as it demands it."

One effective way for the rest of us to help reduce campus disorders is to focus on the unfinished task of striving toward the goals of human life that all of us share and that young people admire and respect.

---

1. We recommend a federal statute of this kind in Chapter III.

X ● CHALLENGING OUR YOUTH*

One key to much of the violence in our society lies with the young. Our youth account for an ever-increasing percentage of crime—greater than their increasing percentage of the population. Arrest rates for violent urban crime are two to three times higher among youth aged 15 to 24 than

---

*An edited version of statement issued November 25, 1969.

among older groups in the urban population. The cutting edge of protest, and the violence which has sometimes accompanied it, has been honed largely by the young in the streets and on the campuses. In cities experiencing ghetto riots, more than half of the persons arrested were teenagers and young adults. Most of the people involved in the violence during the Chicago Convention demonstrations in August of 1968 were under 25 years of age.

Violence by the young, as by persons of all ages, has multiple causes, involving many elements of personality and social environment. Some young people, even those raised in affluence, may rob for the thrill involved, others for what they hope will be material gain. A few maladjusted individuals may engage in wholesale killing; others may commit murder in a particular moment of rage or calculated coolness. Some may engage in violent forms of protest as a deliberate tactic; others may do so out of excitement and response to mob psychology.

Many of the young people in the nation today, however, are highly motivated by the ideals of justice, equality, candor, peace—fundamental values which their intellectual and spiritual heritage has taught them to honor. The youth of today have not been called on by their elders to defend these values by service in causes which young and old alike believe to be urgent and important, such as the war against the Axis power or the struggle to end the Depression of the thirties. Instead, they face the prospect of having to fight in a war most of them believe is unjustified, or futile, or both.

Moreover, they speak eloquently and passionately of the gap between the ideals we preach and the many social injustices remaining to be corrected. They see a nation which has the capacity to provide food, shelter, and education for all, but has not devised the procedures, opportunities, or social institutions that bring about this result. They see a society built on the principle of human equality that has not assured equal opportunity in life. With the fresh energy and idealism of the young, they are impatient with the progress that has been made and are eager to attack these and other key problems. A combination of high ideals, tremendous energy, impatience at the rate of progress, and lack of constructive means for effecting change has led

188

some of today's youth into disruptive and at times violent tactics for translating ideals into reality.

At the same time, our urban slums abound with youths who have few opportunities to perform constructive roles of any kind. They often receive little help from social institutions, or from the equally disadvantaged parents. Too often, in fact, they have no father in the home to provide a male model of acceptable conduct. They are the last to be employed, and the first to suffer social injustices. Recognizing no stake in the values of an orderly society, they often turn to crime, either individually or in gangs. The highest crime rate in the nation is among these young people.

The nation cannot afford to ignore lawlessness, or fail to enforce the law swiftly and surely for the protection of the many against the depredations of the few. We cannot accept violent attacks upon some of our most valuable institutions, or upon the lives of our citizens, simply because some among the attackers may be either idealistically motivated or greatly disadvantaged.

It is no less permissible for our nation to ignore the legitimate needs and desires of the young. Law enforcement must go hand in hand with timely and constructive remedial action. In Chapter IX, the Commission stated its view that students should be given a useful role in shaping the future of the university, as well as responsibility of working directly with faculty members and administrators to develop standards for acceptable student conduct and responses of the institution in the face of deviations from these standards. Whether in the inner city, in a suburb or on a college campus, today's youth must be given a greater role in determining their own destiny and in shaping the future course of the society in which they live.

ONE • YOUTH AND THE POLITICAL PROCESS

Despite their increasing share of the highly educated population—indeed 18-year-olds are now better educated than were 21-year-olds when our nation was born—today's youth remain almost entirely disenfranchised. In 1950, two and a quarter million young men and women were attending college, as compared to the more than seven million

189

today. In the same time span we have seen a decline in farmers and agricultural workers from eight million to less than four million. Yet, the latter exercise considerable political influence, while the growing college population remains excluded from participation in the electoral process. Political realities have changed while our laws and institutions lag behind.

Today only two of our states (Georgia and Kentucky) permit eighteen-year-olds to vote, and two others permit voting before the age of 21. Yet, in virtually every other respect, we expect that eighteen-year-olds behave and assume responsibility as adults. At that age, some are in college, and many are married with families and, along with others, are working taxpayers. In most states, eighteen-year-olds are treated as adults by the criminal law. We demand the ultimate service, the highest sacrifice, when we require them to perform military service. Many young men have become battle-tried veterans and some have died on the battlefield before they could vote. Their way of life—and, for some, even the duration of life itself—is dictated by laws made and enforced by men they do not elect. This is fundamentally unjust. Accordingly:

We recommend that the Constitution of the United States be amended to lower the voting age for all state and federal elections to eighteen.

Presidents Eisenhower, Kennedy, Johnson and Nixon and many elected representatives of both parties have expressed support for such an amendment. In the first session of the 91st Congress, 48 joint resolutions calling for the eighteen-year-old vote were introduced. And over the years, a number of states have raised the issue in popular referenda, but the results have been disappointing.[1]

Today's youth are capable of exercising the right to vote. Statistically they constitute the most highly educated group in our society. More finish high school than ever before and more of them go on to higher education. The mass media —television, news and interpretative magazines, and an unprecedented number of books on national and world affairs—have given today's youth knowledge and perspective and made them sensitive to political issues. We have seen the dedication and conviction they brought to the civil

190

rights movement and the skill and enthusiasm they have infused into the political process, even though they lack the vote.

The anachronistic voting age limitation tends to alienate them from systematic political processes and to drive them into a search for alternative, sometimes violent, means to express their frustrations over the gap between the nation's ideals and actions. Lowering the voting age will not eliminate protest by the young. But it will provide them with a direct, constructive, and democratic channel for making their views felt and for giving them a responsible stake in the future of the nation.

A significant focal point of dissent by the young has been the issue of draft reform. To many, the draft symbolizes the inflexibility of our institutions and all that is wrong with the government's treatment of the young. Further, the inequities of the system have been set in sharp relief by the reality of the on-going war that many youth believe to be immoral and futile. The "oldest-first" order of draft calls produces a period of prolonged uncertainty for young men that profoundly affects their education, career and marriage decisions—a condition which is made more unacceptable by the lack of uniform deferment and exemption standards and by the wide variation in the exercise of discretion by local boards. Draft reform will not take the sting out of student anti-war protest or other manifestations of student discontent, but it could go far to reduce the tensions and frustrations that now lead some young men to seek refuge abroad and others to destroy Selective Service records, burn draft cards, or disrupt induction centers.

A random lottery system which would subject all to equal treatment at age nineteen, would take the youngest rather than the oldest first, and would reduce the period of prime draft vulnerability from the present seven years to one year, appears to be the fairest and most promising alternative to the existing draft system. Undergraduate deferments would be continued, but with the understanding that the year of maximum vulnerability would come whenever the deferment expired. It would be far less disruptive in the lives of young men while fully consistent with national security needs. The President has recommended such a proposal to

191

the Congress. We are pleased to note that the Congress has approved the random lottery feature.

We also strongly endorse the balance of President Nixon's proposals for reform of the draft system, which are similar to those recommended in 1967 by the Marshall Commission and by the Clark Panel.[2] To the extent these proposals require further legislation, we urge the Congress to enact it.

Even with the enactment of a random selection system, however, the area of discretion for local draft boards is enormous and is likely to remain so.

We therefore urge that renewed attention be given to the recommendations of the Marshall Commission for building a greater measure of due process into the exercise of draft board discretion.

Youth should also be given a role on local draft boards.

We therefore recommend that in exercising his power to appoint the members of local draft boards, the President name at least one person under 30 years of age to each local board.[3]

TWO • YOUTH AND PUBLIC SERVICE

At present, the Selective Service System calls only about a third of the eligible young men for the draft each year. Reform of the system will not alter this, but by taking the youngest first and by reducing the period of uncertainty from seven years to one, it will free many young men to make firm decisions about their futures. The federal government should do much more to provide these young men, as well as other young men and women in all walks of life, with the opportunities for service to their communities and the nation. As the Peace Corps and VISTA experiences bear out, many young people are eager to assist the less fortunate to achieve social justice and willing to devote a part of their lives to tasks for which the major reward is the satisfaction of helping others.

We do not suggest that voluntary service of this kind should be an alternative to military service. Rather, we suggest that public service opportunities be made available, regardless of military service, to young men and young women, high school and college graduates, inner-city, suburban, and rural youth—as justified by the Nation's needs.

We are convinced that youth will grasp meaningful opportunities for constructively attacking the problems and injustices that, too often, now drive them to attacks aimed at the destruction of useful institutions rather than at their reform. But we recognize their skepticism of government-sponsored programs and their increasing unwillingness to become involved in social action programs in which they have no voice. Consequently, we believe that a new and flexible approach to youth service opportunities is required, one that is tailored to individual talents and desires.

We urge the President to seek legislation to expand the opportunities for youth to engage in both full-time and part-time public service, by providing federal financial support to young people who wish to engage in voluntary, non-military service to their communities and to the nation.

We do not suggest the creation of another federally-administered program, or set of programs, comparable to the Peace Corps or VISTA. Instead we suggest that a large number of full- and part-time public service options be opened to youth—opportunities which the youths themselves can be expected to seek out and to improve upon, and which can be filled and administered at the local level if federal financial support is made available. We have in mind such possibilities as teaching and reading assistants; tutors and counselors in the elementary and secondary schools; hospital orderlies and nurses' aides; personnel for neighborhood service and recreation centers; auxiliary aides to local law enforcement and social service agencies; and many others.

The service opportunities would be approved by a central federal agency. The authorizing statute should set general standards of agency approval, eligibility, and levels of compensation. The choice of the particular public service opportunity from the large approved list of public and private institutions and groups should be left to the volunteers, and the initiative, direction and control of the activities would remain entirely with the approved local entity.[4]

The program might be launched to recruit 100,000 young people each year for four or five years, as experience was accumulated. The eventual goal might be as high as

1,000,000 active youth volunteers in service at any given time, depending upon experience and developing national needs. As is now true for Peace Corps and similar existing programs, the compensation to be paid should be set at a student subsistence level and should not be financially competitive with other employment opportunities. As a special inducement, however, we recommend that completion of two years of full-time public service entitle the participant to educational assistance comparable to that available to veterans under the GI Bill of Rights, with lesser amounts of assistance for service periods between six months and two years.[5]

Voluntary public service could contribute to reduction of the large backlog of unmet social needs and, thus, could be an important step toward a more humane reordering of national priorities. And youth service could signify to the young that our nation is committed to the achievement of social justice as well as to military security.

THREE ● OPPORTUNITIES FOR INNER-CITY YOUTH

Young people in the inner-city slums often grow up in a stultifying physical environment and in unstable or broken families. They face poverty and racial discrimination. They are trained in overcrowded and inadequate schools, and the failure of the educational process, added to residual racial prejudice, results in thwarted job opportunity. Forced by lack of money and racial exclusion to remain in the most deteriorated part of the city, the ghetto youth's sense of alienation and powerlessness is confirmed and reinforced by the lack of recreational, medical and social services in the community.

Even should his parents wish to leave the slum ghetto, non-ghetto neighborhoods that they can afford to move into are those that tend to be most resistant to them. The Fair Housing Act and the Supreme Court's 1968 decision in *Jones* v. *Alfred H. Mayer Co.* make it illegal to discriminate in housing sales or rentals, but community resistance and the slow process of case-by-case enforcement combine to retard the elimination of housing discrimination in fact.

194

Thus many black parents who try to inculcate values supporting lawful behavior must stay in communities where their children are subjected to the destructive influences of slum life.

Only by a massive effort to improve life in our inner cities and to eliminate private barriers to the dispersal of racial groups beyond the inner city can we begin to root out the basic causes of crime and violence in these concentrated areas. As part of this large effort, we urgently need programs than can effectively intervene at the critical juncture in a slum ghetto youth's life when he is torn between the forces that may lead him into crime and those which may lead him into socially constructive pursuits.[6]

Reaching the alienated slum youth is not easy. To expect youth programs to succeed where parents and schools already have failed is to hope for a great deal. Yet recent experience gives reason for optimism.

Several recently organized youth programs have reached directly into the street and gang culture to draw upon indigenous talent and leadership. In the past, many youth programs, devised and imposed by adults, were alien to the life-styles and problems of the youths they were designed to help. They failed. Youth involvement in the planning and operation of programs characterized several new approaches that commanded the allegiance of the young. These innovative and strikingly successful youth programs may show the way to wider effort.

In Philadelphia, what began in 1966 as a film-making project for the Twelfth and Oxford Street gang—with youths writing, acting, and filming a story depicting the life and death of a gang leader—has bloomed into a full-fledged corporation which is now involved in a wide range of community-oriented projects. Youths who were formerly "warlords," "ministers of defense," and "guardians of weapons" are now the directors of a successful non-profit corporation. Initial financial successes in film-making attracted further assistance from private and governmental sources. Today the Twelfth and Oxford Street Film Corporation own three properties in the neighborhood (one of which has been renovated for rental to five low-income families in the community), several of its members are receiving training in housing rehabilitation from the Philadelphia Housing

195

Corporation and in marketing and survey from Temple University's School of Business, and plans are now being developed for opening the Twelfth and Oxford Restaurant and a Teen Age Record Company, both of which will provide additional opportunities for on-the-job training and utilization of youth's talents and skills.

Throughout the program's three-year development, motivation has remained high, and delinquency rates among the Twelfth and Oxford group have declined. Due to the skill of adult leadership, youths are given genuine responsibility and a sense of fulfillment. Its success thus far is a striking demonstration that the negative influences of the ghetto can be broken; that when urban youths are given a fair opportunity to run their own affairs, to develop their potentials in meaning pursuits, they can become important agents of community change.

The same ingredients of success are evident in another youth program, this one in Washington, D.C. Pride, Inc., which originally began as a modest summer work program for 1,000 inner-city youth to clean up cluttered streets and exterminate rats, has now become a year-round operation with economic and manpower development as its central theme. Pride directors initially hired 21 street-corner leaders as recruiters. Within three days every job was filled and, since then, the organization has reached some of the city's most deprived and alienated youth. It operates a landscaping and gardening division which employs 30 young men and a gasoline station at which fifteen youths are being trained, as well as a program for some 700 participants who work in cooperation with the D.C. Health and Sanitation Departments. Responsibility for supervision and administration of the clean-up programs in various parts of the city is delegated according to ability, and beginners work with the encouragement of knowing that there are possibilities for promotion.

Because Pride, Inc. is recruiting the most difficult of the hard-core unemployed, the organization has had to develop the capacity to deal with young men who are living in a state of crisis and to offer rudimentary supportive services in continuing education, orientation, recreation, health and legal services. On the whole, the results of Pride's efforts to date are good. Evaluations conducted on

196

behalf of the Department of Labor, a major financial supporter of the program, showed that while 67 percent of Pride members had been arrested in the six months prior to joining the program, only 24 percent were arrested during a like period after joining.

Pride, Inc. and the Twelfth and Oxford Street program are by no means unique. Across the country are other youth programs suited to the life-styles of those involved. Program ingredients vary; the key elements to success are the broadened perspective and increased confidence that come with the feeling of responsible participation by the young people.

A number of programs are carried on by residential centers for rehabilitation and treatment of wayward and delinquent youth. One long-established and remarkably successful program of youth rehabilitation, involving young men of high school age, is Boys Republic in Southern California. Many teenage boys, usually from broken families and in difficulty with the law, are offered by the courts the option of attending Boys Republic voluntarily (there are no guards) or being assigned to one of the state's youth rehabilitation institutions. Boys Republic receives ten times as many court-controlled applications for admission as it can accept, for its facilities and funds are limited. The youths who are accepted are intimately involved in all aspects of the operational program, including making of decisions affecting their lives, work and education. A substantial portion of the funds needed to maintain the institution is earned by the boys themselves who operate a large farm and manufacture and sell the famous "Della Robbia" Christmas wreaths. The amazing long-time record of this effort in rehabilitation is that ninety percent of the young men who attend the institution and voluntarily remain until they complete the rehabilitation program never again have trouble with the police.

Examples of some comparable non-governmental residential centers for youth rehabilitation are the Berkshire Farm for Boys, Children's Village, and Lincoln Hall in New York. Of the many state-administered institutions, the Kansas Boys' Industrial School is exemplary.

Junior Achievement, 4–H Clubs, Future Farmers of America, the Boy Scouts, Girl Scouts, YMCA and

197

YWCA, the Catholic Youth Organization, Boys Club, Police Athletic League, Chicago Area Project, and many other youth programs, some church-sponsored, are so well known as to require no comment by this Commission, save perhaps the reminder that all of these stress maximum responsibility by the young people themselves in deciding what is to be done, what policy will govern their actions, how the projects are to be conducted, what will be done with earned funds, if any, and all related questions and policies. Even so, existing programs reach only a fraction of our youth, ghetto youth least of all. This fact emphasizes the importance of the new Philadelphia and Washington, D.C. experimental projects which we have briefly described.

Experience has shown that as youths become involved in meaningful activities such as film-making, housing rehabilitation, landscaping, running a gas station, operating a farm, or making Christmas wreaths, their needs for further education and business skills become apparent to them. All the aspects of running a business or community project—accounting, advertising, financing, marketing, manufacturing, selling, law—can stimulate youth to seek training and advice. This is a solid foundation upon which to develop relevant education or job-training programs, to persuade drop-outs to complete high school, and even to guide the ablest and most highly motivated on to college.

Because some youth programs deal with the most deprived and alienated, special supportive services in drug rehabilitation, legal aid, and health care are sometimes essential. Although youth programs can go far to counteract the negative influences of the street culture, drug abuse, delinquency, and illness remain ever-present possibilities. To some extent existing community services can be reoriented to meet the special needs of youth. But it may prove necessary to establish supportive services linked directly to the over-all program effort. With respect to health care, group health insurance might be made part of any youth program once underway.

We urge the President, the Congress, and the federal agencies that normally provide funding for youth programs—notably the Office of Economic Opportunity, the Department of Labor, and the Department of Health, Education, and Welfare

—to take the risks involved in support of additional innovative programs of opportunity for inner-city youth.

Imagination and flexibility are essential qualities which may be enhanced by greater involvement of young people in the operations of the granting agency.

FOUR • DRUGS AND YOUTH

Our main concern in this chapter is to stress the importance of challenging the young people of the nation to become full partners in the enterprise of building a better society. But we must also add a word on one increasingly acute aspect of the present "generation gap"—the problem of drugs, particularly marijuana.

The development of drug subcultures among many of today's youth is particularly troubling to those who are older. Increased education about the physical and psychological hazards of the use of addictive drugs, LSD, the amphetamines, and other dangerous substances is essential if the health of young people and their children is to be properly safeguarded. In addition, the older generation must answer, in good faith and on the basis of better knowledge, the question raised by many young people as to whether present proscriptions on marijuana use go too far.

The startling recent increase in marijuana use by many young people has intensified the conflict between generations and posed enormous problems in the enforcement of drug laws. Possession and/or use of marijuana is treated severely by the law. In most states such possession or use is a felony, whereas the use or possession of the more dangerous LSD is only a misdemeanor.[7] This lack of elementary logic and justice has become a principal source of frustration and alienation contributing markedly to youth's often bitter dissatisfaction with today's society. We believe that action must be taken to put the whole situation into rational perspective.

Scientific knowledge about marijuana remains sparse, but some of its pharmacological properties have been established: marijuana is not a narcotic or an opiate and is

199

not addicting.[8] There is as yet no evidence as to the relationship it bears to the use of harder drugs.[9]

We recommend that the National Institutes of Health, working with selected universities, greatly expand research on the physical and psychological effects of marijuana use.[10]

The Congress should enact laws and appropriate adequate funds for this purpose. Much remains to be learned about the drug's psychological effects, particularly with respect to the expectation and personality types of users and the total emotional mood of the environment and the persons in it. Many experienced users have had at least one "bad trip" and some cases have been reported of extremely traumatic reactions to marijuana. It may be that marijuana use can be damaging to individuals with a history of mental instability or other personality disorders. Similarly, little is known about its possible psychological effects, including psychological dependency, on adolescents who are in the process of learning to cope with the demands of adult life. And we most assuredly need to know if marijuana users have a predisposition to use harder drugs.

Despite all existing evidence to the contrary, state and federal laws alike treat marijuana as a narcotic, and penalties for its sale and use in some states are extreme. In one state, the penalty is two years to life imprisonment for a first offense of possession. In at least two others, the penalty for an adult convicted of selling marijuana to a minor is death. According to the latest available Justice Department figures, the average length of sentence imposed for violation of state laws was 47.7 months. In 1967 the federal government made 706 arrests for marijuana offenses, as compared to the state of California alone which made 37,513 arrests, 10,907 of them juveniles under eighteen.

Erroneously classifying marijuana as a narcotic, this patchwork of federal and state laws, inconsistent with each other and often unenforceable on their merits, has led to an essentially irrational situation. Respect for the law can hardly be inculcated under these circumstances. Since many of our youths believe marijuana to be relatively harmless and, yet, are faced with legal sanctions, they are led into a practice of law evasion which contributes to general

200

disrespect for the law. Furthermore, enforcement of laws generally deemed harsh and unjust seem nonetheless to encourage police practices—*e.g.,* raids without probable cause, entrapment—which infringe on personal liberties and safeguards. The situation is reminiscent of the problems encountered in enforcement of Prohibition during the 1920s. The present harsh penalties for possession and use of marijuana are a classic example of what legal scholars call "overcriminalization"—treating as a serious crime private personal conduct that a substantial segment of the community does not regard as a major offense; prosecutors, judges and juries tend to moderate the severity of the statutory sanctions, and the resulting hypocrisy of all concerned diminishes respect for the law.

In view of the urgency of the marijuana problem, we believe that legislative reform of the existing marijuana penalty structure should not wait several years until further research is completed.

We recommend that federal and state laws make use and incidental possession of marijuana no more than a misdemeanor until more definitive information about marijuana is at hand and the Congress and state legislatures have had an opportunity to revise the permanent laws in light of this information. (Pending further study, we do not recommend a similar reduction in the penalty for those who traffic in marijuana for profit.)

Instead of the existing inequitable criminal penalties (including imprisonment) for mere possession and use of the drug, interim legislation might well provide only for civil penalties such as the confiscation of the drug and fines. If the interim legislation does provide for prison sentences, it should at least grant wide discretion to the trial judge to suspend sentence or release on probation.

We were heartened by the recommendation recently submitted to the Congress by several leading officials of the Executive Branch of the government—recommendations which seek immediate change in the provisions of federal law affecting drug use. Among other things, these officials indicated that use and incidental possession of marijuana should be declared to be no more than a misdemeanor.

The above recommendations should not, of course, be taken as suggesting either that we approve the use of

201

marijuana, or that we favor any relaxation of society's efforts to discourage the use of the clearly dangerous drugs.

Expert testimony offered to this Commission indicates that the so-called hard drugs, such as heroin, do not in themselves make users prone to commit other crimes, but that the daily use of such drugs involves exorbitant costs; hence users often undertake lives of burglary and armed robbery in order to obtain funds for the continued purchase of drugs. Further, drug importation and distribution, like certain forms of gambling, constitute part of the life-blood of organized crime—an empire of its own, ruthless, rich, pervasive, corrupting, and skillful at avoiding the reaches of the law.

We cannot usefully add to all that has been written by other Commissions, the Department of Justice, and many state authorities about the need for stopping the importation of the hard drugs, and for vigorously prosecuting the traffickers in these drugs. Nor can we add to the urgent recommendations that have been made by others to eliminate from our society the empires of organized crime.

But we do most emphatically declare that classifying marijuana users with the users of the hard drugs is scientifically wrong, a wrong recognized by the young, a wrong that makes them contemptuous of the drug laws and to some extent of all law. They wonder why the federal and state governments do not insist upon more widespread research to establish facts and to change laws in harmony with the facts as developed.

FIVE • THE GENERATION GAP

In this chapter we have stressed the importance of genuinely involving young people in the political process as well as in planning and carrying on useful social projects. In our view, the lack of such alternatives has contributed to the spread of young life-styles which depend on drugs or which stress hustling, vandalism, robbery, and even murder.

In stressing such remedies, we do not mean to suggest that until they are provided, violent behavior by young people would be tolerated or excused. Violent and unlaw-

202

ful conduct must be controlled by vigorous law enforcement at the same time that measures to eliminate the basic causes of violence are vigorously pursued.

We add a final statement on the apparently growing antagonism between young and old.[11]

In a sense, our immortality is our children. Youth represent the next step for our society, since they are the population which will join us in determining our directions and implementing our hopes. Yet we are aware that our youth are at times unstable, unpredictable and engaged in a major struggle to find their place in the world as they assert their adult capacities, physically and emotionally, politically and socially.

The older generation is faced with the challenge of making available to young people adequate opportunities to participate meaningfully in coping with society's problems, and thus facilitating individual emotional growth and maturity. All too often, the society—parents, school and university administrators, law enforcement personnel, community leaders—become identified in the eyes of youth with obstruction and repression, inflexibly protecting the status quo against the "onslaught" of youth.

There are many things each citizen can do to help resolve these problems. The challenge will not be met by new laws alone, or new programs directed to work with problem youth. Each citizen has a responsibility to participate—indeed, only as there is an increasing commitment on the part of all citizens toward understanding the problems of one another can we expect violence to diminish.

Understanding might more readily be achieved by observing the following guidelines:

● It is important to acknowledge openly the existence of problems between the generations when they occur. Too often, people are so threatened by conflict in opinions that they refuse to acknowledge a contrary view, and suppress that challenging view.

● It is imperative for all parties to listen carefully and respectfully to one another, with sincere consideration for differing opinions or ideas. Listening is not an easily practiced art.

● Stated issues are often a red herring. At times, the conflicts cannot be resolved until underlying causal issues are identified and dealt with.

203

- The resolution of any conflict will be profoundly affected by the expectations of the adversaries. If leaders are perceived by youth as unreasonable and are approached with that expectation, the leaders are themselves provoked into being unreasonable, and vice versa.

- All must acknowledge the inevitability of change. The older generation can wear itself out trying to fight the tide or it can turn the energy of youth to advantage for the benefit of all.

- Resolution of conflict depends on finding areas of agreement. Instead of emphasis on differences, which promotes polarization, it is necessary to identify points in common, such as the fact that people seek a voice in determining their destiny and dignity as human beings.

- As a society founded on the principle that every individual has certain inalienable rights and privileges, it is important to keep the value of the individual high, in spite of the population explosion and the complications of modern society. Youth are entitled to full respect as persons. Youth in turn must accord respect to persons they identify as the "older generation."

The older generation has difficulty in dealing with problems of young people because of its awareness that it has not yet created the perfect world. We don't like to be challenged, especially by our juniors. If we are to cope effectively with youth, we must courageously acknowledge our mistakes and recognize that our offspring may surpass us. Indeed, if we have been successful in our child-rearing, they certainly should surpass us. We must take extra effort to understand their criticism of our ways, and be pleased that these suggestions are coming from our most important products, our youth who will prove our ultimate worth.

The younger generation has the difficulties of its impatience and its assumption that all people of a certain age are the same. With all its defects—and today's youth are not the first to criticize those defects—constitutional representative government is still the best form that man has devised. Youth should acknowledge that there are still opportunities for individuals to leave their mark and to prompt change in an orderly manner within our system. At the same time, young people must be aware of the psychological fact that their inner pressures may prompt them to refight childhood battles, artifically appointing

204

well meaning people to play the same adversary role in which a child's parents are cast.

The first step for all of us is to look at ourselves, and to deal understandingly with the problems and conflicts we have with others. It is easier to blame others, and to see violence as being caused by others. But we must look inward as well as outward to the causes and prevention of violence.

1. In referenda on November 4, 1969, voters in Ohio and New Jersey defeated amendments lowering the voting age to nineteen and eighteen, respectively. The unofficial Ohio vote was close; 51 percent against and 49 percent for. In New Jersey, unofficial results show the amendment defeated by a 3 to 2 margin.

Voting participation by 21- to 24-year-olds generally falls below the national average. Of the total population eligible to vote, 67.8 percent did so in the 1968 national elections, as compared to only 51.2 percent of the 21- to 24-year-olds.

2. *In Pursuit of Equity: Who Serves When Not All Serve?*, Report of the National Advisory Commission on Selective Service (Washington, D. C.: Government Printing Office, 1967); U.S., Congress, Senate. *Report of the Civilian Advisory Panel on Military Manpower Procurement*, H Doc. 374 90th Cong., 2d Sess., 1968. Our recommendations, of course, refer only to the present draft system and are intended to apply only so long as it continues. The question of whether the draft should be replaced for the long term by a form of volunteer service in the armed forces is now under consideration by another presidential commission.

3. As suggested by Joseph A. Califano, Jr., in his book, *The Student Revolution* (W. W. Norton & Co., Inc., New York, 1970). The Marshall Commission found that the average age of local board members was 58. One fifth of all the nearly 17,000 board members were over 70. While twelve were over 90, only one was under 30.

4. One considerable virtue of the approach to youth service suggested here is that it involves a "market" strategy rather than a "monopoly service" strategy: the multitude of public and private agencies would have to compete for the services of the federally-supported youth workers by offering them meaningful, satisfying opportunities for achievement of desired goals; less successful, unrewarding programs would fail to attract volunteers and hence would not waste the public funds committed to youth service. *Cf.* the discussion of the importance of market-type incentives for success in public programs in Moynihan, "Toward a National Urban Policy," *The Public Interest* (No. 17, Fall 1969).

5. Depending on the availability of funds, educational assistance could be limited on the basis of demonstrated need.

6. Despite these criminogenic forces, studies show that a large number of ghetto youth never have a police arrest and only a small percentage become repeated offenders.

7. A felony is a serious crime usually punishable by imprisonment for an extended period (under federal law for a year or more); a misdemeanor is a lesser offense punishable by fine or imprisonment of less than a year. In many states, a felony conviction results in a loss of voting rights, jury service, and the right to enter various professional occupations; a misdemeanor conviction does not.

8. Addiction is a physiological and psychological dependence on a drug, with definite symptoms occuring when the drug is withdrawn.

9. In testimony on October 14, 1969 before the House of Representatives Select Committee on Crime, Dr. Robert O. Egeberg, Assistant Secretary of Health, Education and Welfare for Health and Scientific Affairs, stated that "there is no scientific evidence to demonstrate that use of marijuana *in itself* predisposes an individual to progress to 'hard' drugs."

10. A similar provision is contained in H.R. 10019 by Rep. Edward Koch, N.Y.

11. This statement is largely the work of W. Walter Menninger, M.D.

XI ● THE STRENGTHS OF AMERICA

by Louis Heren*

*Since our mandate to examine the causes of violence neces-
sarily concentrates on certain weaknesses of American social
and political structures, the Commission believes that an appraisal of the many strengths of America is essential to view
our institutions in full focus. We therefore asked Mr. Louis
Heren, a distinguished British correspondent who has studied
this nation for many years, to describe it with the perspective
that only a non-American can provide.*

I met many Americans and Europeans in 1968 who won-
dered if the United States could survive that year without
some terrible and lasting damage. For me, there was only
one answer. The United States is not a great nation because
of its political institutions and the spirit of its people. Together, the institutions and people working in creative tension have brought forth an unprecedented social and economic revolution. Great power has been organized without impinging upon personal freedom. The opportunities
for individual and group advancement are unique. The
great Jeffersonian ideals of Life, Liberty, and the pursuit
of Happiness have been sustained through many ordeals
and crises. Whatever the future held, I knew instinctively
that the American political genius would somehow prevail.

To restate these eternal truths is not to ignore the conditions for much of the recent violence, but to remember that the United States is strong enough to deal with
them as it has successfully dealt with far worse problems
in the past. After reading the Commission Reports, I welcome the opportunity, and cherish the honor as a friendly
but critical foreign observer, to remind the world of Amer-

---

*Foreign correspondent of *The Times* (London) for 23 years, nine of them in
Washington. He served in Europe, the Middle East, the Far East, India, and
Africa: he was awarded the Hannan Swaffer Award for International Reporter
of 1967 (the British equivalent of the Pulitzer Prize) and the John F. Ken-
nedy Memorial Award in 1968 for his book *The New American Commonwealth*
(New York: Harper and Row, 1968).

ica's enduring strengths. They are numerous, some less obvious than others, and not all can be given due attention here. For the most part I have confined myself to political strengths because only these can ensure the future well-being, confidence, and unity of a nation of more than 200 million. Last year is an appropriate place to begin.

There were, alas, the murders of Dr. Martin Luther King, Jr. and Senator Robert Kennedy, the riots in Washington and other cities, the pitched street battles in Chicago during the Democratic National Convention, and the ugly brutalities of the campus disorders and anti-war demonstrations. Yet at the end of the year the Presidential election was held, and there was no violence as 69 million Americans went to the polls. The enormous power of the Presidency passed peacefully from one man to another. American political democracy had once again performed its most important function as by law ordained.

Violence continued into the new year; but there was much less of it. President Nixon could not offer quick resolution of the problems assumed to be causes of violence, but he could depend with complete confidence upon sufficient support to govern. He could depart for Europe and Southeast Asia, and remove himself for a working vacation on a distant Pacific promontory. Few national leaders could have acted with such confidence in similar circumstances. The national equilibrium was restored, and was seen to be restored, by what John Bright saw as no finer spectacle in the whole world—the election of the President of the United States.

There is a certain magic in this process of which the British statesman may have been unaware. The peaceful exercise of the sovereign power of the people, their ability to change governments and the direction of the country even in periods of national crisis, is the supreme strength of any democratic society. But because of the special nature of the Presidency—monarch, prime minister, and much else—the Inauguration is more than a swearing-in ceremony. It is a promise of national renewal. Americans can dare to believe that a new day may indeed have dawned; and that with luck the country might within the next four years draw a little closer to the professed ideals that captivate their imagination if not always commend

207

their earnest endeavors. Tensions lessen in times of trouble. The President is allowed a period of grace. The country gives itself another chance.

The magic does not last of course. Problems do not disappear, although they often emerge in better focus. Moreover, this is a country in which individuals and groups freely pursue their destinies, and conflict is more often than not inevitable. Their freedom is ensured by the many jurisdictions essential to federalism, but at the expense of unwieldiness, confusion, and occasionally injustice. Most Americans remain uneasily aware of paradoxes in their national life which appear to belie its promise.

The dictionary definition of paradox is a statement or situation seemingly absurd and self-contradictory, but really true. The immediate one is that this is a violent country but civil strife, apart for the Civil War, has been much less disruptive than in most other countries. There are others. Fiercely dedicated as Americans are to the perhaps impossible proposition of equality—the English more wisely seek individual freedom and liberty—oppression appears to have been accepted with remarkable equanimity. In the richest country in the world a degree of poverty still exists which no democratic government in Western Europe would be permitted to countenance.

These paradoxes and others are disturbing, but each is connected. They are in part the price paid for national unity, again unprecedented. Some Americans have tried to escape it, into the old arcadias and the new hippie communes, but unity is a great strength, the foundation of many others. The benefits are clear, but in dealing with 200 million people its maintenance demands patience. When this is in short supply, when one part of the country moves too slowly for another, violence can follow. Fortunately, the majority instinctively knows the need for patience. Unity also requires political flexibility and inventiveness, and again fortunately there is a surfeit of those qualities due at least in part to the greatest of all American paradoxes. The United States is a very old country when it is supposed to be young.

Let there be no mistakes about this paradox. If the age of a nation is measured by the continuity of its political institutions, and I can think of no better yardstick in this

208

age of territorial and political change, the United States is the second oldest country in the world. Only Britain is older. China, France, Germany and India are all very much younger. None has an uninterrupted political system going back before 1947. In comparison, the United States is a mature, almost ancient land, made immensely stable by established tradition. If the bi-centenary of Independence has yet to be celebrated, the General Assembly of Virginia celebrated its 350th anniversary in 1969. Only two other parliaments are older: Iceland's Althing, which survived the union with Denmark and its dissolution, and the British Parliament. Moreover, the early English settlers in this land brought with them a facility to govern themselves, and political tradition and experience stretching back to de Montfort's Parliament, to Runnymeade, and beyond. The United States Constitution, the distillation of the Anglo-American experience, is the world's oldest written constitution.

Too much can be made of age. Older civilizations and empires have collapsed in violence or from decrepitude, but none with a capacity for renewal and change such as the United States has demonstrated from its colonial beginnings. A perusal of the Constitution would suggest that little has changed since 1787. Many of the later amendments are mutually cancelling or define more specifically rights assumed in the Bill of Rights. Yet merely everything has changed. The founders would not recognize the modern Presidency or the Supreme Court, but there is little in the amendments to suggest the monumental expansion of their authority. The Twenty-second Amendment restricted Presidents to two terms, but the power of the office has continued to expand. Much of this expansion was fundamental if the country was to survive the many transitions from 13 primitive seaboard states to the world's largest democracy, and the legality of this authority is unquestioned except by a few constitutional fundamentalists. Whatever the future holds for the United States, and the authority and scope of the office of the Presidency and the Supreme Court, the past suggests that Americans can assume a realistic response by their leaders as long as they accept the responsibilities and disciplines of representational government.

This capacity for change without offending the spirit of an ancient Constitution is one of the most reassuring of the American paradoxes. Admittedly it has not always been evident or timely. There was the failure of union more than a hundred years ago and the reluctance or refusal to concede political, social, and economic reform: hence the Civil War and the outbursts of violence. The United States is a most violent country compared with modern western Europe, but it is larger and its regions and people much more diverse. Moreover, the American subcontinent has been for the most part successfully governed and developed as a single unit, and western Europe remains divided. No advocate of European unity can afford to ignore the American experience, its triumphs as well as its failures. Certainly none can hope to achieve greater success in unity.

Again, no European country has had to contend with such competing internal forces. Until recently, the nature of British politics was deferential, to use Bagehot's apt description. A majority was prepared to defer to the politicians and assumed betters, on condition that their ancient liberties were preserved. There was also the safety valve of emigration. More than 20 million vexed and troubled Englishmen have gone overseas since the early 19th century. That is the equivalent of nearly half of the present population. To that extent Britain and other European countries unloaded some of their troubles on the United States.

This report states that the myth of the Melting Pot has obscured the great degree to which Americans have identified with their national citizenship through their many ethnic as well as other affiliations, and that this has meant group competition, friction, and conflict. Certainly Israel Zangwell, the English Jewish playwright, assumed too much when he had one of his characters say, "America is God's crucible, the great Melting Pot where all the races of Europe are melting and re-forming! Here you stand, good folk, think I, when I see them at Ellis Island, here you stand in your fifty groups, with your fifty languages and histories, and your fifty blood hatreds and rivalries. But you won't be long like that, brothers, for these are the fires of God you've come to—these are the fires of God.

A fig for your feuds and vendettas! Germans and Frenchmen, Irishmen and Englishmen, Jews and Russians—into the Crucible with you all. God is making the American."

We now know that assimilation is a much more difficult and protracted process, and an occasionally violent one, but in no other country has it been tried on such a scale and with such success. Of the 44 million who have arrived since 1820, when a count was first made, at least 36 million came after 1890. The frontier period had come to an end, but the upheavals of an era of unprecedented industrial expansion were already sweeping the country. Given the circumstances and the diversity of the immigrants, Americans should be amazed by their capacity to accept change with a minimum of violence. A far greater degree of unity has been achieved than in Canada, between the English and the French, and in such mixed societies as Belgium, Finland, India, Malaysia, Spain, and the Soviet Union. There was less violence in Canada, but efforts to protect the interests and culture of French-Canadians have only perpetuated national divisions—a thought for social scientists as well as politicians.

The more or less peaceful absorption of these millions was not achieved by the American equivalent of an imperial edict or *ukase*. The Constitution, of course, provided a dependable and flexible frame. The period of rapid expansion and absorption would surely have ended in disaster without its guarantees, which were given a sanctity rarely accorded nowadays without reservation to the Holy Writ. The Bill of Rights defined and assured for millions of immigrants rights that they had previously not enjoyed. Abundant land and almost limitless opportunity helped, but much of the credit for this extraordinary success must go to the political instincts of individual Americans. Many immigrants had taken refuge in the industrial areas of the East and Middle West, and this coming together fostered differences of culture, language, religion, and politics. It was potentially divisive and dangerous. But a cellular complex of the French-Canadas, or worse, did not become a permanent feature of American life because of the political parties. They recognized that there were no ethnic divisions in the ballot box.

Ethnic politics had its unsavory aspects, but it did largely

211

break down ethnic and religious barriers. Millions of immigrants were brought into political life and across the threshold of American society. It helped to make the United States the largest and most peaceful pluralistic society the world has ever seen. The local politicians were no doubt unconscious of the historical process they were responsible for, but to those with a larger understanding of America's predicament and opportunity the problem was very familiar. Pluralism, in this sense, assumes separation and division which must be accommodated, a process by no means novel for American politicians. The Constitution separates power, and federalism divides the country into fifty states. Pluralism therefore is no more than a further complication in the quest for national unity which brings political power. That they succeeded is surely proof of the political experience that is one of the benefits of great age.

The process of accommodation worked both ways. For instance, the Roosevelt coalition of ethnic groups, labor, the intellectuals and the South paid political dividends. The ethnic groups in turn found an active and honorable role in American politics and society. Take one example. There were very few foreign names in the Fifty-second Congress which was elected at the end of the frontier period. There were in fact only a few Irish-Americans and Anthony Caminetti, a native-born Californian. But the roster of the Ninety-first Congress reads like a gazetteer: Addabbo, Conti, Derwinski, Galifianakis, O'Konski, Zablocki, and of course Mrs. Patsy Mink from Hawaii. The House of Representatives is now clearly representative of the American pluralistic society. The Senate has its Fong and Pastore, and if the names remain overwhelmingly Anglo-American it is because the Senate represents states and the demographic mix is not evenly spread from sea to shining sea. The dominance of the WASPs in the White House was broken by President John F. Kennedy. Mr. Spiro T. Agnew, the son of an itinerant Greek fruit seller, was elected Vice-President in 1968.

The ethnic balance is well maintained in the world of appointed politics. This goes far beyond the old concept of jobs for the boys, although this must be a consideration and is also part of the assimilating process. It is seen to be necessary in achieving the balance and unity of the parties,

212

and in turn the country. The political good sense of Americans can hardly be better demonstrated than in the acceptance of the consequences of pluralism, and the confidence in political and social accommodation. Something splendid has emerged from the early mire of ethnic politics for the United States, and perhaps the world. Pluralism is surely essential for peace in the world and domestic tranquility in a number of countries, and the American experience, incomplete as it is, has demonstrated that accommodation is not beyond the wit of man. As far as white Americans are concerned, a very stable and peaceful society exists, and the wonder of it is that the original Anglo-American traditions, as well as the English language, have survived intact. They may be observed and spoken in some odd ways, but the character of those traditions remain fundamentally unchanged. No matter what his ethnic background or religion, the average American identifies himself with those traditions, even sartorially down to Brooks Brothers suits and button-down shirts. He may remember old national heroes, but Miles Standish, George Washington, and Abraham Lincoln are claimed as his own. Thus political, social, and cultural assimilation have gone hand in hand.

Group competition continues, regional and industrial as well as ethnic and racial. It is the very stuff of politics everywhere, but is much more intense in the United States. The reason is clear when we consider the federal government. In spite of what Edmund Burke said to the voters of Bristol in 1774, congressmen are not representatives of independent judgment. To reverse his election address, the Senate and the House of Representatives are a congress of ambassadors for different and (occasionally) hostile interests, which each must maintain, as an agent and advocate, against other agents and advocates. It cannot be otherwise, because Congress is the final cockpit of group competition.

This does not mean that congressmen are oblivious of the national interest. Nothing could be further from the truth, and some critics tend to forget that this is a union of sub-continental proportions. Singly or in groups, the states encompass, and their politics defend, interests and regions as diverse and as numerous as can be found in all Europe. The prime function of Congress is to reconcile the internal

213

differences. For a member of Congress it is rather like a game of three-dimensional chess played under the most demanding rules. As the delegate of his state or electoral district, he must try to satisfy the demands of his constituents, which is the first dimension. The second is to serve the national interest, and the third to strike a balance with state and regional interests. It is a hard game to play, which helps to explain why American politicians are as a body the most sophisticated in the democratic world. The variation of compromise is infinite. The moves are often hard to follow, but there can be no party discipline in the British sense when constituency and regional interests of members of the same party are in conflict. Political scientists regret it, but they fail to understand the true purpose of Congress. The crossing of party lines to form loose coalitions in order to defend common interests is inevitable. Confusion and frustration can be considerable, but one majority leader in the House of Representatives said that it was the lesser of two evils. The larger was splinter parties, and perhaps the eventual Balkanization of the United States.

In reconciling internal interests, Congress maintains the Union but three-dimensional politics often leads to indecision and the avoidance of urgent problems. There are many examples in American history, and this report has explored some of the violent consequences, but political flexibility has fended off disaster. In separating powers the founders, unwittingly one must assume, provided alternative sources of leadership. Alexander Hamilton said of the House of Representatives at the New York Convention: "Here, Sir, the people govern." George Dewey added later, "I am convinced that the office of the President is not such a difficult one to fill, his duties being mainly to execute the laws of Congress." We now know that this is no longer the case, and not because, as some constitutional fundamentalists would have it, the power of Congress has been usurped. The constitutional authority of the Presidency has been legitimately developed and extended of necessity, and often with congressional approval.

Both recognized, reluctantly or otherwise, the new imperative of solving nationwide problems at the national level. Only the President could act in many cases: hence his increased power. The shift is dramatically evident in

214

the President's war powers. He is the Commander-in-Chief, and is responsible for foreign affairs, but there are constitutional checks and balances. Only Congress can declare war and appropriate money to wage it, and there is the advice and consent clause. But Congress recognized the dangers of the nuclear age, and gave the President sufficient authority to act in an emergency. The history of the modern Presidency is also to a large extent the history of American social and economic reform. This does not mean that Congress is oblivious of social and economic ills. Many reforms originated there, and often it has improved and gone beyond Presidential proposals, but for the reasons stated Congress cannot always act promptly. The new imperative demands Presidential activism. This brought about a new kind of politics in the United States, and it is largely Presidential politics.

The consequences can be seen in the bureaucratic ramifications of the Executive Office. There is the Bureau of the Budget, the Central Intelligence Agency, and the councils for economic, national security, aeronautics and space, and urban affairs. Special offices have proliferated: economic opportunity, emergency planning, science and technology, and trade negotiations. The legislative program now for the most part originates in the White House. The President can actually reach up to the moon and stars and down to the gutters of the slums of New York and Chicago. He can personally command the most powerful military forces in history and negotiate the price of wheat with the European Economic Community. He can influence the direction of scientific research and help to create another million jobs and build tens of thousands of dwellings.

Some Americans believe that this accumulation of Presidential power has gone too far. It is possible. Certainly Congress grumbles from time to time, and there is talk of returning some of the power to the states. Clearly the federal bureaucracy has become cumbersome, but the point I am trying to make here is that within the American system power tends to flow where it can best be used. There is a response to national need and requirements. Today, no group, no problem or reasonable demand is overly long ignored, and both of the political parties can share the credit. President Franklin D. Roosevelt must be regarded

215

as the first of the modern Presidents, but his relative, President Theodore Roosevelt, and President William Taft and President Woodrow Wilson helped to pave the way. It was President Theodore Roosevelt who expounded the theory of the President as the Steward of the People.

He wrote in his Autobiography: "I declined to adopt the view that what was imperatively necessary for the Nation could not be done by the President unless he could find some specific authorization to do it. My belief was that it was not only his right but his duty to do anything that the needs of the Nation demanded unless such action was forbidden by the Constitution or by the laws. Under this interpretation of executive power I did and caused to be done many things not previously done by the President and the heads of the Departments. I did not usurp power, but I did broaden the use of executive power. In other words, I acted for the public welfare, I acted for the common well-being of all our people, whenever and in whatever manner was necessary, unless prevented by direct constitutional or legislative prohibition."

The parties have also tended to accept and proceed from each other's policies and reforms. The Democrats were long concerned with the condition of the cities, but President Nixon established the Council for Urban Affairs. He also proposed to return some revenue and administrative functions to the states, but such is the imperative of solving nationwide problems at the national level that the National Governors Conference insisted that welfare programs should be run from Washington. Thus it would seem that the powers of the modern Presidency are not likely to diminish in the near future.

Whatever happens, the nation is immeasurably strengthened by this free flow of power and responsibility between the different levels and branches of government. In Washington, the Presidency is not the only coequal branch which can exert leadership as required. Witness the activism of the Supreme Court during the last 15 years. Again, there are Americans who believe that it went too far. They question the right of the Court to wield such authority, but it did no more than try to formulate answers for fundamental problems that the executive and legislative branches could not resolve. The Court responded to the pressures of the times, and in so doing again demonstrated the flexibility and resilience of the American system.

The Supreme Court is a very American institution, the like of which exists nowhere in the world. After years of close study, it is for me still one of the inner mysteries of American life. It is eternally aware of the spirit and the verities of the past, especially the long struggle for human liberty and dignity. This, with its sensitive awareness of the present, helps to explain its grandeur. Its uniqueness lies elsewhere. It is the final appellate court, but is also a political institution because of the power to hold unconstitutional and judicially unenforceable any act of the President, the Congress, and the states. The power is not expressly granted by the Constitution, but rests on what is known as logical implication. I prefer to see it as yet another example of the American ability to change when change is necessary. History would seem to bear me out.

The implied logic was first seen and established by Chief Justice John Marshall, one of the last of the Federalists who was determined to combat what he saw as the populist excesses of Jacksonian democracy. He acted in defence of property, but a century later the sanctity of property was not the only imperative. The protection of human rights and liberties was of equal importance, and they were protected under Marshall's implied logic. Thus the wheel turned, more or less smoothly within the constitutional framework as it had turned before. In 1964, a decade after the *Brown* v. *Board of Education* decision, the annual report of the American Bar Association said, "The new trend is not back to an exaggerated individualism, which has been corrected in part by the notion of a sociological jurisprudence. Neither is it a re-affirmation of the 'jurisprudence of interests', which was a positivistic effort to spell out in jurisprudential terms the property and power priorities of society. The new jurisprudence constitutes, rather, a recognition of human beings, as the most distinctive and important feature of the universe which confronts our senses, and the function of law as the historic means of guaranteeing that pre-eminence. . . ."

The wheel will turn again, because one can be sure that the Court will remain alert to the problems and priorities of the time. It will intervene in the states when the civil

217

rights of citizens are seen to be offended. It will intervene when the three-dimensional politics of Congress make reasonable compromise impossible. The balance in the Court will change, from liberal to conservative (to use misleading political labels) and back again, but it will continue to intervene because it cannot do otherwise. When contradictions have to be resolved, when Congress and the state legislatures fail, there is only the Court or the streets.

These, as I see them, are the structural strengths of the American political system. It is complicated. Little wonder that harassed men in Washington occasionally look enviously across the Atlantic to Britain, where there is a unitary form of government. Parliament is supreme. The Magna Carta and constitutional statutes can be repealed, as the monarchy can be changed—by a simple majority vote. At least this is the constitutional theory. But, history apart, the United States is not a tight little island. It must pay a price for bigness. Sheer size is the basic dilemma of American government and society, as the Europeans will realize when they eventually achieve unity. More than 200 million people cannot be ruled, democratically, under a unitary form of government, and their differences create immense problems when they have to be resolved by 51 governments working under 51 constitutions. There are critics who argue that those differences will eventually prove irreconcilable.

Americans are unlikely to accept this, even after the recent decade of national distemper and violence. I am certain that the system will continue to be flexible and, if necessary, new arrangements will be made without doing damage to the Constitution, but it will take time, more time than in man-sized countries such as Britain with unitary systems. The majority of Americans appear instinctively to understand this, at least when their group interests have been generally recognized. Now the time has come for the recognition of Negro interests, and those of the Puerto Ricans and Mexican-Americans, and the question is whether their legitimate goals can be achieved without violence much greater than that which marked organized labor's fight for recognition. The question demands complete honesty because the challenge the Negro poses for the American system is unprecedented.

Americans do not have to be told why, but it is worth

218

remembering that racial prejudice is not the only problem. There is no American monopoly of racial prejudice. The evidence is painfully obvious. The Indian word for caste means color, which suggests that the sanctified segregation and discrimination of the caste system are fundamentally racial. The English were found to be only too human when colored immigrants from the Commonwealth came crowding in after the Second World War. The same prejudice exists even in deepest, darkest Africa. Ethiopia comes readily to mind. Only countries without minorities of another world appear to be free of racial prejudice. Nevertheless, the peculiarity of the condition of American Negroes is that they have been denied participation in the political processes I have mentioned. Indeed, in the South exclusion became the foundation of politics. To a large extent, Southern politics remains a reversal of ethnic politics in that courthouse politicians combine to exclude Negroes rather than seek their votes and thus bring them across the threshold of American political and social life.

The legal barriers to political participation and representation have been removed. The subsequent violence was proof that legislation is not enough, but some progress has been made. There are now 10 black Members of Congress. The Institute for Black Elected Officials has 1,200 members, 490 of them in the South. Black mayors have been elected in Cleveland, Ohio, Gary, Indiana, and Fayette, Mississippi. Few Americans anticipated such progress when I began to report from Washington in 1960. Even President Kennedy was chary of doing much in the first months of his tragically short Administration. Some progress has also been made elsewhere. Professions and trades once more or less closed are now beginning to accept Negro recruits. There are more black factory and construction workers, office and store clerks, truck and bus drivers. Similar progress is evident in the academic world and the front offices of the large corporations. Tokenism is suspected, but this is a process that can hardly be stopped. Negroes are proving themselves everywhere. There is an easier acceptance of them in public places and transport. Of equal significance, the average Negro has a new racial pride. Black can indeed be beautiful, as model agencies now recognize. The universities have discovered black culture.

219

These advances have both relaxed and increased tensions. The militant black can be overly assertive in his new pride. Often only a thin line separates aggressiveness from confidence when confidence is still new and uncertain. Many whites continue to defend their trades, neighborhoods, and schools from the black advance, but resistance is not entirely racial. Some are defending traditional skills which are their only working capital. Homes are their one major investment, and local schools are their children's main hope of advancement. The bad attracts more attention than the good, but clearly much more time is required. Most Negroes are not the black equivalents of the old immigrants from eastern and southern Europe. Very few have comparable skills. Unlike the Irish, they have little experience of politics. More than justice for Negroes is required in the South. A whole way of life must be changed. Gradualism is a dirty word for black militants, but it is essential if more terrible violence is to be avoided. The North is also beginning to realize that race is not only a Southern problem. Prejudice crosses the Mason-Dixon line as well as the Atlantic and Indian Oceans.

Given time, there is no reason for despair. If the problem is greater here, the United States is in many ways better equipped than most countries to reach an acceptable accommodation. There is the resilience of the political system, and the long acceptance of pluralism. The white backlash vote in 1968 was much smaller than expected. There is also American youth. Who can doubt that the majority of today's youngsters are willing to come to terms? The black community is also blessed with first-rate leadership from the National Association for the Advancement of Colored People to the Southern Christian Leadership Conference. The young militants make the headlines, but none has survived for very long. The Stokely Carmichaels come and go, but the Roy Wilkins and Whitney Youngs remain towers of strength.

There is probably more time available than is generally imagined. Subterranean movements within the black community can be sensed, among them the defensive withdrawal which this report establishes as an historical reaction of groups discontented with their social environment. It has gone far beyond the Black Muslim movement, and appears to be a reaction from violence as well as the goal of integration. I doubt that it is permanent, but tension has been relaxed. Confrontation will continue, but so will the small advances and adjustments. There is time for new thinking on both sides, and time has not been wasted. President Nixon's welfare program, with its guaranteed income levels, is of immense promise because poverty is as much a cause of violence as prejudice and injustice. This has been amply proved in Britain. About one million colored immigrants— proportionally the equivalent of 4 million in the United States—have been peacefully settled, and one reason is the welfare state programs.

The future is uncertain, but the United States faces it with many great strengths, and now is the time to count the blessings. The American experience is unparalleled. Apart from the blessings of Life, Liberty, and the pursuit of Happiness, unity on a sub-continental scale has been achieved and maintained, and with it the great American common market. To that extent, the United States is nearly 200 years older than Western Europe, including Britain.

I refer to the stumbling European movement towards unity. There, thirteen countries, as there were once thirteen American states, are interested in varying degrees of unity, but only the six of the European Economic Community have made much progress. If I can switch historical periods for comparison, the seven countries of the European Free Trade Area are a sort of confederacy, which is not likely to have much more influence upon the future shape of a United States of Europe than the Southern Confederacy had upon the Union. History rarely repeats itself, as those well-meaning Americans who tried to apply their national experience to Europe have discovered. I can recall no American parallel for President de Gaulle's rejection of Britain, but one can be fairly certain that behind the tariff wall of the Common Market, perhaps in Holland or Belgium, a second Calhoun is growing up. Nullification may eventually be translated into Dutch or Walloon. If complete European economic unity has yet to be achieved, political unity remains a dream. Britain, renowned for its political sagacity, is still an offshore Massachusetts anxious for its mercantile trade and connections across the sea. Sweden is perhaps comparable to colonial Rhode Island,

221

content with its rather special democracy and reluctant to consider union.

Beyond the Elbe, the future is more uncertain than it once was beyond the Mississippi, in spite of all the once grand talk of a Europe reaching to the Urals. There are many pamphleteers, but not a single Hamilton or Jefferson. In these circumstances, I am inclined to regard the United States as the old world, and not the new. I certainly know many Europeans who would like their continent to be as old as the United States, to have done with all the trials and tribulations of early union, and with a secure political future based on continuity, stability, maturity, and the habit of union. Despite the violence that has attended its recent progress, the United States remains the envy and the model for much of the world.

Unity has made possible the enormous industrial expansion which impresses so many Europeans, but there is more to America than that. It has absorbed more than 40 million immigrants from many lands and cultures, and in so doing has enriched itself. It has given them freedom to develop in their own manner—to chase an honest buck, build, aim at the moon, build a bomb, and dream their dreams. If there is an American Dream the one distinction, for most men dream, is that Americans can hope to realize their dreams regardless of race, color, and creed. That phrase has an unpleasant connotation for some Americans, but it is true for most of them as it will be one day for the black minority.

That much is clear. What is not so certain is whether Europe has the strengths that made all this possible. Most do not have a fraction of the American political genius for compromise and flexibility. My own people are beginning to realize that they are not free of racial prejudice, and this year British troops once again faced angry Irishmen across smoking barricades. The differences in language and political and juridical institutions would appear to deny reasonable compromise. Will Englishman have to give up *habeas corpus* in order to sell more cars and sweaters in a united Europe? It seems a heavy price to pay. I am by nature an optimist, but it is quite likely that the strengths that make the United States great are peculiarly American, the fruits of an experience, a history and geography that cannot be

222

duplicated elsewhere. It gives me no pleasure to admit this, but Americans, even those still waiting to be fully accepted, can count their blessings and look to the future with the greatest confidence in their own strengths.

XII ● RELIGION AND THE PROBLEM OF VIOLENCE

A Concluding Statement by Terence Cardinal Cooke

I join my fellow members of the Commission in this Report and in commending it to the American people. I believe the Commission and its staff have done an outstanding job of investigating one of the most difficult and distressing phenomena that our nation faces—acts of violence by individuals and by groups.

This Report and the reports of the Commission's Task Forces mention some of the excellent service programs religious groups have developed in youth work and acknowledge the necessity for involving our religious institutions in the future prevention of or the diminution of the recent level of violence in America.

Yet the solution to the problem of violence requires that we go beyond the recognition of what has been done by religious organizations, or what they should do in the future, to a recognition of the religious and moral dimensions of this problem of individual and group violence.

The Task Force Reports and the transcripts of the public hearings and conferences suggest that the Commission has been dealing not just with violence but with a growing national situation which has elements of apathy and indifference, of frustration and alienation. The evidence also indicates that many violent disturbances are rooted to a significant extent in a basic conflict between society and the individual person—between larger groups and minority groups.

It is not new to say that, historically, discontent in society comes either from the failure of the individual to respect the rights and human dignity of other individuals in the social group or from the failure of those in the social group to respect the rights and human dignity of the individual. Whether you speak of social control or social change, you are implicitly referring to the brotherhood of men under the fatherhood of God. You are speaking of human persons, whether individually or in groups, who are members of one human family.

Religion and religious leaders have something to say about the basic human problem of violence within the human family. For religion is inescapably a social virtue. It is a virtue which strengthens the individual not only in his relationship with God but also in his relationship with his fellow man. It is the God-given power a person acquires realistically to know himself, his society and his world. Religion—that virtue by which man gives to God the love, the service and the honor which are due to God—does have a unifying effect on men. Since it puts man in relation to his Maker, it puts him in a relationship of love, service and honor to all men who are, like him, God's children.

Man is disposed to be at one not only with the members of his own religious community, but with all men because of his religious belief in the equal dignity and worth of each individual made in God's image. Each man has a right from God and by nature to the conditions of life and work which permit him to exercise his function as a person, husband, and father; worker, neighbor and citizen. Light and air, cleanliness, safety, and a certain amount of privacy should characterize his housing. Job training and job opportunity and job performance should be worked out by the agencies of society and by him to produce equitable remuneration from society's economic activity. Education should be provided to equip him for life in his society and also to help him to develop a quality and style of life. Equal and effective participation in government should be assured through our political processes.

Government should not only forbid transgression of these rights but must encourage the development of positive programs to see that these human rights can be exercised. The churches and the synagogues proclaim these concepts and should on every level implement these teach-ings by their witness. That is why church and synagogue are involved in the specific concerns of people for housing, jobs, education, and self-determination. For if man does not have these for himself and for his family, he is never truly free—free to live his life in peace with himself, his neighbor and his God; if he has not these indispensible requisites to full human dignity, he cannot be fully committed to God and to the human family.

I wish to affirm my strong belief that when I witness violence which involves individual persons or social groups, I think that religion and religious leaders must be concerned. For violence is a moral and social evil. Church and synagogue can play a strong and positive role in its prevention and in the preservation of social peace. For if they do not, the task may be left undone. As our pluralistic society has grown larger and more complex, it has become almost a pattern of thinking to assume that government will solve all the ills of society. But government alone can never solve all our problems. And it can never, under our Constitution, produce a complete solution to any problem which is rooted to a certain extent in religion and morality. It can control one man's social relations with another by its laws and sanctions. But it can never touch the hearts, the free wills and the minds of men as religion can. Social persuasion can go only so far. It is the role of religion to stimulate change in attitudes and to promote peace and understanding among men.

What then are the roles of religion in the prevention and diminution of violence? What are the roles of the ministers of religion? What is the function of those citizens of religious faith who believe in the brotherhood of man under the fatherhood of God? I believe there are three roles, three functions that must be fulfilled if we are to see the dawn of an age of domestic peace following our present decade of violence. The first role is that of peacemaker; the second is that of prophet; the third is that of bridge-builder.

It is not an easy task to be a peacemaker, to be in the middle, to be the mediator with whom neither person or group really wants to agree. It is difficult to bring together persons with opposing viewpoints, to help each to learn where the other is right or fair in his position, to soften demands into requests, to make negotiable that which is

225

stated as "non-negotiable." None of these is easy. Yet all of these are the role of the peacemaker who has faith in God, in his fellow men, and in himself.

Religious groups are probably among the few who enjoy some possibility of working toward an assertion of national values in such a way that conflicting groups and alienated groups may be brought to a level of unity. Repeatedly in the past, the religious group has succeeded in acting as a bond between different social classes, different ethnic groups, different interest groups around common religious beliefs and values, or around religious practices. It is true that the interpretation of these values and beliefs by people in different classes varies greatly and can become the cause of division. But the possession of some common beliefs provides a basis of unity from which the churches can work toward understanding on other levels. The fact that conflicting groups at least accept the belief that all men are children of God is a fulcrum toward unity on other matters which would be much more difficult if there were no belief in the common human family of God.

To so particularize the role of the peacemaker in our society almost of necessity involves the role of the prophet —he who will give effective witness to truth. For the man of religion cannot stand in the middle believing each side is totally right. He may concede that they honestly think they are. But he who witnesses to justice and goodness must be free to speak the truth—and this is the role of the prophet. He must challenge; he must question; he must make clear. In calling attention to the violence of individuals and groups, he must speak the truth about such basic concepts as "good" and "evil." The strains of evil lie within each of us and must be fought there. But the inclinations to good lie there also and must be nurtured.

There is a need to speak the truth about good and evil to today's radical militants. In their confrontations, in their attempt to dehumanize their opponents by their rhetoric, they are projecting the fatal illusions that some people are wholly good, others wholly bad and that all people can be compelled by fear and force. They must learn what our political, social and religious organizations have learned or are swiftly learning—that neither imposition nor dictation will turn the tide of evil. We must search out together

226

the strains of evil and combat them wherever they are found. But hatred of persons, indeed hatred itself, must be seen as an irrationality because it assumes what is rarely found—the pure wickedness of an antagonist. The instincts for good must be sought out and evoked in every man. We must learn again to live amicably and cooperatively with each other. We must end the "up against the wall" attitude towards those in disagreement; and we must end the conditions that produce the frustrations and despair productive of this reaction.

It is a natural concomitant of functioning as peacemaker and prophet that church and synagogue are uniquely qualified for what I would call the role of "bridge-builder." In any period of rapid social change in society there are always dangers. There is the danger, on the one hand, of confusing permanence and stability with inflexibility and thus stifling progress. There is the equal danger, at the opposite extreme, of ignoring the past in dealing with the present.

Change is not a new phenomenon in this age, although it is more rapid. We must not forget that the human condition itself assumes continual and gradual change. But as universal as is the need for change, equally universal is the need for continuity and relatedness. We all need a bridge from past to present and from present to future. Deep within the human spirit lies the need for continuity, for roots. Just as deep with that same spirit lies the need for change, for responsiveness to the demands of the present and the future.

Religion does provide continuity among the various stages of life. Its religious services give solemnity to and celebrate the major points of birth, marriage, and death, and to a host of other key moments in our lives. These celebrations provide a climate and capacity for reverence and mutual respect. They are contact points between the generations. Religion provides a setting in which a man can put himself together, can sense something of whence he comes and where he goes, and can be aware of the continuity of his life and his relatedness to others. Out of this sense of continuity and relatedness and responsibility towards others comes the love so well described as "affection and respect, encouragement, order, and support."

227

In the effort to achieve a blend of permanence and progress in peace, two significant features of the religious experience of the United States support the hope of favorable activity by religious groups in the prevention of individual and group violence. In the first place, the experience of religious pluralism in the nation has developed a tradition of understanding and accommodation among the religious groups. Differences have been serious, and hostility often present, but there has been a strong and growing tendency to examine religious differences and differences of values with a high degree of intelligent objectivity. A second promising feature of religious experience is the spirit of ecumenism which has developed remarkably in the past few years. This has emerged from a large number of sources. But one significant source has been the recognition by religious leaders that their common values are more important at a given time than their differences.

In conclusion and in summary, our task is not only to try to prevent or diminish individual and group violence. We must go further and join in a national effort to help people to live together in unity and peace and human dignity. Under God we can achieve a renewed sense of faith in American and Americans, a firm hope for the fulfillment of our personal destinies and the dreams enshrined in the preamble to our Constitution, and an ever-increasing love and respect for our fellow citizens.

APPENDIX 1 ● SUMMARY OF RECOMMENDATIONS

The Commission recommends

INTRODUCTION

1. that "the time is upon us for a reordering of national priorities and for a greater investment of resources in the fulfillment of two basic purposes of our Constitution—to establish justice and to insure domestic tranquility."

2. that "when our participation in the Vietnam War is concluded, we recommend increasing annual general welfare expenditures by about 20 billion dollars (stated in 1968 dollars), partly by reducing military expenditures and partly by use of increased tax revenues resulting from the growth of the Gross National Product."

3. that "as the Gross National Product and tax revenues continue to rise, we should strive to keep military expenditures level (in constant dollars), while general welfare expenditures should continue to increase until essential social goals are achieved."

4. that, to aid in the reordering of national priorities, consideration should be given to establishing a counterpart of the Council of Economic Advisers to develop tools for measuring the comparative effectiveness of social programs, and to produce an "Annual Social Report," comparable to the present Annual Economic Report.

CHAPTER II ● VIOLENT CRIME

5. that "we double our national investment in the criminal justice process, that central offices of criminal justice be created at the metropolitan level, and that complementary private citizen groups be formed." (See Chapter VI for detail.)

6. that cities provide "increased day and night foot-patrols of slum ghetto areas by interracial police teams, in order to discourage street crime against both blacks and whites; improved street lighting to deprive criminals of hiding places from which to ambush victims; increase in numbers and use of community neighborhood centers that provide activity so that city streets are not deserted in early evening hours."

7. that cities undertake "increased police-community relations

activity in slum ghetto areas in order to secure greater understanding of ghetto residents by police, and of police by ghetto residents."

8. that there be "further experimentation with carefully controlled programs that provide low cost drugs such as methadone to addicts who register, so that addicts are not compelled to resort to robbery and burglary in order to meet the needs of their addiction; increased education about the dangers of addictives and other drugs in order to reduce their use."

9. that we devise means of "identification of specific violence-prone individuals for analysis and treatment in order to reduce the likelihood of repetition; provision of special schools for education of young people with violence-prone histories, special psychiatric services and employment programs for parolees and released offenders with a history of violent criminal acts."

10. that "concealable handguns, a common weapon used in violent crimes, must be brought under a system of restrictive licensing." (See Chapter VII for detail.)

11. that we "meet the 1968 Housing Act's goal of a decent home for every American within a decade."

12. that we "take more effective steps to realize the goal, first set in the Employment Act of 1946, of a useful job for all who are able to work."

13. that the Congress "act on current proposals that the federal government pay a basic income to those American families who cannot care for themselves."

14. that "a more sophisticated understanding and appreciation of the complexity of the urban social system is required—and this will in turn require the development of new, dependable and lasting partnerships between government, private industry, social and cultural associations and organized groups of affected citizens."

15. that "the President might profitably convene an Urban Convention of delegates from all the states and major cities, as well as the national government, to advise the nation on the steps that should be taken to increase urban efficiency and accountability through structural changes in local government."

16. that "a primary object of federal urban policy must be to restore the fiscal vitality of urban government, with the particular object of ensuring that local governments normally have enough resources on hand or available to make local initiative in public affairs a reality."

17. that "federal urban policy should seek to equalize the provision of public services as among different jurisdictions in metropolitan areas."

18. that the federal government "assert a specific interest in the movement of people, displaced by technology or driven by poverty, from rural to urban areas, and also in the movement from densely populated central cities to suburban areas."

19. that the federal government must work with state governments to encourage a more progressive, responsible exercise of the state role in the management of urban affairs.

20. that the federal government should "sponsor and subsequently evaluate alternative—in a sense 'competing'—approaches to problems whose methods of solution are imperfectly understood, as is increasingly being done in the areas of medical and legal services for the poor and educational assistance for disadvantaged children."

21. that the federal government should "provide more and better information concerning urban affairs, and should sponsor extensive and sustained research into urban problems."

22. that the federal government discourage further "unrestrained technological exploitation of the resources of land, air and water" and take the lead in encouraging and acting consistently with "a new conservation ethic more appropriate to a crowded urban society."

CHAPTER III • GROUP VIOLENCE

23. that "those of us who find authoritarianism repugnant have a duty to speak out against all who destroy civil order. The time has come when the full weight of community opinion should be felt by those who break the peace or coerce through mob action."

24. that "when group violence occurs, it must be put down by lawful means, including the use of whatever force may be required. But when it occurs—better still, before it occurs—we must permit aggrieved groups to exercise their rights of protest and public presentation of grievances; we must have the perception to recognize injustices when they are called to our attention, and we must have the institutional flexibility to correct those injustices promptly."

25. that police departments throughout the nation "improve their preparations for anticipating, preventing and controlling group disorders, and to that end to study the approaches that have been employed successfully on the three most recent occasions in Washington and Chicago."

26. that "the President seek legislation that would confer jurisdiction upon the United States District Courts to grant injunctions, upon the request of the Attorney General or private persons, against the threatened or actual interference by any person, whether or not under color of state or federal law, with the rights of individuals or groups to freedom of speech, freedom of the press, peaceful assembly and petition for redress of grievances."

27. that "private and governmental institutions encourage the development of competing news media and discourage increased concentration of control over existing media."

231

28. that "the members of the journalism profession continue to improve and re-evaluate their standards and practices, and to strengthen their capacity for creative self-criticism, along the lines suggested in the staff report of our Media Task Force."

CHAPTER V ● ASSASSINATION

29. that there be a "selective expansion of the functions of the Secret Service to include protection of any federal officeholder or candidate who is deemed a temporary but serious assassination risk."

30. that state and local governments provide "improved protection of state and local officeholders and candidates, and strengthened ties between those holding this responsibility and the appropriate federal agencies."

31. that Congress enact legislation requiring the restrictive licensing of handguns. (See Chapter VII for detail.)

32. that the federal government encourage the "development and implementation of devices to detect concealed weapons and ammunition on persons entering public meeting places."

33. that the President (and presidential candidates) minimize the risk of assassination "by carefully choosing speaking opportunities, public appearances, his means of travel to engagements, and the extent to which he gives advance notice of his movements."

34. that the Congress enact "a law that would grant free television time to presidential candidates during the final weeks preceding the national election" in the interest of the safety of Presidents and presidential candidates.

35. that the news media clearly present the complexities of the institutions of government, fully and fairly report the issues these institutions face, and delve into the issues deserving governmental attention.

36. that the news media lessen the attention given to the personal lives of the President and his family and give greater attention to the working nature and limitations of the presidency.

37. that the nation's schools emphasize in American history and social studies the complexities and subtleties of the democratic process; shun the myths by which we have traditionally made supermen of Presidents, "founding fathers," and other prominent persons; and restore to history books a full and frank picture of violence and unrest in America's past, in the hope that children can be educated to repudiate violence and recognize its futility.

CHAPTER VI • VIOLENCE AND
LAW ENFORCEMENT

38. that "the Legal Services Program of the Office of Economic Opportunity, which already has won the strong support of the organized Bar and the enthusiasm of graduating law students across the country, should be continued and expanded."

39. that all states "should provide compensation to attorneys appointed to represent indigent criminal defendants in the state and local courts."

40. that the federal government and states "should provide adequate compensation for lawyers who act in behalf of the poor in civil cases."

41. that the federal government "allocate seed money to a limited number of state and local jurisdictions demonstrating an interest in establishing citizens' grievance agencies."

42. that there should be "extension and vigorous enforcement of the 1965 Voting Rights Act, and intensified efforts to persuade all qualified citizens to vote."

43. that "we should give concrete expression to our concern about crime by a solemn national commitment to double our investment in the administration of justice and the prevention of crime, as rapidly as such an investment can be wisely planned and utilized."

44. that "the Law Enforcement Assistance Administration and the state planning agencies created pursuant to the Omnibus Crime Control and Safe Streets Act take the lead in initiating plans for the creation and staffing of offices of criminal justice in the nation's major metropolitan areas."

45. that we should create and support, with private and public funding, "private citizens' organizations to work as counterparts of the proposed offices of criminal justice in every major city in the nation."

CHAPTER VII • FIREARMS AND VIOLENCE

47. that the National Rifle Association and other private organizations devoted to hunting and sport shooting aid in undertaking a public education campaign to "stress the duties and responsibilities of firearms ownership so that a new awareness of the proper role of firearms in American life can prevail in the more than 30 million homes which possess firearms."

48. that because of the risks of firearms accidents, individual

233

citizens "reflect carefully before deciding that loaded firearms are necessary or desirable for self-defense in their homes."

49. that "further research be undertaken on the relationships between firearms and violence and on the measures that can reduce firearms violence."

50. that "research should be intensified on devices to assist law enforcement personnel in detecting the presence of concealed firearms on the person."

51. that "the federal government should join with private industry to speed the development of an effective non-lethal weapon."

52. that federal legislation be enacted "to encourage the establishment of state licensing systems for handguns. The federal legislation would introduce a federal system of handgun licensing, applicable only to those states which within a four-year period fail to enact a state law that (1) establishes a standard for determining an individual's need for a handgun and for the licensing of an individual who shows such a need and (2) prohibits all others from possessing handguns or buying handgun ammunition."

53. that "a system of federal administrative or judicial review be established to assure that each state system is administered fairly and does not discriminate on the basis of race, religion, national origin, or other unconstitutional grounds."

54. that federal legislation be enacted "to establish minimum standards for state regulation of long guns under which (1) an identification card would be required for long gun owners and purchasers of long gun ammunition (a system similar to that recommended by gun manufacturers) and (2) any person 18 and over would be entitled to such a card, except certain classes of criminals and adjudicated incompetents."

55. that "persons who transfer long guns be required to fill out a single card giving the serial number, type, make, and model of the weapon, the transferee's social security and firearms identification card numbers, the transferor's name and social security number, and the date of the transaction."

56. that "the Gun Control Act of 1968, which is intended to curtail the import of firearms unsuitable for sporting use, should be extended to prohibit domestic production and sale of 'junk guns.' "

57. that "a federal firearms information center should be established to accumulate and store information on firearms and owners received from state agencies; this information would be available to state and federal law enforcement agencies."

58. that "licensed gun dealers should be required by federal statute to adopt and maintain security procedures to minimize theft of firearms."

CHAPTER VIII • VIOLENCE IN TELEVISION ENTERTAINMENT PROGRAMS

59. that "the broadcasting of children's cartoons containing serious, non-comic violence should be abandoned."

60. that "the amount of time devoted to the broadcast of crime, western and action-adventure programs containing violent episodes should be reduced."

61. that "more effective efforts should be made to alter the basic context in which violence is presented in television dramas."

62. that "the members of the television industry should become more actively and seriously involved in research on the effects of violent television programs, and their future policies, standards and practices with regard to entertainment programs should be more responsive to the best evidence provided by social scientists, psychologists, and communications researchers."

63. that "adequate and permanent financing, in the form of a dedicated tax, should be provided for the Corporation for Public Broadcasting so that it may develop the kind of educational, cultural, and dramatic programming not presently provided in sufficient measure by commercial broadcasting."

64. that "parents should make every effort to supervise their children's television viewing and to assert their basic responsibility for the moral development of their children."

65. that parents "should express to the networks and to the local stations both their disapproval of programs which they find objectionable and their support for programs they like. We believe that most families do not want large doses of violence on television, and thus we urge them to make the weight of their opinion felt."

66. that there be "an evaluation of the effectiveness of the new movie-rating system with an emphasis on the question of the validity of the ratings as they relate to violence and the enforcement of the admission standards regarding minors."

CHAPTER IX • CAMPUS DISORDER

67. that in "the university community a consensus should be achieved among students, faculty and administration, and embodied in a code of conduct, concerning both the permissible methods of presenting ideas, proposals and grievances and the responses to be made to deviations from the agreed-upon standards."

68. that "universities should prepare and currently review contingency plans for dealing with campus disorders."

69. that procedures for campus governance and constructive reform should be developed especially by the faculties, to permit more rapid and effective decision-making.

70. that "faculty leaders and administrative officers need to make greater efforts to improve communications both on the campus and with alumni and the general public."

71. that the American people do not let their understandable resentment for the few students who foment and engage in campus disorders lead them to support legislation or executive action which would withhold financial aid from students or universities.

72. that the American people recognize that the campus is a mirror of the "yearnings and weaknesses of the wider society" and that their focus ought to be on "the unfinished task of striving toward the goals of human life that all of us share and that young people admire and respect."

CHAPTER X • CHALLENGING OUR YOUTH

73. that "the Constitution of the United States be amended to lower the voting age for all state and federal elections to eighteen."

74. that there be implementation of all of "President Nixon's proposals for reform of the draft system, which are similar to those recommended in 1967 by the Marshall Commission and by the Clark Panel."

75. that "renewed attention be given to the recommendations of the Marshall Commission for building a greater measure of due process into the exercise of draft board discretion."

76. that "in exercising his power to appoint the members of local draft boards, the President name at least one person under 30 years of age to each local board."

77. that the President "seek legislation to expand the opportunities for youth to engage in both full-time and part-time public service, by providing federal financial support to young people who wish to engage in voluntary, non-military service to their communities and to the nation."

78. that "the President, the Congress, and the federal agencies that normally provide funding for youth programs—notably the office of Economic Opportunity, the Department of Labor, and the Department of Health, Education, and Welfare—take the risks involved in support of additional innovative programs of opportunity for inner-city youth."

79. that "the National Institutes of Health, working with selected universities, greatly expand research on the physical and psychological effects of marijuana use."

80. that "federal and state laws make use and incidental possession of marijuana no more than a misdemeanor until more definitive information about marijuana is at hand and the Congress

and state legislatures have had the opportunity to revise the permanent laws in light of this information."

81. that all our citizens, young and old, try to bridge the "generation gap" by observing the guidelines for understanding and communicating with one another as set forth in Chapter 10.

APPENDIX 2 ● PROGRESS REPORT

submitted by
the National Commission on the Causes and
Prevention of Violence
to President Lyndon B. Johnson,
January 9, 1969.

INTRODUCTION

Mr. President, your charge to this Commission was, in your words, "simple and direct." It was also demanding. You said:

I ask you to undertake a penetrating search for the causes and prevention of violence—a search into our national life, our past as well as our present, our traditions as well as our institutions, our culture, our customs and our laws.

We submit this progress report not as the mature product of our deliberations, with findings and recommendations, but rather as a first look at the multifaceted problem of violence in our nation.

This report will tell you how we have conducted, and are continuing to conduct, our search into the causes and prevention of violence. The organized research effort that we have mounted under your auspices is one which has never before been made in the area of violence by a single entity on a comparable scale.

Our labor is far from finished, and we offer no final judgments or conclusions at this time: the contents of this report are entirely tentative in nature and subject to later revision in light of fuller consideration. But we can at least share with you some of the knowledge we have gained about violence, and we can reaffirm our commitment to carry on our work in a manner consistent with your trust.

237

VIOLENCE IN AMERICA TODAY

The people of America are deeply concerned about violence. They have seen a President struck down by an assassin's bullet, and then seen the assassin himself slain while in police custody. They have seen other assassinations of national figures, and none more devastating than the killings earlier this year, first of a major leader of the civil rights movement, and then the brother of the dead President.

Americans have seen smoke and flames rising over the skylines of their cities as civil disorder has spread across their land—holocausts of rioting, looting, firebombing, and death—a pattern of disorder and destruction repeated in city after city.

Americans have seen students disrupt classes, seize buildings and destroy property at institutions of learning. They have seen young people confronting police at the Pentagon and at draft induction centers across the country. They have seen them heckling, vilifying and even physically abusing public officials. They have heard them shouting obscenities and the strident rhetoric of revolution.

Americans have also come to know the fear of violent crime. They know robberies and assaults have increased sharply in the last few years. They know that only a small fraction of all such crimes is solved.

For many Americans this is the sum and substance of violence.

But many Americans see additional kinds of violence. They see the violence of overseas war. At home, they see the violence of terrorist murders of civil rights workers, of four little black girls bombed to death in a Sunday school class, the violence of police dogs, fire hoses and cattle prods; others see "violence" in discrimination and deprivation, disease, hunger, and rats. They see the violence of capital punishment, of slaughter on the highways, of movies, of radio and television programs, of some professional sports.

In the minds of some Americans all these different sorts of violence overlap. To some, the scourge of rats excuses robberies and riots. To others, the Vietnam War justifies attacks on Selective Service facilities. Others say looting justifies shooting those who seek to escape arrest.

We as a Commission must take into account all these kinds of violence. There are, of course, moral, social, and legal distinctions which can and must be drawn among the different kinds of violence. We cannot intelligently make these vital distinctions by studying only what we would personally regard as "illegitimate

238

violence. We have thus had to find a vantage point from which we can see all the forms of violence and their causes in a perspective broader than that of our individual day-to-day concerns.

VIOLENCE IN PERSPECTIVE

Man, said Aristotle, is a social animal. Man's ability to create social order has enabled him to embrace for human purposes the challenges and opportunities of the environment. The condition of social order came in time to be known as the state, and the rules of its maintenance, the law.

But interwoven in human history with the strand of social order and cooperative behavior is the strand of violence. From *Genesis* and the *Iliad* to this morning's newspaper, the story of civilization has also included the story of man's violence toward other men.

Historically men have not acted on the principle that all violence is to be avoided. Our nation is no exception. Like all others, our society has recognized some uses of violence as necessary and legitimate and some as unacceptable and illegitimate.

All societies must draw moral and legal distinctions between legitimate and illegitimate violence. One traditional and vital function of social order, of the state and its laws, has been to determine in particular cases when violence is legitimate (as in self-defense, discipline of children, maintenance of public order or war against an enemy) and when it is illegitimate (as in violent crime, civil disorder, rebellion or treason).

History records a persistence of challenge to any given social order's determinations of the legitimacy or illegitimacy of violence —sometimes by other social orders, sometimes by individuals within the social order. To most of our forefathers and to virtually all of us today, for example, the American revolution was an act of courage, patriotism, and honor. To most of the English at that time, however, it was treason and revolution. Even the phenomenon of assassination is subject to this relativity of values: our judgment of the wartime plot to murder Hitler is utterly different from our reaction to the murder of the Head of State in our own open and democratic society.

There is, therefore, no universal agreement on a definition of the term "violence" which makes it mean something that is always to be condemned. For purposes of commencing our study, we have defined "violence" simply as the threat or use of force that results, or is intended to result, in the injury or forcible restraint or intimidation of persons, or the destruction or forcible seizure of property.

There is no implicit value judgment in this definition. The maintenance of law and order falls within it, for a policeman may

239

find it necessary in the course of duty to threaten or use force, even to injure or kill an individual. Wars are included within this definition, as is some punishment of children. It also includes police brutality, the violence of the Nazis, and the physical abuse of a child.

This definition has important implications for our understanding of the causes and prevention of the illegitimate violence that our society condemns. For example, it helps us to recognize that illegitimate violence, like most deviant behavior, is on a continuum with and dynamically similar to legitimate violence. The parent who spanks a child may be engaging in legitimate violence, but for the parent to break the child's arm would be illegitimate violence.

A neutral definition of violence also helps us to recognize that some minimum level of illegitimate violence is to be expected in a free and rapidly changing industrial society. Maintaining a system of law enforcement capable of eliminating all illegitimate individual and group violence might so increase the level of legitimate violence that the harm to other values would be intolerable. A totalitarian police state, however efficient its use of violence might be in preserving order, would destroy the freedom of all.

The elimination of all violence in a free society is impossible. But the better control of illegitimate violence in our democratic society is an urgent imperative, and one within our means to accomplish.

The observations return us to a basic point about violence. Violence is but one facet of man living with his fellow men. Throughout history men have sought to control violence, to institutionalize it and to regulate the forms it takes, to make some forms of violence serve their collective needs and desires and to place other forms of violence beyond the pale. Violence becomes sharply separated into the basic categories of "legitimate" and "illegitimate" primarily in the context of a particular human society or cultural tradition.

Man's effort to control violence has been one part, a major part, of his learning to live in society. The phenomenon of violence cannot be understood or evaluated except in the context of that larger effort.

The wisdom of your mandate to us, Mr. President, is confirmed: this Commission's study of violence in contemporary America must, if it is to reach meaningful conclusions, include the study of American society itself, past and present, and the traditions and institutions which accept or condemn the various forms that violence takes in our society.

THE NATIONAL COMMISSION

In planning our work we have thus acted on the premise that to reach an understanding of the social context of contemporary domestic violence, we must conduct a broad-ranging inquiry into many seemingly unrelated subjects. Aware of the dangers of an over-ambitious approach, we have nonetheless concluded that this broad inquiry is the only way to achieve an appropriate perspective on violence in America and a national consensus about the means of its control. That is our task, and our effort must be commensurate with it.

We wish we could promise solutions to all of the problems of illegitimate violence. We cannot. There is no simple answer to the problem of illegitimate violence: no single explanation of its causes, and no single prescription for its control.

The phenomena of illegitimate violence—from robbery to murder, from civil disorder to larger conflicts, from child abuse to suicide—are enormously complicated.

An awesome complexity is concealed in such simple questions as who is violent, when, why, under what conditions, and with what consequences. Recognizing this complexity, however, may well be the first step toward understanding—and toward convincing the American people that they must be uncommonly thoughtful, open-minded, and persevering if the challenge of illegitimate violence in our society is to be met.

Accordingly, we have divided our research work into seven basic areas of detailed inquiry. We have created a staff Task Force to conduct the research effort and produce a staff report in each area. Our Task Forces are:

(1) TASK FORCE ON HISTORICAL AND COMPARATIVE PERSPECTIVES. An overview of the causes, processes and consequences of violence in American history and in other societies.

(2) TASK FORCE ON GROUP VIOLENCE. An analysis of the nature and causes of the violence accompanying contemporary student unrest, opposition to overseas war, and racial militancy, together with a consideration of the responses of social and political institutions to these phenomena.

(3) TASK FORCE ON INDIVIDUAL ACTS OF VIOLENCE. A study of the patterns of violent crime and other individual acts of violence and of the role of biological, psychological, and sociocultural factors.

(4) TASK FORCE ON ASSASSINATION. A world-wide study of violence directed toward politically prominent persons.

(5) TASK FORCE ON FIREARMS. An investigation of the role of firearms in accidents, suicides and crime, and an evaluation of alternative systems of firearms control.

241

(6) TASK FORCE ON THE MEDIA. An investigation of the effects of media portrayals of violence upon the public and of the role of the mass media in the process of violent and non-violent social change.

(7) TASK FORCE ON LAW AND LAW ENFORCEMENT. An assessment of the strengths and weaknesses of our system of justice, and of the steps that can be taken to increase respect for the rule of law.

The dimensions of the research are suggested by the fact that the personnel of the Task Forces and the central staff numbers approximately 70, and that more than 140 research projects and special analyses have been undertaken for the Task Forces by outside experts and scholars.

In addition to these seven basic Task Forces, an eighth Task Force consisting of a number of Study Teams, has been investigating recent violent events on which no other adequate factual record has yet been made. The reports of these Teams become part of the research base of the relevant Task Force and ultimately of the Commission itself.

While the work of the Task Forces has been proceeding, the Commission has met almost weekly, has studied scores of reports and articles, and has held a series of hearings and conferences in which we received the views of more than 150 public officials, scholars, experts, religious leaders and private citizens. The testimony and discussions have been valuable; from them we have gained a deeper understanding of attitudes and motivations than we would otherwise have had.

THEMES OF CHALLENGE

Attached to this progress report is a staff memorandum describing the work of our Task Forces in carrying out the research assignments we have set forth.* The final reports of our Task Forces are now becoming available for study by the Commission along with other materials. We will present our final conclusions and recommendations in the spring of the year.** Meanwhile, however, from preliminary reports, testimony, and consultation, we have identified certain themes of challenge for the leaders and the people of America. Among these are the following:

First: As we have noted, not all violence in our society is illegitimate. Indeed, a major function of society is the organization and legitimation of violence in the interest of maintaining society itself. Unfortunately, however, the existence of legitimate violence—from a shooting in lawful self-defense through international violence in the form of warfare—sometimes provides rationalization for those

---

*Not reprinted. 50 pp.
**The Commission's life was subsequently extended to December 10, 1969.

who would achieve ends or express grievances through illegitimate violence.

Second: Violence by some individuals may result in part from a deranged mind or abnormal biological make-up. Experts agree, however, that most persons who commit violence—criminal or non-criminal—are basically no different from others, and their behavior is the result of the complex interaction of their biology and life experience. Scholars observe that man has no instinct or trait born within that directs aggression in a specific way. He does have, from birth, the potential for violence. He also has the capacity for creative, constructive activity and for the rejection of violence. Insofar as life experience teaches individuals violence, the incidence of violence is subject to modification, control, and prevention through conscious changes in man's environment.

Third: Historically, when groups or individuals have been unable to attain the quality of life to which they believe they are entitled, the resulting discontent and anger have often culminated in violence. Violent protest today—from middle-class students to the inhabitants of the black ghettos and the white ghettos—has occurred in part because the protesters believe that they cannot make their demands felt effectively through normal, approved channels and that "the system," for whatever reasons, has become unresponsive to them.

Fourth: Progress in meeting the demands of those seeking social change does not always reduce the level of violence. It may cause those who feel threatened by change to engage in counter-violence against those seeking to shift the balance. And the pace of change may be slower and more uneven than the challenging group is willing to tolerate. We see these social forces at work in our country today. After several decades of rapid social change, we have better housing, education, medical care and career opportunities for most groups in our society than at any time in the past. Nonetheless, these advances have been uneven, and what we have so far achieved falls short of the needs or expectations of many. Impatience is felt on all sides, and our social order is subject to escalated demand both from those who desire greater stability and from those who desire greater social change.

Fifth: The key to much of the violence in our society seems to lie with the young. Our youth account for an ever-increasing percentage of crime, greater than their increasing percentage of the population. The thrust of much of the group protest and collective violence—on the campus, in the ghettos, in the streets—is provided by our young people. It may be here, with tomorrow's generation, that much of the emphasis of our studies and the national response should lie.

Sixth: The existence of a large number of firearms in private hands and a deep-seated tradition of private firearms ownership are complicating factors in the task of social control of violence.

243

Seventh: Additional complications arise from the high visibility of both violence and social inequalities, resulting from the widespread impact of mass communications media. The powerful impact of the media may aggravate the problems of controlling violence; on the other hand, the media may be one of our most useful social agents for explaining all elements of our society to another and achieving a consensus as to the need for social change that may help to reduce levels of violence.

Eighth: Social control of violence through law depends in large measure on the perceived legitimacy of the law and the society it supports. Persons tend to obey the law when the groups with which they identify disapprove those who violate it. Group attitudes about lawful behavior depend, in turn, on the group's views of the justice provided by the legal order and of the society which created it. The justice and decency of the social order thus are not simply desirable embellishments. On the contrary, a widespread conviction of the essential justice and decency of the social order is an indispensable condition of civil peace in a free society.

Ninth: Our system of criminal justice suffers from an under-investment of resources at every level—police, courts and corrections. Partly because of this accumulated deficit, the criminal justice system is neither as strong nor as fair as it should be—and consequently it has failed to control illegitimate violence as well as it should.

Tenth: The social control of violence does not depend merely on the conduct of those who attack or defend the social order. It depends also on the attitudes, cooperation, and commitments of the community—of our political, religious, educational, and other social institutions and of citizens in every walk of life. Violence in our society affects us all. Its more effective control requires the active engagement and commitment of every citizen.

STEPS TOWARD CONTROL

Facing these challenges, we as a nation have been taking important additional steps to improve the ability of our social order to control violence. Previous commissions and study groups which you appointed, Mr. President, have provided much of the knowledge the nation needs to move ahead. Fundamental contributions have already been made by the President's Commission on Law Enforcement and Administration of Justice and the National Advisory Commission on Civil Disorders. Moreover, acting in response to your initiatives, the Congress has begun to lay the legislative foundation for effective action on a number of fronts critical to the complex problem of violence.

Title I of the Omnibus Crime Control and Safe Streets Act of 1968 provides the groundwork for substantial research and financial

244

assistance in aid of local law enforcement. The Juvenile Delinquency Prevention and Control Act will stimulate and support expansion of youth opportunity and youth rehabilitation programs. The Gun Control Act of 1968 makes a necessary contribution to effective firearms control. The Model Cities Act, the Housing Act of 1968, the Civil Rights enactments of recent years and the employment program of the National Alliance of Businessmen have accelerated the process of social change believed necessary to remove some of the causes of violence in our midst.

All these measures are important steps along the road to a more peaceful, prosperous and equitable society. They confirm the judgment of the Commission on Law Enforcement and Administration of Justice that the Nation can, if it will, take steps to control crime and other forms of violence. Much more, of course, remains to be done. We hope the work of our Commission will make an equally significant contribution toward the completion of this unfinished task.

APPENDIX 3 ● CONSULTANTS TO THE COMMISSION

1 ● ADVISORY PANEL

Professor Orville Brim, Jr.	Russell Sage Foundation
Professor Morris Janowitz	University of Chicago
Professor Benjamin Quarles	Morgan State College
Professor Leon Radzinowicz	Cambridge University, Great Britain
Professor Neil J. Smelser	University of California at Berkeley
Professor John P. Spiegel	Brandeis University
Professor James Vorenberg	Harvard University
Professor Richard C. Wade	University of Chicago
Professor Stanton Wheeler	Yale University
Professor James Q. Wilson	Harvard University

245

Berkowitz, Leonard	University of Wisconson, Madison
Bettelheim, Bruno	Orthogenic School, Chicago
Blumstein, Alfred	Institute for Defense Analysis
Brown, Bertram	Deputy Director, NIMH
Burdman, Milton	California Department of Corrections
Conrad, John	Department of Justice, Washington, D.C.
Cressey, Donald R.	University of Washington, Seattle
Daniels, David N.	Stanford University
Donald, David	The Johns Hopkins University
Delgado, Jose M. R.	Yale University
English, Joseph	Office of Economic Opportunity
Etzioni, Amitai	Columbia University
Frantz, Joe B.	White House Staff
Freedman, Lawrence Z.	University of Chicago
Goldstein, Joseph	Yale University Law School
Gude, Edward W.	Northwestern University
Gurr, Ted Robert	Princeton University
Hackney, Sheldon	Princeton University
Horn, Daniel	United States Public Health Service
Janowitz, Morris	University of Chicago
Janis, Irving	Yale University
Klapper, Joseph T.	CBS Research Department
Kornhauser, William	University of California, Berkeley
Larsen, Otto N.	University of Washington, Seattle
Mark, Vernon H.	Boston City Hospital, Boston, Mass.
Martin, John M.	Fordham University
Menninger, Karl	Menninger Clinic
Morris, Norval	University of Chicago Law School
Ottenberg, B. Perry	Group for the Advancement of Psychiatry, Philadelphia, Pa.
Pool, Ithiel deSola	Massachusetts Institute of Technology
Potter, David M.	Stanford University
Redl, Fritz	Wayne University, Detroit
Rossi, Peter H.	The Johns Hopkins University
Rostow, Edna	Office of Economic Opportunity
Rubenstein, Richard E.	Adlai E. Stevenson Institute
Ruth, Henry S., Jr.	University of Pennsylvania
Satten, Joseph	Menninger Foundation, Topeka, Kansas
Selznick, Philip	University of California, Berkeley
Shah, Saleem	National Institute of Mental Health
Spiegel, John	Brandeis University
Taft, Philip	Brown University
Tilly, Charles	University of Toronto, Toronto, Canada

Toch, Hans	State University of New York, Albany
Vorenberg, James	Harvard University
Wade, Richard C.	University of Chicago
Wilson, James Q.	Harvard University
Wolfgang, Marvin E.	University of Pennsylvania

3 • WITNESSES—HEARINGS

September 18, 1968

Ramsey Clark, Attorney General
John Edgar Hoover, Director, Federal Bureau of Investigation
Benjamin Quarles, Professor of History, Morgan State College
James Q. Wilson, Professor of Government, Harvard University
Seymour L. Halleck, Professor of Psychiatry, University of Wisconsin

September 19, 1968

Albert Bandura, Professor of Psychology, Stanford University
Neil Smelser, Professor of Sociology, University of California at Berkeley
Clarence Schrag, Chairman, Sociology Department, University of Southern California
Leonard Berkowitz, Chairman, Department of Psychology, University of Wisconsin
Robin Fox, Professor of Anthropology, Rutgers University

September 25, 1968

Nicholas Katzenbach, Under-Secretary of State, former Attorney General
James Vorenberg, Director, President's Commission on Law Enforcement and Administration Justice
Daniel Glaser, Professor of Sociology, Rutgers University
Ronald H. Beattie, Chief, California Bureau of Criminal Statistics
Jerome J. Daunt, Criminal Records Division, Federal Bureau of Investigation

September 26, 1968

Leon Radzinowicz, Institute of Criminology, Cambridge, England
Herbert J. Miller, District of Columbia Crime Commission
Howard Willens, District of Columbia Crime Commission
Joseph Satten, M.D., Menninger Foundation

October 2, 1968

James Kirkham, Co-Director, Task Force on Assassination
Ivo Feierabend, San Diego State College

247

James J. Rowley, Director, United States Secret Service

Thomas Kelly, Protective Intelligence, United States Secret Service

Charles Humpstone, Deputy Special Assistant to the Secretary of the Treasury

October 3, 1968

David Abrahamsen, M.D., Psychiatrist

David A. Rothstein, M.D., Psychiatrist

Richard Maxwell Brown, Professor of History, College of William and Mary

Dore Schary, National Chairman, Anti-Defamation League

October 9, 1968

Sheldon Cohen, Commission, Internal Revenue Service

Norval Morris, Professor of Law, University of Chicago

Arthur Sills, Attorney General, State of New Jersey

Luis Neco, New York Police Department

October 10, 1968

Elliot Richardson, Attorney General, Massachusetts

Franklin E. Zimring, Jr., Director of Research, Task Force on Firearms

Paul A. Beuke, President, Colt's Firearms Division, Colt Industries, Inc.

Philip H. Burdett, Vice President, Remington Arms Company, Inc.

October 16, 1968

Bradley Greenberg, Professor of Journalism, Michigan State

Joseph Klapper, Director, Office of Social Research, Columbia Broadcasting System

Leonard Berkowitz, Professor of Psychology, University of Wisconsin

Percy Tannenbaum, Annenberg School of Communication, University of Pennsylvania

George Gerbner, Dean, Annenberg School of Communication, University of Pennsylvania

October 17, 1968

Otto Larsen, Professor of Sociology, University of Washington

Alfred R. Schneider, Vice President, American Broadcasting Company

Robert Kasmire, Vice President, National Broadcasting Company

Dr. Leo Bogart, American Newspaper Publishers Association

October 23, 1968

Henry Mayer, Co-Chairman of the Faculty-Student Committee, University of California at Berkeley

248

Tom Hayden, Students for a Democratic Society

Kingman Brewster, President, Yale University

Sam Brown, Youth coordinator for Senator Eugene McCarthy's presidential campaign

Irving L. Horowitz, Editor, *Trans-Action*

October 24, 1968

Gordon Misner, Acting Associate Professor of Criminology, University of California at Berkeley

John Harrington, President, Fraternal Order of Police, Philadelphia

David Craig, Public Safety Commissioner, Pittsburgh

David Ginsburg, Former Executive Director, National Advisory Commission on Civil Disorders

October 25, 1968

Louis J. Masotti, Director, Cleveland Study Team

Herman Blake, Assistant Professor of Sociology, University of California at Santa Cruz

Price Cobbs, M.D., Psychiatrist, San Francisco

Sterling Tucker, Director of Field Services, Urban League

October 30, 1968

Patrick V. Murphy, Former Administrator, Law Enforcement Assistance Agency

Arlen Specter, District Attorney, Philadelphia

Myrl Alexander, Director, United States Bureau of Prisons

William T. Gossett, President, American Bar Association

Francis Allen, Dean, University of Michigan Law School

October 31, 1968

Norman Dorsen, Professor of Law, New York University Law School

Robert Carter, General Counsel, NAACP

Anthony Amsterdam, Professor of Law, University of Pennsylvania Law School

Paul Chevigny, American Civil Liberties Union

Ronald Dworkin, Professor of Law, Yale University Law School

November 1, 1968

Carl E. Sanders, Former Governor of Georgia

Richard Hatcher, Mayor of Gary, Indiana (submitted statement)

Joseph L. Alioto, Mayor of San Francisco (submitted statement)

December 18, 1968

Robert MacNeil, British Broadcasting Corporation

Ben H. Bagdikian, Director, News Media Study, RAND Corporation

Norman Isaacs, Executive Editor, *Louisville Courier-Journal and Times*
John F. Dille, Jr., President, Communicana Group

December 19, 1968

Jack Valenti, President, Motion Picture Association of America
Rosel H. Hyde, Chairman, Federal Communications Commission
Lawrence S. Kubie, M.D., Psychiatrist, Baltimore
Nicholas Johnson, Commissioner, Federal Communications Commission
James J. Casey, Assistant U.S. Attorney for the Northern District of Illinois
Thomas A. Foran, U.S. Attorney for the Northern District of Illinois

December 20, 1968

Leonard H. Goldenson, President, American Broadcasting Company, Inc.
Elmer W. Lower, President, American Broadcasting Company News
Frank Stanton, President, Columbia Broadcasting System Inc.
Richard Salant, President, Columbia Broadcasting System News
Julian Goodman, President, National Broadcasting Company, Inc.
Reuven Frank, President, National Broadcasting Company News
Donald Durgin, President, National Broadcasting Company Television Network

4 • CONFERENCE ON YOUTH AND VIOLENCE

November 6, 1968

Dr. Max Bear	B'Nai B'rith Youth Organization
Rabbi Ervin Blank and Rabbi Hirsch	Synagogue Council of America
Monsignor Laurence Corcoran	National Conference on Catholic Charities
Father Joseph Fitzpatrick	Fordham University
Moe Hoffman	National Jewish Welfare Board
Ernest A. Villas	Greek Orthodox Archdiocese of North and South America
Dr. Elmer Witt	Church Youth Research
Jack Agueros	Urban Association, New York City
Rev. Jesse F. Anderson	Washington, D.C.
Robert L. Brooks	Boy Scouts of America
Marshall Brown	Neighborhood Development Youth Programs, Washington, D.C.
Frederick D. Carl	YMCA
Mrs. C. E. Cortner	Girl Scouts of America

Rev. David Eaton	Federal City College
A. Boyd Hinds	Boys' Club of America
Barbara McGarry	American Parents Committee
Monsignor James J. Murray	Catholic Archdiocese of New York
Theodore Parrish	Youth Opportunities Center, Boston, Mass.
William W. Barr	Department of Public Welfare
Aaron Bodin	Department of Labor
Virginia Burns	Department of Health, Education and Welfare
Dr. Joseph Douglas	1970 White House Conference on Children and Youth
Daniel Lang	Department of Health, Education and Welfare
Lawrence Pierce	New York State Narcotics Addiction Control Center
Dennis Porter	Office of Economic Opportunity
Dr. Catharine V. Richards	Children's Bureau, Department of Health, Education and Welfare
Gerald Whitman	Department of Health, Education and Welfare
John Irving	National Council of Juvenile Court Judges
George Jones	Task Force on Urban Education

5 ● CONFERENCES WITH UNIVERSITY PRESIDENTS

Spring, 1968

Dr. Morris Abram	Brandeis University
Dr. Kingman Brewster	Yale University
Dr. Mary Bunting	Radcliffe College
Dr. James P. Dixon	Antioch College
Dr. Ralph A. Dungan	Chancellor, Department of Education, New Jersey
Dr. Gaylord P. Harnwell	University of Pennsylvania
Dr. Richard A. Harvill	University of Arizona
Dr. Vivian W. Henderson	Clark College
Dr. David Henry	University of Illinois
Rev. Theodore Hesburgh	University of Notre Dame
Dr. Roger Heyns	Chancellor, University of California at Berkeley
Dr. Martin Jenkins	Morgan State College
Dr. Howard Johnson	Massachusetts Institute of Technology
Dr. William Rea Keast	Wayne State College
Dr. Edward Levi	University of Chicago
Dr. Maurice B. Mitchell	University of Denver
Dr. James Perkins	Cornell University

251

Dr. Kenneth D. Roose   Vice President, American Council on Education

Dr. Keith Spalding   Franklin & Marshall College

Rev. Michael P. Walsh   Fordham University

APPENDIX 4 ● TASK FORCE REPORTS

PREFACE*

From the earliest days of organization, the Chairman, Commissioners and Executive Director of the National Commission on the Causes and Prevention of Violence recognized the importance of research in accomplishing the task of analyzing the many facets of violence in America. As a result of this recognition, the Commission has enjoyed the receptivity, encouragement and cooperation of a large part of the scientific community in this country. Because of the assistance given in varying degrees by scores of specialists here and abroad, these Task Force Reports represent some of the most elaborate work ever done on the major topics they cover.

The Commission was formed on June 10, 1968. By the end of the month, the Executive Director had gathered together a small cadre of capable young lawyers from various federal agencies and law firms around the country. That group was later augmented by partners borrowed from some of the nation's major law firms who served without compensation. Such a professional group can be assembled more quickly than university faculty because the latter are not accustomed to quick institutional shifts after making firm commitments of teaching or research at a particular locus. Moreover, the legal profession has long had a major and traditional role in federal agencies and commissions.

In early July a group of fifty persons from the academic disciplines of sociology, psychology, psychiatry, political science, history, law and biology were called together on short notice to discuss for two days how best the Commission and its staff might proceed to analyze violence. The enthusiastic response of these scientists came at a moment when our nation was still suffering from the tragedy of Senator Kennedy's assassination.

It was clear from that meeting that the scholars were prepared to join research analysis and action, interpretation and policy. They

*This Preface appears in each of the staff research reports.

were eager to present to the American people the best available data, to bring reason to bear where myth had prevailed. They cautioned against simplistic solutions, but urged application of what is known in the service of sane policies for the benefit of the entire society.

Shortly thereafter the position of Director of Research was created. We assumed the role as a joint undertaking, with common responsibilities. Our function was to enlist social and other scientists to join the staff, to write papers, act as advisors or consultants, and engage in new research. The decentralized structure of the staff, which at its peak numbered 100, required research coordination to reduce duplication and to fill in gaps among the original seven separate Task Forces. In general, the plan was for each Task Force to have a pair of directors, one a social scientist, one a lawyer. In a number of instances, this formal structure bent before the necessities of available personnel but in almost every case the Task Force work program relied on both social scientists and lawyers for its successful completion. In addition to our work with the seven original Task Forces, we provided consultation for the work of the eighth "Investigative" Task Force, formed originally to investigate the disorders at the Democratic and Republican National Conventions and the civil strife in Cleveland during the summer of 1968 and eventually expanded to study campus disorders at several colleges and universities.

Throughout September and October and in December of 1968 the Commission held about thirty days of public hearings related expressly to each of the Task Force areas. About one hundred witnesses testified, including many scholars, government officials, corporate executives as well as militants and activists of various persuasions. In addition to the hearings, the Commission and the staff met privately with scores of persons including college presidents, religious and youth leaders and experts in such areas as the media, victim compensation and firearms. The staff participated actively in structuring and conducting those hearings and conferences and in the questioning of witnesses.

As Research Directors, we participated in structuring the strategy of design for each Task Force, but we listened more than directed. We have known the delicate details of some of the statistical problems and computer runs. We have argued over philosophy and syntax; we have offered bibliographical and other resource materials, we have written portions of reports and copyedited others. In short, we know the enormous energy and devotion, the long hours and accelerated study that members of each Task Force have invested in their labors. In retrospect we are amazed at the high caliber and quantity of the material produced, much of which truly represents the best in research and scholarship. About 150 separate papers and projects were involved in the work culminating in the Task Force Reports. We feel less that we have

253

orchestrated than that we have been members of the orchestra, and that together with the entire staff we have helped compose a repertoire of current knowledge about the enormously complex subject of this Commission.

That scholarly research is predominant in the work here presented is evident in the product. But we should like to emphasize that the roles which we occupied were not limited to scholarly inquiry. The Directors of Research were afforded an opportunity to participate in all Commission meetings. We engaged in discussions at the highest levels of decision-making, and had great freedom in the selection of scholars, in the control of research budgets, and in the direction and design of research. If this was not unique, it is at least an uncommon degree of prominence accorded research by a National Commission.

There were three major levels to our research pursuit: (1) summarizing the state of our present knowledge and clarifying the lacunae where more or new research should be encouraged; (2) accelerating known on-going research so as to make it available to the Task Forces; (3) undertaking new research projects within the limits of time and funds available. Coming from a University setting where the pace in research is more conducive to reflection and quiet hours analyzing data, we at first thought that completing more meaningful new research within a matter of months was most unlikely. But the need was matched by the talent and enthusiasm of the staff, and the Task Forces very early had begun enough new projects to launch a small university with a score of doctoral theses. It is well to remember also that in each volume here presented, the research reported is on full public display and thereby makes the staff more than usually accountable for their products.

One of the very rewarding aspects of these research undertakings has been the experience of minds trained in the law mingling and meshing, sometimes fiercely arguing, with other minds trained in behavioral science. The organizational structure and the substantive issues of each Task Force required members from both groups. Intuitive judgment and the logic of argument and organization blended, not always smoothly, with the methodology of science and statistical reasoning. Critical and analytical faculties were sharpened as theories confronted facts. The arrogance neither of ignorance nor of certainty could long endure the doubts and questions of interdisciplinary debate. Any sign of approaching the priestly pontification of scientism was quickly dispelled in the matrix of mutual criticism. Years required for the normal accumulation of experience were compressed into months of sharing ideas with others who had equally valid but differing perspectives. Because of this process, these volumes are much richer than they otherwise might have been.

Partly because of the freedom which the Commission gave to

254

the Directors of Research and the Directors of each Task Force, and partly to retain the full integrity of the research work in publication, these Reports of the Task Forces are in the posture of being submitted to and received by the Commission. These are volumes published under the authority of the Commission, but they do not necessarily represent the views or the conclusions of the Commission. The Commission is presently at work producing its own Report, based in part on the materials presented to it by the Task Forces. Commission members have, of course, commented on earlier drafts of each Task Force, and have caused alterations by reason of the cogency of their remarks and insights. But the final responsibility for what is contained in these volumes rests fully and properly on the research staffs who labored on them.

In this connection, we should like to acknowledge the special leadership of the Chairman, Dr. Milton S. Eisenhower, in formulating and supporting the principle of research freedom and autonomy under which this work has been conducted.

We note, finally, that these volumes are in many respects incomplete and tentative. The urgency with which papers were prepared and then integrated into Task Force Reports rendered impossible the successive siftings of data and argument to which the typical academic article or volume is subjected. The reports have benefited greatly from the counsel of our colleagues on the Advisory Panel, and from much debate and revision from within the staff. It is our hope that the total work effort of the Commission staff will be the source and subject of continued research by scholars in the several disciplines, as well as a useful resource for policy-makers. We feel certain that public policy and the disciplines will benefit greatly from such further work.

To the Commission, and especially to its Chairman, for the opportunity they provided for complete research freedom, and to the staff for its prodigious and prolific work, we, who were intermediaries and servants to both, are most grateful.

James F. Short, Jr.,
Marvin E. Wolfgang,
Co-Directors of Research

Violence in America:
Historical and Comparative Perspectives

(Washington, D.C.: Government Printing Office, 1969)
(Vols. 1 & 2, NCCPV Staff Study Series)

(Available in commercial editions
from Frederick A. Praeger (cloth) and Bantam Books (paperback)

Report of the Task Force on Historical and
Comparative Perspectives; Hugh Davis Graham
and Ted Robert Gurr, Co-Directors.

STAFF
Frances L. Adams
Susan G. Lipsitch
Carol J. Voit

CONTRIBUTORS

Robin Brooks	Roger Lane
Richard Maxwell Brown	Sheldon G. Levy
George Carstairs	Kenneth Lynn
James P. Comer	John M. Martin
James C. Davies	August Meier
Ivo K. Feierabend	Betty A. Nesvold
Rosalind L. Feierabend	Ben C. Roberts
Joe B. Frantz	Philip Ross
Fred P. Graham	Elliot Rudwick
Edward W. Gude	Bernard J. Siegel
Sheldon Hackney	Philip Taft
Louis Hartz	Raymond Tanter
Michael C. Hudson	Charles Tilly
Morris Janowitz	

CONTENTS

256

257

The Politics of Protest:
Violent Aspects of Protest and Confrontation

(Washington, D.C.: Government Printing Office, 1969)
(Vol. 3, NCCPV Staff Study Series)

Report of the Task Force on Group Violence; Jerome H. Skolnick, Director.

STAFF

GENERAL COUNSEL
Ira M. Heyman

ASSOCIATE DIRECTOR
Anthony Platt

ASSISTANT GENERAL COUNSEL
Edmund C. Ursin

ASSISTANT DIRECTOR
Elliott Currie

ACCOUNTANT
Herbert Kalman, C.P.A.

RESEARCH ASSISTANT TO DIRECTOR
Richard C. Speiglman

RESEARCH ASSISTANTS

Charles Carey
Howard Erlanger
Nancy L. Leonard

Sam McCormick
Alan Meyerson

SUPPORTING RESEARCH ASSISTANTS

Susan Currier
Howard Schechter

Nelson Soltman
H. Frederick Wilkie, III

SUPPORTING OFFICE STAFF

Mary Alden
Jayne Craddock
Judy Dewing
Sally Duensing
Sue Feinstein

Judy Foosaner
Vera Nielson
Elizabeth Okamura
Melba Sharp
Betty Wallace

OFFICE STAFF

Kathleen Courts
Gabriella Duncan
Emily Knapp

Wendy Mednick
Sharon Overton
Charlotte Simmons

258

STAFF CONSULTANTS

CONTENTS

Crimes of Violence

(Washington, D.C.: Government Printing Office, 1970)
(Vols. 11, 12 & 13, NCCPV Staff Study Series)

Report of the Task Force on Individual Acts of Violence; Donald J. Mulvihill and Melvin Tumin, Co-Directors; Assistant Director, Lynn A. Curtis.

STAFF

RESEARCH STAFF

Elizabeth M. Schweitzer
Candice H. Conrad
Kenneth E. DeMario
Patricia D. Gurne
Olympia T. Kollias
James H. McGregor

Peter J. Ognibene
Marguerite C. Pellerin
Robert S. Tigner
Richard A. Weiner
Judith A. Winston

SECRETARIAL STAFF

Patricia Horan
Loretta A. Wilbourn
Delores L. Hampton
Evelyn S. Spaulding

Nancy L. Clarke
Mary M. Greeley
Mamie L. Hale

STAFF CONSULTANTS

Seymour Baxter
Richard Blum
Paul Bohannon
Richard Bucher
Virginia Burns
Bernard Chodorkoff
Jonathan O. Cole
Robert L. Conner
Herbert L. Costner
Jose M. R. Delgado
Ithiel de Sola Poole
Laurence Dizmang
LaMar Empey
Frank R. Ervin
Clinton Fink
Mark Furstenberg

Gilbert Geis
David G. Gil
Eli Ginzberg
Robert Gold
William Goode
Mark Haller
James Johnson
Robert Johnston
Samuel Klausner
Malcolm Klein
Seymour Levine
John R. Lion
Perry London
Gerald McClearn
Turner McLardy
Edwin I. Megargee

260

CONTENTS

261

262

Assassination and Political Violence

(Washington, D.C.: Government Printing Office, 1969)
(Vol. 8, NCCPV Staff Study Series)

*Report of the Task Force on Assassination; James F.
Kirkham, Sheldon G. Levy, and William J. Crotty,
Co-Directors*

STAFF

Vicky M. Clinton
Anne S. Crossman
Robert C. Herr

James McEvoy, III
Robert C. Nurick
Linda G. Stone

CONSULTANTS

David Abrahamsen
Henry S. Alberts
Inkeri Auttila
Jerome Bakst
Joseph Bensman
Rae L. Blumberg
Richard Maxwell Brown
Harold Deutsch
Ivo K. Feierabend
Rosalind Feierabend
Lawrence Z. Freedman

Jerry A. Gaines
Clinton E. Grimes
Judith H. Grimes
Feliks Gross
Murray C. Havens
Lynne Iglitzin
Franz N. Jaggar
Carl Leiden
Seymour M. Lipset
Klas Lithner
Betty A. Nesvold

Harold L. Nieburg
David A. Rothstein
Richard E. Rubenstein
Dore Schary
Carl Scheingold
Karl M. Schmitt
Rita J. Simon
James R. Soukup

Joyce A. Sween
Denis Szabo
Daniel Tretiak
Seymour D. Vestermark, Jr.
Doris Y. Wilkinson
Peter B. Young
Edward A. Ziegenhagen

CONTENTS

Firearms and Violence In American Life

(Washington, D.C.: Government Printing Office, 1969)
(Vol. 7, NCCPV Staff Study Series)

Report of the Task Force on Firearms;
George D. Newton, Jr., Director;
Franklin E. Zimring, Director of Research

264

STAFF

Harry Barnett
E. Asa Bates, Jr.
Vivian S. Bullock
Joan A. Burt
Margaret S. Enright
Leigh S. Hallingby
William Helmer

Jean M. Horan
James G. Hunter, Jr.
Joel Koford
Elizabeth F. Koury
Harry G. Sklarsky
Susan Watts
Claire M. Whitaker

STAFF CONSULTANTS

C. David Anderson
Jack J. Basil
William D. Behan
Thomas F. Casey
Mary A. Chorba
Jerome J. Daunt
Barnes Ellis
Robert H. Haynes
Richard Hallman

John M. Linsenmeyer
Lawrence Margolis
Jack W. Osburn, Jr.
Peter Rothenberg
R. Dean Smith
Quinn Tamm
Cecil M. Wolfe
Frederick S. York
Hans Zeisel

CONTENTS

265

Mass Media and Violence

(Washington, D.C.: Government Printing Office, 1969)
(Vol. 9, NCCPV Staff Study Series)

Report of the Task Force on the media;
Robert K. Baker and Sandra J. Ball, Co-Directors;
David L. Lange, General Counsel.

STAFF

F. Clifton Berry, Jr.
Paul L. Briand, Jr.
Jewel I. Boyd
Deborah N. Cutler
Steffen W. Graae

Carolyn M. McClelland
Jean C. Peterson
Linda J. Schacht
Philip W. Tone, Special Counsel

STAFF CONSULTANTS

Gary L. Amo
Leonard Berkowitz
Monica Blumenthal
Leo Bogart
William R. Catton, Jr.
Peter Clarke
I. William Cole
Seymour Feshbach

George Gerbner
Walter Gerson
Bradley Greenberg
Richard Goranson
Jack B. Haskins
Jay W. Jensen
Harry Kalven
Otto Larsen

Jack Lyle
Eleanor Maccoby
Richard H. Nagasawa
Marsha A. O'Bannon
Theodore Peterson

William L. Rivers
Milton Rokeach
Arline H. Sakuma
Alberta E. Siegel

CONTENTS

267

Hearings On Mass Media and Violence

(Washington, D.C.: Government Printing Office, 1969)
(Vol. 9–A, NCCPV Staff Study Series)

Edited by *Paul L. Briand, Jr.*

Included is the testimony of:

Professor Bradley Greenberg, Department of Communications, Michigan State University

Dr. Joseph Klapper, Director of Social Research, CBS

Professor Leonard Berkowitz, Department of Psychology, University of Wisconsin.

Dr. Percy Tannenbaum, Annenberg School of Communications, University of Pennsylvania

Dean George Gerbner, Annenberg School of Communications, University of Pennsylvania

Professor Otto Larsen, Department of Sociology, University of Washington

Alfred R. Schneider, Vice-President and Assistant to the Executive Vice-President, ABC

Robert D. Kasmire, Vice-President, Corporate Information, NBC

Dr. Leo Bogart, Executive Vice-President and General Manager, Bureau of Advertising, American Newspaper Publisher's Association

Robert MacNeil, BBC

Ben H. Bagdikian, Director, News Media Study at RAND

Normal E. Isaacs, Vice-President and Executive Editor, *Louisville Courier-Journal and Times*

John F. Dille, Jr., President, Communicana Group

Jack Valenti, President, Motion Picture Association of America

Rosel Hyde, Chairman, FCC

Lawrence S. Kubie, MD, Psychiatrist

Nicholas Johnson, Commissioner, FCC

James J. Casey, Assistant U.S. Attorney, Northern District of Illinois

268

Thomas A. Foran, U.S. Attorney, Northern District of Illinois
Leonard Goldenson, President, ABC
Elmer Lower, President, ABC News
Frank Stanton, President, CBS
Richard Salant, President, CBS News
Julian Goodman, President, NBC
Reuven Frank, President, NBC News
Donald Durgin, President, NBC Television Network

Law and Order Reconsidered

(Washington, D.C.: Government Printing Office, 1969)
(Vol. 10, NCCPV Staff Study Series)

Report of the Task Force on Law and Enforcement;
James S. Campbell, Joseph R. Sahid, and
David P. Stang, Co-Directors.*

CONTRIBUTORS

Richard Bonnie	Shlomo Shoham
Jose Luis Cuevas	Arthur B. Shostak
William A. Dobrovir	Linda R. Singer
Jon Ellertson	Judith Toth
Dorsey D. Ellis, Jr.	Ralph W. Tyler
Joseph P. Fitzpatrick, S.J.	Patricia M. Wald
Daniel J. Freed	Robert F. Wald
Monrad G. Paulsen	Charles Whitebread
David J. Saari	Ronald A. Wolk

ADVISORS

Silvia Bacon	Herbert L. Packer
John Conrad	Val Peterson
Sanford H. Kadish	James Q. Wilson
Yale Kamisar	

RESEARCH ASSISTANTS

Dale L. Smith, Chief Assistant	Robert A. Crittenden
Danial J. Boyle	Thomas R. Jolly
Thomas R. Callahan	John Lawrence Manning, Jr.
William Edward Callis	

*During the first part of the Commission's existence this Task Force was directed by George L. Saunders, Jr. and Leroy D. Clark.

269

SECRETARIAL ASSISTANTS

Carol A. Honus, Chief Assistant
Frances L. Adams
Mildred F. Dolan

Cecelia Roots
Martha Ann Younger

CONSULTANTS

Henry J. Abraham
Jeffrey N. Albert
Herbert E. Alexander
Francis A. Allen
Gerald Anderson
David H. Bayley
Timothy James Bloomfield
Alfred Blumstein
Albert M. Bottoms
Paul L. Briand, Jr.
Jerome Carlin
William Chambliss
Samuel Chapman
Karl O. Christiansen
Christine Clark
Thomas A. Clingan, Jr.
George A. Codding
Fred Cohen
Henry Cook
Herbert L. Costner
Barbara Curran
Roger H. Davidson
Alan Dershowitz
Norman Dorsen
Martin Eden
Harvey F. Friedman
Warwick R. Furr
Albert C. Germann
Jean D. Grambs
John J. Guidici

J. Archie Hargraves
Jane Harmon
Robert Johnston
George Jones
Richard J. Kendall
Randolph C. Kent
Luis Lastra
L. Harold Levinson
Theodore Lowi
Thomas Lumbard
Donal MacNamara
Bernard W. Marschner
Donald McIntyre
Theodore Miller
Charles Monson
George W. O'Connor
Vincent I. O'Leary
Irving Piliavin
Gustav Rath
Rev. David Romig
Eugene V. Rostow
Arnold and Louise Sagalyn
Ralph F. Salerno
William A. Scott
Rev. Donald W. Seaton, Jr.
Jan Smith
Arlene Ulman
Marvin G. Weinbaum
William D. Zarecor

CONTENTS

270

B. SPECIAL INVESTIGATION REPORTS

Rights in Conflict: the Violent Confrontation of
Demonstrators and Police in the Parks
and Streets of Chicago during the week of
the Democratic National Convention of 1968

*(Available in commercial editions from E. P. Dutton (cloth)
and Bantam Books (paperback))*

*Report of the Chicago Study Team;
Daniel Walker, Director*

STAFF

ASSISTANT DIRECTOR   *Assistant*

Victor R. deGrazia   Patricia Oakley

271

272

- MEDIA

Michael C. Johnson and John A. Koten, *Co-Directors*

William E. Beringer
Geoffrey Davis
Ronald Grais
Mike Lerner

Edward Small
Robert Storozuk
Sydney Weisman

Assistants:

Joseph Feldman
William Lempke

Nancy Lynn

- EVENTS OF THURSDAY AND FRIDAY

James Barr and Gary Nelson, *Co-Directors*

Carroll Cihlar
Richard Cochran

High Griffin
John Pendergast

- ISOLATED INCIDENTS OF VIOLENCE

James Keffler, *Director*

Robert Berendt
William B. Sawtell

David S. Tatel

Assistants

Arthur Benson
James F. Devitt
James A. Maland

Marietta Marcin
Walter E. Young

Assistant to the Director

Mary Parrilli

Librarian

Judy Pedersen

Administrative Assistant

Carla Z. Pierson

Visual Aid Co-ordinators

Paul Levy
Leslie R. Korshak

Accountants

James Raim
Richard Zeder
Julia Odishoo

Organization Consultants

Interview Co-ordinator

Deborah Long

Booz, Allen & Hamilton, Inc.:
Maurice J. Walker
Danial T. Carroll
Lynn F. Chandler

Typing Co-ordinator

Kathy Raad

Design Consultants

Staff Assistants

Adrian Foster
Shirley Johnson
J. Vernon Lloyd
Gary Pollack

Latham-Tyler-Jensen Inc.:
Charles G. MacMurray
Howard W. Knight

273

Patricia A. Avants   Judith R. Moseley
Beverly J. Berni   Lynne M. Wright
Judith K. Kolina   Mary Ann Fahrberger

CONTENTS

Miami Report: Civil Disturbances in Miami, Florida, during the week of August 5, 1968

(Washington, D.C.: Government Printing Office, 1969).

Report of the Miami Study Team; Louis J. Hector and Paul L. E. Helliwell, Co-Directors.

STAFF

Terry Cueto   David Fincher
Ralph C. Datillio   Robert C. Josefsberg
Arden Doss, Jr.   James W. Matthews
Melville Dunn   Jerome S. Reisman
Wilkie Ferguson   James Simmons

CONTENTS

274

Shoot-out in Cleveland:

Black Militants and the Police, July 23, 1968

(Washington, D.C.: Government Printing Office, 1969)
(Vol. 5, NCCPV Staff Study Series)

*(Available in commercial editions from Frederick A. Praeger (cloth)
and Bantam Books (paperback))*

Report of the Cleveland Study Team; Louis H. Masotti, and Jerome R. Corsi, Co-Directors.

EDITORIAL CONSULTANT: Anthony E. Neville
PICTORIAL CONSULTANT: Judith Harkison

STAFF

Kermit Allen, III
Timothy Armbruster
Mr. Robert Bauerlin
Ellen Cummings
Mrs. Robert Dickman
Sharon Dougherty
Robert Farlow
John Krause, Jr.

Forrester Lee
Lauren McKinsey
James Monhart
Mrs. Yoram Papit
Julie Reinstein
Estelle Zannes
Mrs. Jeffrey Zerby

CONSULTANTS

Jeffrey K. Hadden   Charles McCaghy

CONTENTS

275

Rights in Concord: The Response
to the Counter-Inaugural Protest Activities in
Washington, D.C. January 18–20, 1968

(Washington, D.C.: Government Printing Office, 1969)
(Vol. 4, NCCPV Staff Study Series)

*A Special Staff Study by the Task Force on Law and
Law Enforcement; Joseph R. Sahid, Study Director.*

CONTENTS

Shut it Down! a College in Crisis:

San Francisco State College, October, 1968–April, 1969

(Washington, D.C.: Government Printing Office, 1969)
(Vol. 6 NCCPV Staff Study Series)

A Special Staff Report; William H. Orrick, Jr., Director.

STAFF

Jack Abbott   Michael Parker
James Brann   Bruce Pollock
Janet Brune   Robert Young
Douglas Haydel   William Zeidler

CONTENTS

276